12   Y29422

LONDON BOROUGH OF LEWISHAM
LIBRARY SERVICE

Author

_____

Title

_____

Books or discs must be returned on or before the last date stamped on label or on card in book pocket. Books or discs can be renewed by telephone, letter or personal call unless required by another reader. After library hours use the Ansafone Service (01-698 7347). For hours of opening and charges see notices at the above branch, but note that all lending departments close   on Wednesday and all libraries are closed on Sundays, Good Friday, Christmas Day, Bank Holidays and Saturdays prior to Bank Holidays.

Rover 3500 SD1 1976-77 Autobook

By Kenneth Ball

Associate Member, Guild of Motoring Writers
and the Autobooks Team of Technical Writers

Rover 3500 SD1 1976-77

Autobooks Ltd. Golden Lane Brighton BN1 2QJ England

The AUTOBOOK series of Workshop Manuals is the largest in the world and covers the majority of British and Continental motor cars, as well as the majority of Japanese and Australian models.

Whilst every care has been taken to ensure correctness of information it is obviously not possible to guarantee complete freedom from errors or omissions or to accept liability arising from such errors or omissions.

CONTENTS

ISBN 0 85147 707 0

First Edition   1978

© Autobooks Ltd 1978

921

Illustrations reproduced by kind permission of the manufacturers © British Leyland UK Limited.

Printed in Brighton England for Autobooks Ltd by G. Beard and Son Ltd
Bound in Hove England for Autobooks Ltd by Jilks Ltd

A

ACKNOWLEDGEMENT

My thanks are due to British Leyland Motor Corporation Limited for their unstinted co-operation and also for supplying data and illustrations.

Considerable assistance has also been given by owners, who have discussed their cars in detail, and I would like to express my gratitude for this invaluable advice and help.

Kenneth Ball
Associate Member, Guild of Motoring Writers

Ditchling Sussex England.

INTRODUCTION

This do-it-yourself Workshop Manual has been specially written for the owner who wishes to maintain his vehicle in first class condition and to carry out the bulk of his own servicing and repairs. Considerable savings on garage charges can be made, and one can drive in safety and confidence knowing the work has been done properly.

Comprehensive step-by-step instructions and illustrations are given on most dismantling, overhauling and assembling operations. Certain assemblies require the use of expensive special tools, the purchase of which would be unjustified. In these cases information is included but the reader is recommended to hand the unit to the agent for attention.

Throughout the Manual hints and tips are included which will be found invaluable, and there is an easy to follow fault diagnosis at the end of each chapter.

Whilst every care has been taken to ensure correctness of information it is obviously not possible to guarantee complete freedom from errors or omissions or to accept liability arising from such errors or omissions.

Instructions may refer to the righthand or lefthand sides of the vehicle or the components. These are the same as the righthand or lefthand of an observer standing behind the vehicle and looking forward.

CHAPTER 1

THE ENGINE

1:1 Description

A cross-section through the engine is shown in **FIG 1:1**. It is an eight cylinder V-type engine with the cylinders arranged in two banks of four. The banks are disposed at 90° to each other. The aluminium alloy cylinder block is fitted with dry cylinder liners and carries the crankshaft which runs in five main bearings. A flanged type centre bearing controls the crankshaft axially. The forward extension of the crankshaft caters internally for the camshaft, distributor and oil pump drives and externally for a torsional vibration damper and two pulley drives for the water pump, the cooling fan and the alternator and for the power steering hydraulic pump. An electronic diagnostic sensor operates in conjunction with a sensing pip which is incorporated into the periphery of the damper. The crankshaft rear oil seal is carried in the cylinder block and the forward oil seal is carried in the front cover which encloses the camshaft, oil pump and distributor drives and incorporates the water pump casing.

Two connecting rods run on each of the four crankpins. The big-end bearings are thin shell type as also are the main bearings. The alloy pistons each carry two compression rings and a single composite oil control ring. The gudgeon pins have a running fit in the pistons but have an interference fit in the connecting rod small-ends. The alloy cylinder heads are provided with valve seat inserts and inserted valve guides. Each valve is provided with a single valve spring which is retained conventionally by a collar and split collets.

The single camshaft is located centrally above the crankshaft and runs in plain bearings. It is driven by an inverted tooth type chain and 2:1 chainwheels. The spiral gear which drives the distributor and oil pump is keyed to a forward extension of the camshaft. The camshaft operates the valves through self-adjusting tappets, pushrods and rockers which oscillate on rocker shafts mounted on the cylinder heads. Rocker covers enclose the rocker gear and the breather inlet air filter and oil filler on the lefthand side and the breather outlet flame trap on the righthand side.

The sump encloses the bottom of the cylinder block/crankcase. The oil pump is located in the lower part of the front cover and the fullflow disposable canister oil filter is screwed to the pump body. The oil pickup in the sump incorporates a gauze strainer. The induction

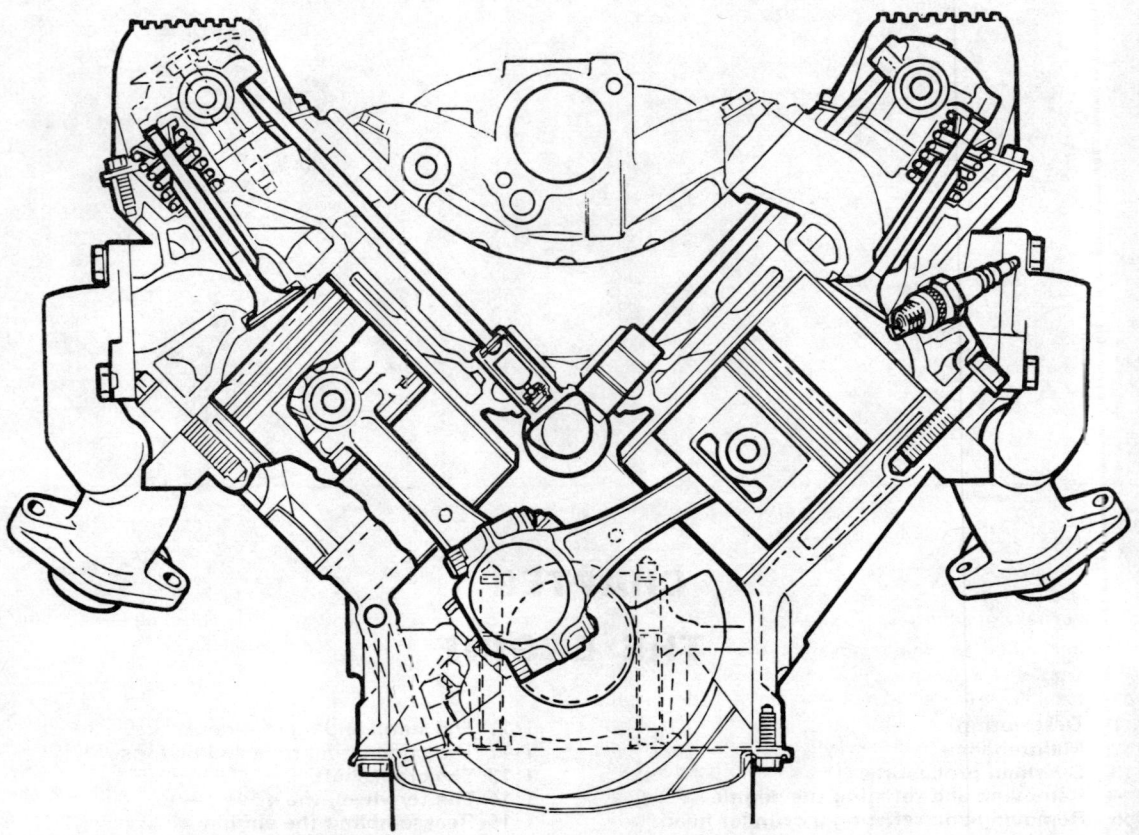

FIG 1:1 A cross-section through the engine

manifold gasket and casing enclose the upper section of the block between the two banks of cylinders. The flywheel or, in the case of automatic transmission models, the torque converter drive plate, is attached to the rear of the crankshaft. In the case of manual transmission models, the clutch operates directly on the rear face of the flywheel.

The engine and the transmission casings form a unit which is supported in the vehicle by three mountings. One of these is located forwards on each side of the engine and the third is located at the rear of the gearbox.

1:2 Maintenance

Oil level:

Check the oil level with the car on level ground and, if the engine has been running, wait for at least a minute after the engine has stopped. Remove the dipstick, wipe it dry, re-insert fully, withdraw and check the level. If necessary add oil to bring the level up to the top mark. Use the same grade and brand of oil as that already in use. If the brand is to be changed, do so when the engine oil is being changed.

Changing engine oil:

Change the oil every 6000 miles (10,000km). Drain off the old oil when the engine is hot. The drain plug is in the lefthand side of the sump. Refill with new oil up to the dipstick top mark and recheck the level after running the engine. Use an oil of reputable brand to the specification relevant to the ambient temperature as quoted in **Section 1:10**.

Oil filter renewal:

At the same time that the engine oil is being changed, that is every 6000 miles (10,000km), renew the oil filter as described in **Section 1:10**.

Drive belts:

Every 6000 miles (10,000km), check and adjust the drive belt tensions as described in **Chapter 10, Section 10:4** and **Chapter 12, Section 12:5**.

Breather system:

Every 12,000 miles (20,000km), clean the breather flame trap and renew the breather inlet air filter. The procedures are described in **Section 1:16**.

General:

Maintain regular checks for oil, fuel, breather and exhaust system leaks and rectify any fault without delay.

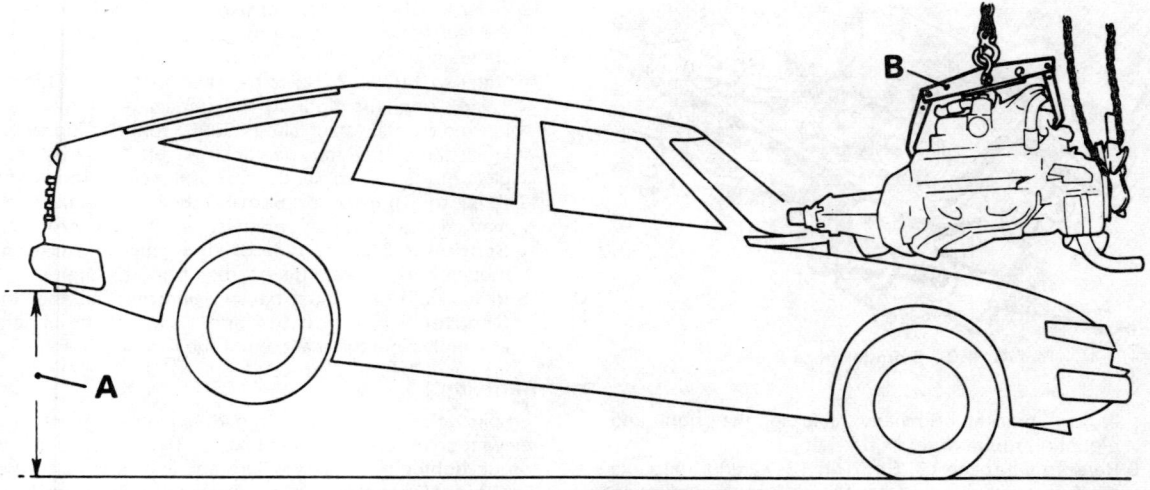

FIG 1:2   Removing the engine and gearbox

Key to Fig 1:2   A 700mm (28in)   **B** Lifting sling 600963

1:3 Overhaul procedures

The procedure for the removal of the engine and gearbox as a unit is described in **Section 1:4** but, except when dealing with the cylinder block, crankshaft and main bearings, it is not essential for the engine to be removed and other assemblies can be serviced or renewed with the engine in the car. To allow access for these procedures to be carried out in situ, however, does require varying amounts of preliminary work involving the removal or dismantling of relevant systems and, in some instances, working on an engine which is partially supported by a jack or by overhead lifting tackle. This preliminary access dismantling ranges from removal of the radiator to allow the front of the engine to be worked on, removal of the propeller shaft and gearbox to give access to the flywheel, to raising the engine out of its mountings to allow removal of the sump for access to the connecting rod big-ends. To give additional working space, an operator may decide to remove units which it is not strictly necessary to disturb and, in such cases, reference should be made to the text of the relevant chapter(s) for removal and refitment instructions.

In the case of a vehicle which has seen very considerable mileage it may be prudent to decide to remove the engine and gearbox for a complete overhaul rather than to begin piecemeal repairs and find later that, say, the main bearings require attention. Whatever plan is adopted, **Hints on maintenance and overhaul** in the **Appendix** should be read before proceeding.

Recommended torque tightening figures are given in the **Technical Data** section of the **Appendix**. Where specific figures are not quoted, use normal automobile engineering practice for the size, location and type of fastening being tightened.

1:4 Removing and refitting the engine

If either the engine or the gearbox is to be dismantled, it will be found convenient to drain off the old lubricant before removing the unit from the car. To ensure correct and speedy refitting, identify all cables, pipes and wiring connections as they are uncoupled.

Removal:

1 Disconnect the battery. Refer to **Chapter 4, Section 4:3** and remove the radiator. Refer to **Chapter 13, Section 13:2** and remove the bonnet.

2 Refer to **Chapter 2, Sections 2:3** and **2:4** and remove the air cleaner and the temperature control system. Refer to **Chapter 3, Sections 3:4** and **3:5** and disconnect the HT and LT leads from the coil and the plug from the heat-sink.

3 Refer to **Chapter 12, Sections 12:2** and **12:5**. Disconnect the battery earth lead from the alternator bracket. Uncouple the alternator harness plug and release the harness from the engine clip.

4 Refer to **Section 1:10** and disconnect the leads from the oil pressure switch and from the oil pressure transmitter. Refer to **Section 1:18** and disconnect the brown lead to the diagnostic sensor at the connector. On automatic transmission models, refer to **Chapter 7, FIG 7:2** and disconnect the leads from the starter inhibitor/reversing light switch. Refer to **Chapter 12, FIG 12:19** and disconnect the leads from the coolant temperature transmitter.

5 Refer to **Chapter 2, Section 2:7** and disconnect the throttle cable from the carburetter linkage, the throttle return spring and the choke cable. Uncouple the brake servo hose from the induction manifold.

6 Remove the two bolts which secure the kickdown cable bracket to the rear of the induction manifold and withdraw the shaft from the throttle shaft.

7 Refer to **Chapter 10, Section 10:4** and dismount the power steering pump from the engine. Secure the pump to one side leaving the hoses connected. Remove the air heater chamber from the righthand exhaust manifold including the backplate.

8 Refer to **Section 1:18**. Remove two nuts and bolts and release the lefthand mounting rubber from its

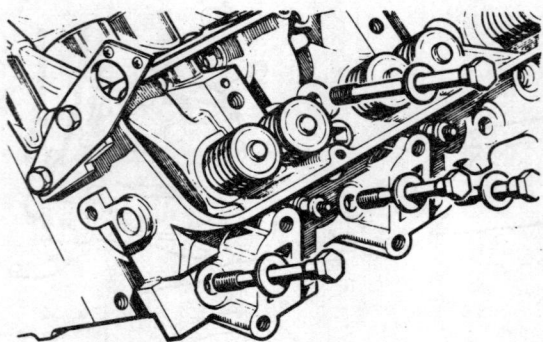

FIG 1:3 Cylinder head bolts

engine bracket. Similarly, release the righthand mounting rubber from its bracket.

9 Refer to **Chapter 13, Section 13:12** and uncouple the two heater hoses from the rear of the induction manifold. Raise the front of the car, position stands and lower the car onto them. Ensure that they are firm.

10 Refer to **Section 1:17**. Disconnect the front exhaust pipes from the manifolds and from the crossmember brackets. Disconnect the exhaust branch pipe from the intermediate pipe.

11 In the case of manual transmission models, refer to **Chapter 6, Sections 6:3** and **6:7** and remove the gear lever assembly. Raise the rear of the car, position stands and lower the car onto them. Ensure that they are firm.

12 Refer to **Chapter 8, Section 8:3** and uncouple the propeller shaft from the gearbox. Uncouple the speedometer drive cable from the gearbox. In the case of automatic transmission models, refer to **Chapter 7, Section 7:8** and remove the gear selector rod.

13 In the case of manual transmission models, refer to **Chapter 5, Section 5:3**, remove the two bolts which secure the clutch slave cylinder to the bellhousing, withdraw the cylinder and secure it to one side.

14 Refer to **Section 1:18**. Remove the two nuts which secure the gearbox mounting to the crossmember. Release the locknut and unscrew the centre bolt from the gearbox casing leaving the bolt and locknut in the crossmember.

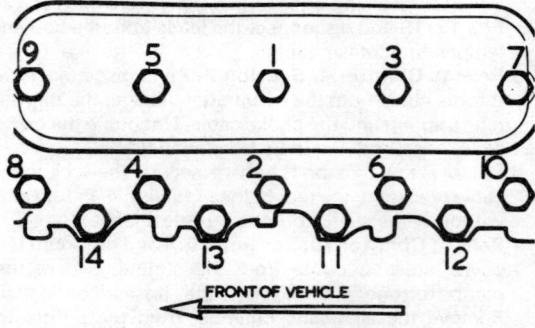

FIG 1:4 Bolt tightening sequence

Key to Fig 1:4   1, 3 and 5 Long bolts   2, 4, 6, 7, 8, 9 and 10 Medium bolts   11, 12, 13 and 14 Short bolts

15 Refer to **Chapter 12, Section 12:4** and disconnect the leads from the starter motor. Raise the car off the stands and lower the car onto the floor.

16 Refer to **FIG 1:2**. Raise the rear of the car 700mm (28in) from the floor to the underside of the rear jacking points. Attach sling 600963 to the lifting eyes. Hoist the engine and gearbox unit up, forwards and clear of the car. Lower the rear of the car to the floor.

17 Refer to **Chapter 6, Section 6:3** in the case of manual transmission models or to **Chapter 7, Section 7:5** in the case of automatic transmission models and separate the gearbox from the engine.

18 In the case of manual transmission models, refer to **Chapter 5, Section 5:4** and dismount the clutch assembly from the rear face of the flywheel.

Refitting:

Follow the reverse of the removal sequence. Refer to the relevant chapter and section texts and, for recommended torque tightening figures where applicable, refer to the **Technical Data** section of the **Appendix**. Refilling of the cooling system is covered in **Chapter 4, Section 4:3**. Refilling the engine sump is covered in **Section 1:11**. Refilling the gearbox is covered in **Chapter 6, Section 6:2** (manual transmission) and in **Chapter 7, Section 7:2** (automatic transmission). If work was carried out on any of the hydraulic systems, refer to the relevant chapter sectional texts and refill and bleed the systems. Tension the power steering pump belt drive as described in **Chapter 10, Section 10:4**.

1:5 Removing and refitting a cylinder head

Compression pressures:

With an engine at normal operating temperature, the compression pressure should be approximately 9.5kg/sq cm (135lb/sq in). To measure this, remove **all** the sparking plugs, secure the throttle in the fully open position and, using a suitable pressure gauge connected with each sparking plug position in turn, crank the engine on the starter motor. Note the highest reading obtained. If the pressure is appreciably less than that specified earlier, worn piston rings, leaking valves or an unserviceable cylinder head gasket should be suspected and the head(s) should be removed for investigation.

Cylinder head removal:

1 Remove the induction manifold as described in **Chapter 2, Section 2:10**. Refer to **Section 1:7** and remove the rocker gear cover, the rocker shaft assembly, the pushrods and the tappets. Keep the pushrods and tappets identified to their positions

2 Uncouple the front exhaust pipe from the manifold. In the case of a lefthand cylinder head on an automatic transmission model, disconnect the tranmission dipstick and, on all models, the oil sump dipstick from the head.

3 Refer to **Chapter 12, Section 12:5** and dismount the alternator. Slacken the cylinder head bolts (see **FIG 1:3**). Work in the reverse of the tightening sequence shown in **FIG 1:4** by starting at bolt numbered 14 and proceeding in sequence to bolt numbered 1.

4 Remove the cylinder head bolts and immediately wire brush wash them in 3M Solvent No. 2. If this solvent is

not available, immerse and clean them in petrol or paraffin to preclude old sealant air hardening and becoming difficult to remove.

5 Lift off the cylinder head complete with its exhaust manifold. Discard the joint gasket and place the head face down on a surface which will not damage the joint face.

Cylinder head bolts:

Ensure that old sealant is cleaned off without delay. Reject bolts after four reassemblies and obtain new replacements. Check the lengths of the bolts against the following specification lengths: long, 97.03mm (3.820in); medium, 66.55mm (2.620in); short, 54.86mm (2.160in). Renew all the bolts if more than two bolts exhibit evidence of elongation. If only one or two bolts are elongated, renew only these.

Cylinder head refitment:

Check that the faces of the block and head are clean. Fit a new joint gasket to the block with TOP uppermost. Do not use sealant on the gasket nor on the joint faces. Locate the head on the block dowels. Coat the bolt threads with 3M EC 776 sealant and immediately insert them into their correct locations (see **FIG 1 : 4**). Tighten the bolts little by little following the numerical sequence shown in **FIG 1 : 4** to the torque figures quoted in the **Technical Data** section of the **Appendix**. The remaining operations are the reverse of the removal sequence. Refer to the relevant chapter sectional texts for descriptions of the procedures.

1 : 6 Servicing a cylinder head

Removal of the head(s) is described in **Section 1 : 5**. When servicing a head, take great care not to damage the joint face.

Dismantling:

Using a suitable valve spring compressor (the official tool is 276102), remove the collets, springs and valves. Keep them identified to the positions to which they were fitted. Clean the combustion chambers with a soft wire brush. Clean the valves and the bores of the valve guides.

Valves:

Valves which are only slightly worn or pitted may be lapped to their seats. If this treatment is inadequate, the valves may be reground and the seats recut. Refer to **FIG 1 : 5**. The correct angle for the valve face **A** is 45°. Reject any valve which has had to be ground to a knife-edge as at **B**. The valve to seat witness should be towards the outer edge as at **C**.

Valve guides:

Valve stems are slightly tapered. Valve guide bores are parallel. Stem to guide bore clearances are quoted in the **Technical Data** of the **Appendix**. They differ between the inlet and the exhaust. Excessively worn guides should be removed using drift 274401 applied at their combustion chamber ends.

Replacement guides are 0.025mm (0.001in) larger than original guides to ensure an interference fit. Refer to **FIG 1 : 6**. Lubricate and fit new guides 3 using drift 4 (600959)

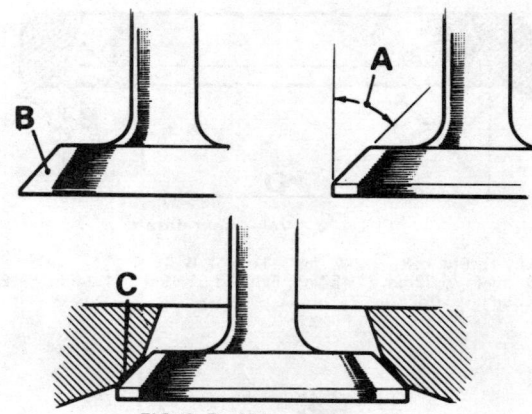

FIG 1 : 5   Valve head seats

Key to Fig 1 : 5   See text

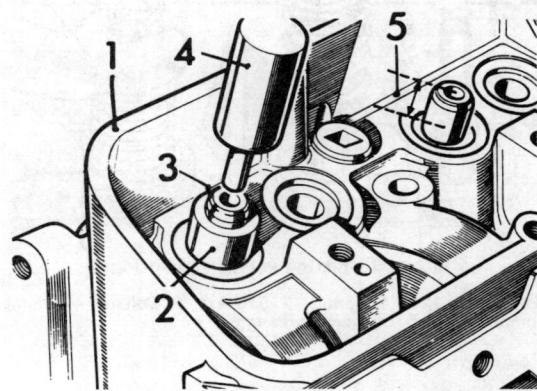

FIG 1 : 6   Fitting new valve guides

Key to Fig 1 : 6   1 Cylinder head   2 Distance piece 605774   3 New valve guide   4 Drift 600959   5 19mm (0.75in)

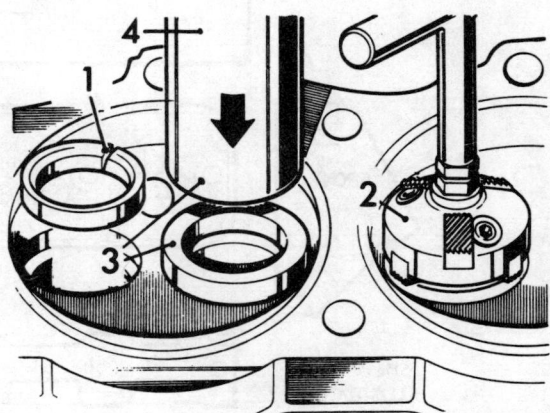

FIG 1 : 7   Fitting new valve seat inserts

Key to Fig 1 : 7   1 Old seat insert   2 Seat angle cutter 3 New seat insert   4 Press mandrel

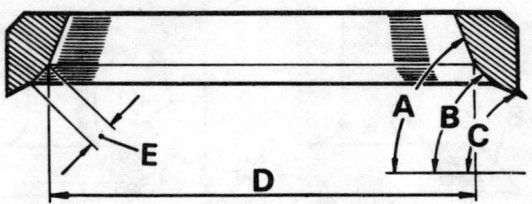

FIG 1:8   Valve seat data

Key to Fig 1:8   **A** 56 ± 1°   **B** 46 ± $\frac{1°}{4}$ **C** 20°
D Inlet: 36.93mm (1.454in); Exhaust 31.49mm (1.240in)   **E**
1.59mm (0.062in)

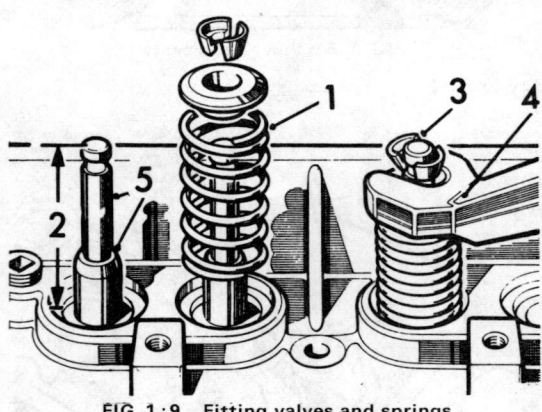

FIG 1:9   Fitting valves and springs

Key to Fig 1:9   1 Spring   2 See text   3 Collets   4 Spring
compressor   5 Lubricate with engine oil

and distance piece 2 (605774). Drive the guides into the
heads until the drift bottoms on the distance piece. The
dimension 5 for a fitted guide should be 19mm (0 750in).

Valve seats:

Valve seat inserts which will not clean up without
excessive recutting should be renewed. The outside
diameter of standard valve seat inserts is: inlet, 42.768—
0.033mm (1.6838—0.0013in); exhaust, 36.944—
0.025mm (1.4545—0.0010in). Replacement inserts are
available in two oversizes, 0.25mm (0.010in) and 0.50mm
(0.020in) larger on the outside diameter than standard to
ensure an interference fit. Refer to **FIG 1:7**. Grind an old
seat away until it is thin enough to be cracked and prised
out. Heat the cylinder head evenly to approximately 65°C
(150°F) and press in the new insert 3. If necessary use
cutter 2 on the valve seats. Seat diameters, angles and
width are shown in **FIG 1:8**. If the seat width exceeds
2.00mm (0.078in) it should be reduced to the specified
width of 1.590mm (0.062in) by the use of 56° stones in
cutter 2 in **FIG 1:7**.

Fit the valves and check the dimension 2 in **FIG 1:9**
from the valve stem tip to the valve spring seat surface.
This must not exceed 47.63mm (1.875in). If necessary,
correct by grinding the end of the valve(s) or by fitting new
parts.

Valve springs:

Check that the loads required to compress the springs to
the following specified lengths are within limits. 40.05mm
(1.577in) under a load of 31.78kg ± 5% (70lb ± 5%),
34.29mm (1.350in) under 59kg ± 5% (130lb ± 5%),
30.15mm (1.187in) under 80kg ± 5% (176lb ± 5%).
Reject weak springs and obtain new replacements.

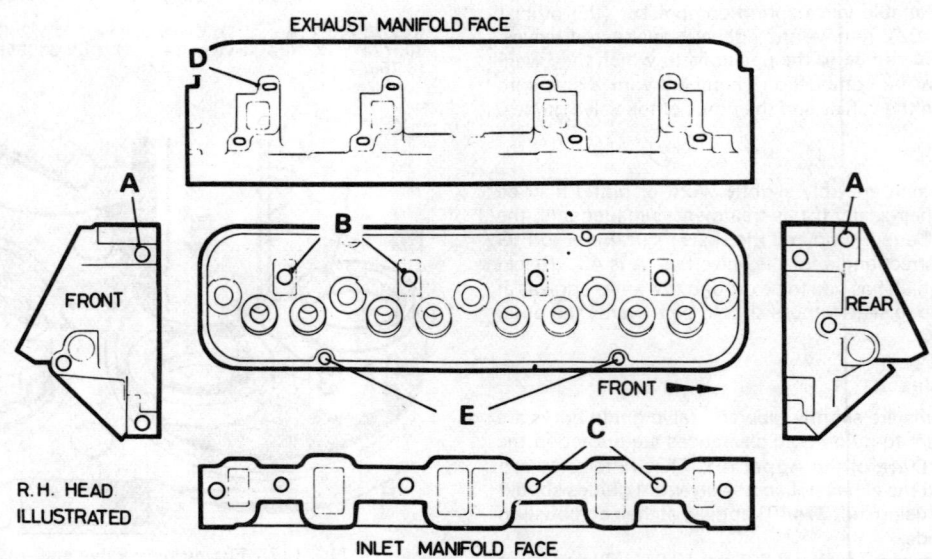

FIG 1:10   Salvaging by fitting thread inserts

Key to Fig 1:10   See text

Cylinder head thread inserts:

The cylinder head threads indicated in **FIG 1:10** may be salvaged by fitting inserts. The three holes **A** front and rear, the four holes **B** and the six holes **C** may be drilled 0.3906in dia. by 0.937 + 0.040in deep, tapped Helicoil No 6CPB or 6CS by 0.875in (min) deep for $\frac{3}{8}$UNC 1$\frac{1}{2}$D inserts. The eight holes **D** may be drilled 0.3906in dia. by 0.812 + 0.040in deep, tapped Helicoil No 6CBB by 0.749in (min) deep for $\frac{3}{8}$UNC 1$\frac{1}{2}$D inserts. The four holes **E** two at each side may be drilled 0.261in dia. by 0.675 + 0.040in deep, tapped Helicoil No 4CPB or 4CS by 0.625in (min) deep for $\frac{1}{4}$UNC 1$\frac{1}{2}$D inserts.

Do not attempt to salvage sparking plug hole threads. This may result in breaking through into the coolant jacket.

Reassembly:

Refer to **FIG 1:9**. Lubricate the stems and guide bores 5 with engine oil. Check that dimension 2 does not exceed 47.63mm (1.875in). Fit and compress the valve springs 4, fit the collets 3, release the spring compressor and check that the collets are correctly seated.

1:7 Servicing the rocker gear

1 Remove the induction manifold and gasket as described in **Chapter 2, Section 2:10**. Detach the sparking plug leads from the rocker cover clips. Remove the retaining bolts and washers and lift off the rocker covers.
2 Identify each rocker shaft assembly and note which way round each is fitted. One end of each shaft is notched on one side only. Note that the notches are uppermost and that the notched end is forwards on one bank and rearwards on the other. Note which is which.
3 Remove the bracket retaining bolts and lift off the rocker shaft assemblies. Refer to **FIG 1:11**. Withdraw the pushrods 1 and tappets 2 and identify them to the positions to which they were fitted.
4 If a tappet cannot be withdrawn, it will be necessary to remove the camshaft as described in **Section 1:8** and withdraw the tappet downwards.
5 Refer to **FIG 1:12**. Dismantle a rocker shaft assembly by removing a splitpin 8 from one end. Withdraw the components and retain them in their correct sequence.

Pushrods:

Reject any pushrod which is bent or has a rough or damaged ball end or seat.

Hydraulic tappets:

Inspect the inner and outer surfaces of the bodies for blow holes, scoring etc. Reject tappets which are roughly scored or grooved or if blow holes through the wall could allow oil to leak from the lower chamber. The prominent wear pattern just above the lower end of the body is acceptable unless it is definitely grooved or scored. Inspect the cam contact surface and reject a tappet if this surface is excessively worn. **Tappets must rotate** and a round wear pattern is normal; a square pattern, indicating that the tappet has not been rotating, is not acceptable. Non-rotating tappets should be rejected and the relevant camshaft lobes should be specially suspected of being

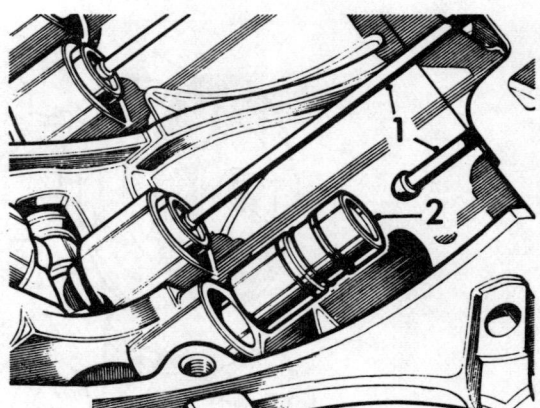

FIG 1:11   Pushrods and tappets

Key to Fig 1:11   1 Pushrod   2 Tappet

excessively worn. Reject tappets if the pushrod contact area is rough or damaged. Check that all new tappets rotate freely in their cylinder block locations.

Rocker arms:

Check that the pushrod and valve tip contact areas are smooth and undamaged. Note that there are two shapes of arms and, if replacements are required, check that the correct arms are obtained. If new arms are being fitted ensure that the protective coating is removed from the oil feed hole and from the pushrod seat.

Rocker shafts:

Check that the rocker arm bearing areas are not excessively worn or scored and that the oil holes are clear.

Rocker covers:

If necessary, renew the rocker cover gaskets. Remove the old gasket and clean the mounting face with Bostic 6001 cleaner. Dry thoroughly. Apply an even film of Bostik

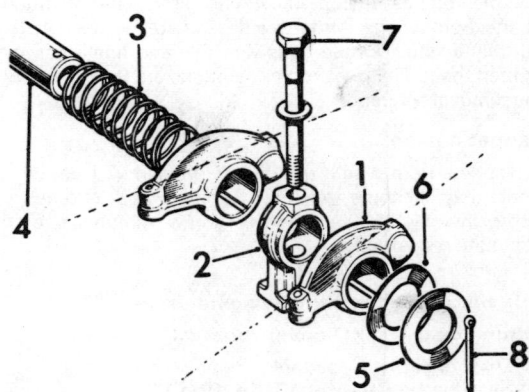

FIG 1:12   Rocker gear components

Key to Fig 1:12   1 Rocker arm   2 Bracket   3 Spring
4 Shaft   5 Plain washer   6 Wavy washer   7 Bolt
8 Splitpin

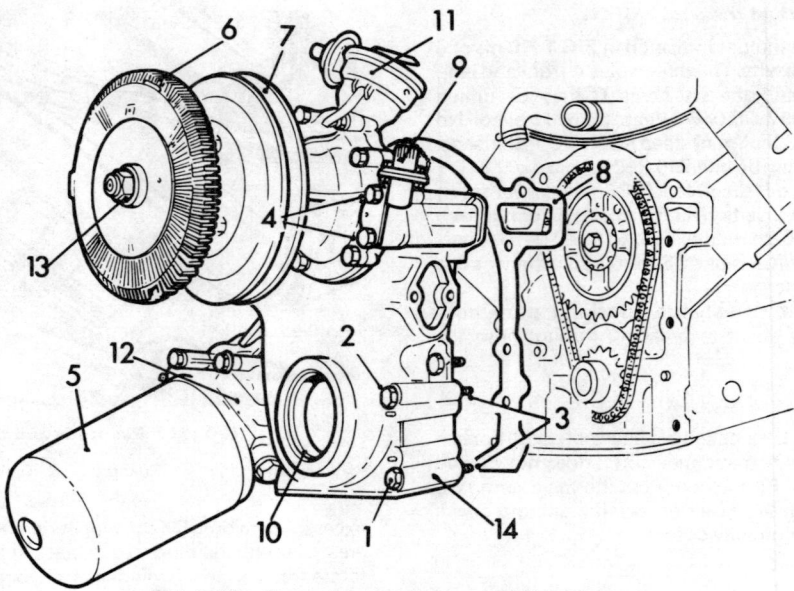

FIG 1 :13   Removing the timing gear (front) cover

Key to Fig 1:13   1 Bolt   2 Bolt   3 Bolt threads   4 Bolts   5 Oil filter   6 Fan drive viscous coupling   7 Water pump/
fan drive pulley   8 Gasket   9 Diagnostic socket   10 Oil seal   11 Distributor   12 Oil pump   13 Coupling retaining nut
14 Timing gear cover

1775 impact adhesive to the rocker cover and gasket faces, allow the adhesive to become touch-dry before attaching the gasket. **The gasket fits one way round only and must be located and attached accurately first time.** Leave for at least 30 minutes before fitting the cover to the cylinder head,

Reassembly:

Follow the reverse of the dismantling sequence. Lubricate all working surfaces with engine oil. Use new splitpins 8 in **FIG 1:12**. Ensure that each rocker shaft assembly is the correct way round as noted on removal and that the notches are uppermost. The baffle plates are fitted to the front of the lefthand side and to the rear of the righthand side. Tighten bolts 7 evenly and finally torque tighten them. The remaining operations are the reverse of the removal sequence.

Tappet noise:

Tappets from which the oil has drained will be noisy until they become refilled. Running the engine at approximately 2500rev/min for a few minutes should eliminate tappet noise.

1:8 Servicing the camshaft and drive

Timing gear (front) cover removal:

1 Disconnect the battery. Remove the bonnet as described in **Chapter 13, Section 13:2.** Remove the radiator and cooling fan as described in **Chapter 4, Sections 4:3** and **4:4**. Dismount the alternator as described in **Chapter 12, Section 12:5**. Turn the engine to TDC of No 1 cylinder firing stroke.

2 Remove the power steering pump as described in **Chapter 10, Section 10:4.** Refer to **Section 1:19** and dismount the transducer from its bracket. Remove the bolt and washer which retains the crankshaft pulley. Withdraw the crankshaft and power steering pump drive pulleys complete with the vibration damper.

3 Disconnect the sparking plug leads and remove the distributor cap. Disconnect the vacuum pipe from the distributor. Refer to **FIG 1:13** and remove the timing cover bolts 1 and 2. Remove the transducer and steering pump brackets. Clean the threads of the bolts as described in **Section 1:5** for cylinder head bolts.

4 Disconnect the following: the brown wire to the transducer at the connector; the coolant temperature transmitter lead; the diagnostic socket leads from the ignition coil; the electronic ignition leads from the distributor and coil and the plug from the heat-sink; the leads from the oil pressure switch and from the oil pressure transmitter.

5 Remove the thermostat by-pass hose and the heater return hose from the water pump. Remove the two bolts which secure the sump to the timing cover. Remove the remaining five bolts and one nut which secure the cover to the cylinder block. Clean the threads of the bolts as described for cylinder head bolts in **Section 1:5**.

6 Clean the cylinder block and cover joint faces and the bottom edge of the cover where it contacts the sump gasket after withdrawing the cover. If the units which remain attached to the cover are to be removed, refer to the relevant chapter or sectional texts for procedure descriptions.

Timing chain and gears:

With the timing gear cover removed, confirm that No 1 piston is still at TDC of the firing stroke. Refer to **FIG 1:14**. Remove bolt and washer 1 and 2, withdraw the distributor drive gear 4 and the spacer 5. Withdraw both chain wheels complete with chain 6. **Do not rotate the engine if the rocker shaft assemblies are in position** or the valve gear and pistons will be damaged. If other operations require the engine to be rotated, **remove both rocker shaft assemblies** as described in **Section 1:7**.

Renew worn or damaged chain wheels. Renew a chain which is worn or stretched.

If the engine has not been rotated, refitment of the chain and chain wheels will be the reverse of the removal sequence. Refer to **FIG 1:15**. Note the timing marks 1 and 2 and the crankshaft chain gear marking 3. Ensure that the distributor drive gear 4 (see **FIG 1:14**) is fitted with its annular groove face in contact with the flanged face of the spacer 5. Torque tighten bolt 1. If the engine has been rotated, follow the procedure described in operations 1, 2 and 3 of the reassembly sequence.

Camshaft removal:

Remove both rocker shaft assemblies and all the pushrods and tappets as described in **Section 1:7**. Remove the timing gear cover and the camshaft drive chain and chain wheels as described earlier. Carefully withdraw the camshaft as shown in **FIG 1:16**.

When inspecting the camshaft, check particularly any cam lobe on which it was found (see **Section 1:7**) that a non-rotating tappet was operating. Slight scuffing of cam lobe faces may be corrected by judicious stoning. Note that the space between the key 2 and the keyway in the camshaft drive gear acts as a lubrication oilway. Check that the overall dimension 1 over the shaft and key does not exceed 30.15mm (1.187in).

Reassembly:

Lubricate all working surfaces with engine oil. Fit the camshaft and time its drive before refitting the rocker shaft assemblies. The camshaft timing procedure is as follows:

1 Set No 1 piston at TDC noting that, on completion of the timing operations, this will be the firing stroke. Temporararily fit the camshaft chain wheel with the FRONT marking outwards as shown in **FIG 1:15**.

2 Turn the camshaft until the timing mark 2 is at the 6 o'clock position. Withdraw the chain wheel without disturbing the camshaft. Fit the chain wheels to the chain with the timing marks 1 and 2 aligned and the FRONT mark 3 outwards.

3 Fit the wheels and chain. Fit the spacer, distributor drive gear, washer and retaining bolt (5, 4, 2 and 1 in **FIG 1:14**) as described earlier. Torque tighten the retaining bolt.

The timing gear cover may now be refitted. The procedure is basically the reverse of the removal sequence but note the following.

Coat both sides of the new gasket 8 in **FIG 1:13** with Hylomar PL 32/m. Set the distributor rotor arm approximately 30° before its final position and fit the cover. The remaining operations are the reverse of the removal sequence. Refer as necessary to the relevant

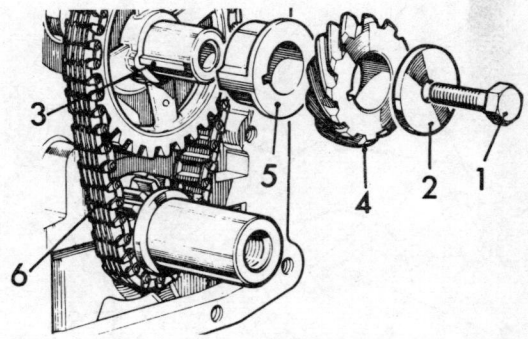

FIG 1:14   The camshaft drive

Key to Fig 1:14 1 Bolt 2 Washer 3 Key 4 Distributor drive gear 5 Spacer 6 Camshaft drive chain

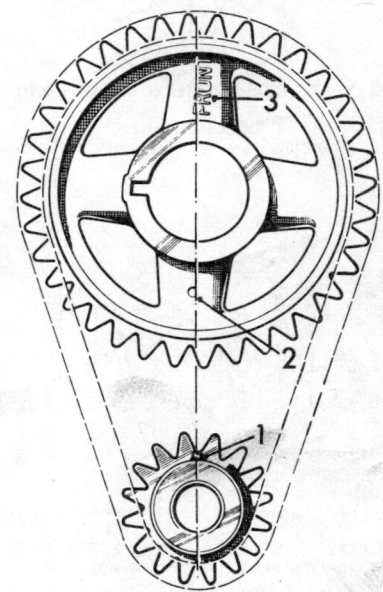

FIG 1:15   Camshaft drive marks

Key to Fig 1:15   1 Crankshaft wheel timing mark 2 Camshaft wheel timing mark   3 FRONT mark (fitted outwards)

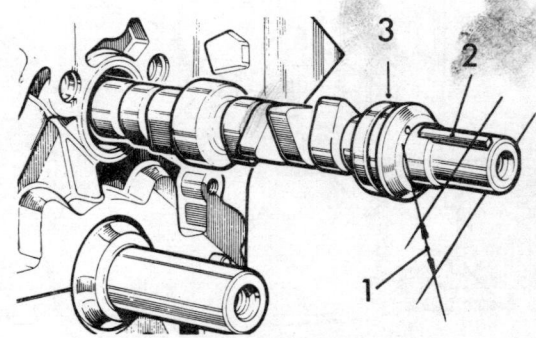

FIG 1:16   Removing the camshaft

Key to Fig 1:16 1 30.15mm (1.187in) maximum   2 Key 3 Camshaft

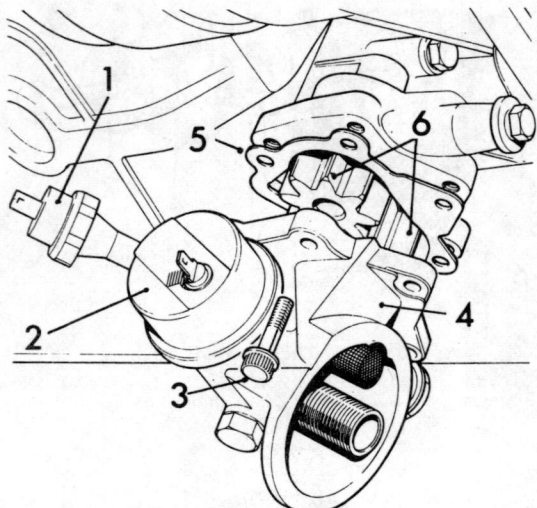

FIG 1:17 Components of the oil pump

Key to Fig 1:17 1 Oil pressure switch 2 Oil pressure transmitter 3 Pump cover retaining bolt 4 Pump cover 5 Gasket 6 Pump gears

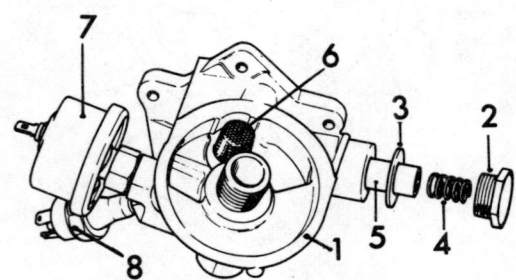

FIG 1:18 Components of the pump cover

Key to Fig 1:18 1 Pump cover 2 Plug 3 Washer 4 Spring 5 Relief valve 6 Bypass strainer 7 Oil pressure transmitter 8 Oil pressure switch

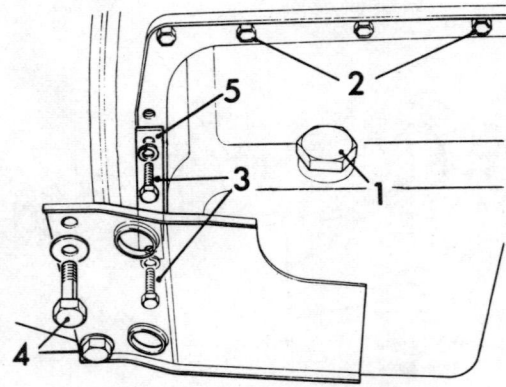

FIG 1:19 Removing the sump

Key to Fig 1:19 1 Drain plug 2 Side bolts 3 Rear bolts 4 Coupling plate bolts 5 Reinforcing plate

chapter and sectional texts and, when the engine can be run, refer to **Chapter 3, Section 3:6** and check and adjust the ignition timing dynamically.

Timing cover oil seal:

This seal is 10 in **FIG 1:13** and may be renewed, if necessary, after removing the crankshaft and power steering pump drive pulleys and the vibration damper (see operation 2 of the timing gear cover removal procedure described earlier). Note which way round the seal is fitted and take care, when prising it out, not to damage the timing cover. Lubricate the outer diameter and the lip of the new seal and fit it the correct way round. Using a straightedge across the diameter, check that it is square in its housing.

1:9 The distributor drive

The distributor is driven by the spiral gear 4 in **FIG 1:14**. This gear is mounted on the forward extension of the camshaft and engages with a skew gear which is pinned to the distributor shaft and is shown in **Chapter 3, FIG 3:1**. Removal of the spiral gear is covered in **Section 1:8**. Removal of the skew gear is covered in **Chapter 3, Section 3:5**.

1:10 The lubrication system

The gear type oil pump is driven by a dog on the lower end of the distributor shaft (see **Chapter 3, FIG 3:6**). Suction oil is taken from the sump via a gauze strainer. Pressure oil is delivered via a fullflow filter 5 in **FIG 1:13** to the cylinder block and is distributed to the major assemblies. Splash oil lubricates the piston and cylinder bores.

Oil specifications:

Only use oil of reputable brand. Select an oil viscosity to suit the ambient temperature of the region in which the car will operate. Recommendations are: below −12°C (10°F) use a 5W/20, 5W/30 or 5W/40; above −22°C (−8°F) use a 10W/30, 10W/40 or 10W/50; above −12°C (10°F) use a 15W/40 or 15W/50 and above 0°C (32°F) use a 20W/40 or 20W/50.

Renewing the oil filter:

Unscrew the canister. Use a strap spanner if necessary. Discard the old sealing washer. Lightly lubricate the new washer, and screw on the new canister without delay so as to avoid the need to prime the pump. Screw on the canister until the seal touches the pump cover face. Tighten by hand by a further half turn only. **Do not overtighten.**

Oil pump:

To dismantle the pump, refer to **FIG 1:17** and proceed as follows. Remove the oil filter canister as described earlier, remove the leads from the pressure switch 1 and from the pressure transmitter 2, remove the cover retaining bolts 3, withdraw the cover 4, lift off the gasket 5 and remove and clean the gears 6. Refer to **FIG 1:18**. Remove and clean the plug 2, washer 3, spring 4, relief valve 5 and strainer 6.

With the gears fitted to the timing gear cover, place a straightedge across them and using feelers, measure the clearance between the straightedge and the cover face. This should not be less than 0.05mm (0.0018in).

Reassemble the internal parts wetted with engine oil. Torque tighten the cover retaining bolts and the relief valve plug.

1:11 The sump and oil strainer

Sump removal and fitment:

With the car on a ramp or over a pit, remove the sump plug 1 in **FIG 1:19** and drain off the engine oil. Raise the bonnet, disconnect the battery and, to give access to the crankshaft damper, remove the underbelly panel as described in **Chapter 13, Section 13:4**. Position a jack in support under the crankshaft damper (keep it clear of the sensor pip). Refer to **Section 1:18** and remove the bolts from the lefthand engine mounting. Checking that the air cleaner does not foul the bulkhead, raise the engine until the mounting bracket holes are approximately 38mm (1.5in) apart. Remove the power steering hose clamp bolt. Remove 14 sump retaining bolts 2 from the front and sides. Remove two retaining bolts 3 and reinforcing plate 5 from the rear of the sump and remove two coupling plate bolts 4. Dismount the sump and discard the joint gasket.

Refitment is the reverse of this sequence. Clean the joint faces and apply Hylomar PL 30/m to both sides of a new gasket. Torque tighten the sump retaining bolts and the drain plug. Refill with approved oil.

Oil strainer and sump baffle plate:

The oil strainer and pick-up pipe and the sump baffle plate are shown in **FIGS 1:20** and **1:21**. Access to these components requires removal of the sump as described earlier.

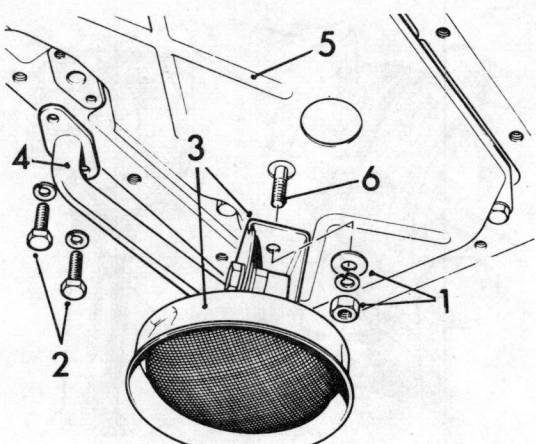

FIG 1:20 The oil strainer and sump baffle plate

Key to Fig 1:20   1 Central retaining nut and washers 2 Oil pick-up pipe retaining bolts and washers   3 Oil strainer and bracket assembly   4 Oil pick-up pipe   5 Baffle plate 6 Central stud

1:12 The connecting rods and pistons

Removing connecting rods and pistons:

1 Remove the cylinder heads as described in **Section 1:5**. Remove the oil sump, oil pick-up pipe and baffle plate, see **Section 1:11**.
2 Remove the connecting rod cap retaining nuts. Remove the caps and identify them to their own connecting rods. Note that the rib on the edge of each cap is fitted on the same side as the domed boss 1 (see **FIG 1:22**) on the connecting rod and that the domed

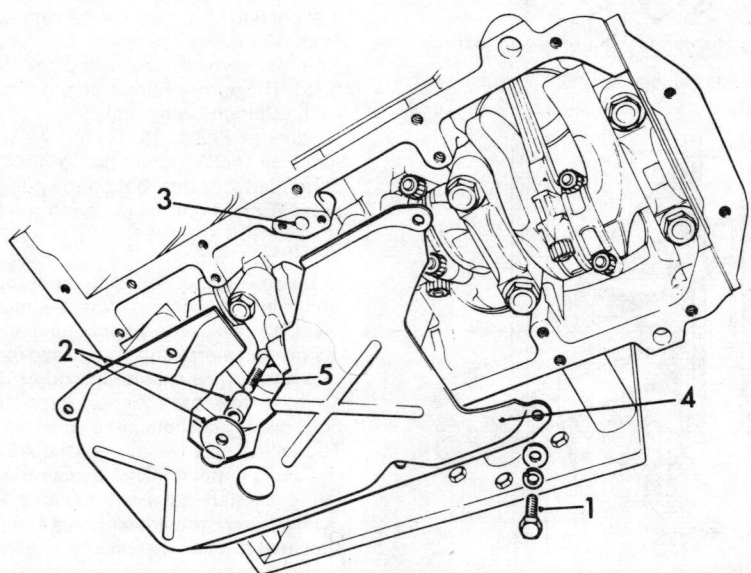

FIG 1:21 Removing the baffle plate

Key to Fig 1:21   1 Baffle plate retaining bolts and washers location   4 Baffle plate   5 Central stud   2 Plain washer and distance piece   3 Pick-up pipe flange

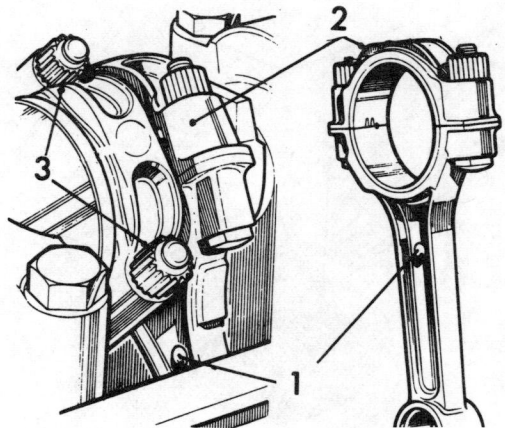

FIG 1 : 22   The connecting rods

Key to Fig 1 : 22   1 Domed boss   **2** Connecting rod cap
3 Cap retaining nuts

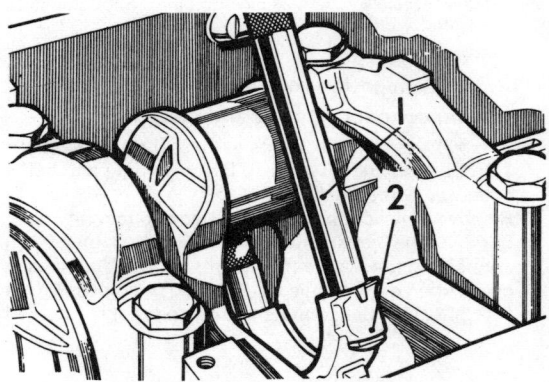

FIG 1 : 23   Removing the connecting rods and pistons

Key to Fig 1 : 23   1 Guide bolt 605351   **2** Connecting rod

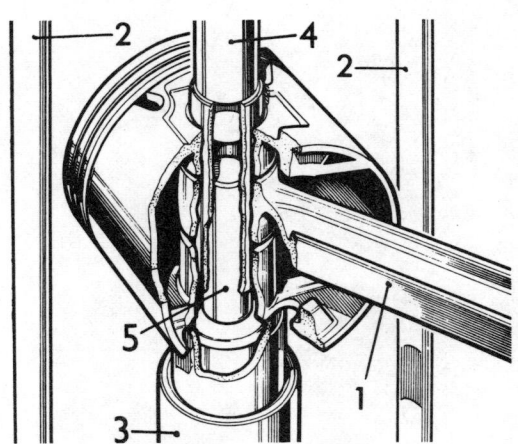

FIG 1 : 24   Removing a gudgeon pin

Key to Fig 1 : 24   1 Connecting rod   **2** Press frame   **3** Tool
605350 (lower section)   **4** Tool 605350 (upper section)
5 Gudgeon pin

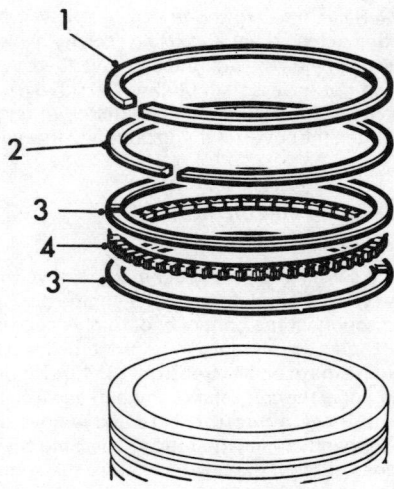

FIG 1 : 25   Piston rings

Key to Fig 1 : 25   1 Top compression ring   **2** Second
compression ring   **3** Oil control rail rings   **4** Oil control
expansion ring

boss faces forwards on the righthand bank of cylinders
and rearwards on the left. Screw guide bolts 605351
onto the connecting rod bolts as shown in **FIG 1 : 23**.
3 Push each connecting rod and piston up the cylinder
bore and withdraw the assembly from the top. Retain
each connecting rod and piston in sequence together
with its own cap. Remove the guide bolts.

Separating a piston from a connecting rod:

Gudgeon pins have an interference fit in the connecting
rod little-ends and have to be pressed out under a hydraulic
press of 8 tons capacity. If the same piston is to be refitted,
mark which way round and in which bore it was located.
Note also which way round the connecting rods were
fitted. The domed bosses on the connecting rods will face
each other on each crankpin.

Refer to **FIG 1 : 24**. Locate the piston and connecting
rod 1 on tool 3 (lower part of tool 605350). Locate the
upper part 4 of this tool on the gudgeon pin and, under a
press 2, press out the gudgeon pin 5.

Piston:

Remove carbon deposits from the pistons, particularly
from the ring grooves. With the pistons and the cylinder
block at the same temperature, measure the bore and
piston diameters at right angles to the axes of the gudgeon
pins and, in the case of the bores, 90 to 100mm (3.5 to
4.0in) from the cylinder head face. The ranges of
bore/piston acceptable clearances are quoted in the
Technical Data section of the **Appendix**.

A single standard of oversize piston is available for
fitting to standard bores. This is 0.025mm (0.0010in)
oversize and the cylinder bores must be honed to give the
specified running clearances.

Piston rings:

There are two compression rings and one (composite)
oil control ring. The top compression ring 1 is chrome

FIG 1:26   Removing the crankshaft

Key to Fig 1:26   1 Rear oil seal   2 Cruciform face seals   3 Location for jointing compound   4 End piece and rear main bearing cap   5 Rear cap retaining bolts   6 Pilot bearing   7 Main bearing caps   8 Flanged bearing shell   9 Connecting rod cap retaining nuts   10 Connecting rod big-end caps   11 Crankshaft   12 Main bearing cap retaining bolts

parallel faced. The second compression ring 2 has an L-profile and is marked T or TOP to ensure that it will be fitted the correct way up. The composite oil control ring comprises three sections 3 and 4 as shown in **FIG 1:25**.

Using feeler gauges, check the ring gaps with the rings square in the upper part of the cylinder bore. Gap widths are quoted in the **Technical Data** section of the **Appendix**. Compression ring gaps which are below limits may be widened with a fine-cut file. If new piston rings are to be fitted, the cylinder bores must be deglazed by honing to a crosshatch finish. The clearance of the compression rings in their grooves should be within 0.08 to 0.13mm (0.003 to 0.005in).

Gudgeon pins:

Gudgeon pins must have an interference press fit with their connecting rod little-ends. Their clearance in the piston bores should be within the range of 0.0025 to 0.0076mm (0.0001 to 0.0003in).

Connecting rods:

Do not attempt to salvage bent, twisted or damaged connecting rods but obtain new replacements. Reject bearing shells which are scored or excessively worn. If a bearing failure has occurred, examine the crankpin for transfer of bearing metal and ensure that all oilways are clean and clear. Crankpins may be salvaged by regrinding

undersize. One non-standard size of big-end shells is available (see **Section 1:13**).

Connecting rod to crankpin clearances (and crankshaft journal to main bearing clearances) are best measured by using Plastigage, which is a proprietary plastic 'thread', as follows:

1 Select the diameter of Plastigage which covers the clearance to be measured. Place a length of the thread on the journal along its full width.

2 Fit the bearing shell and cap. Torque tighten the retaining nuts or bolts. The Plastigage will be squeezed down to the clearance dimension of the bearing and its width will increase. **Do not turn the connecting rod or crankshaft while the plastigage is in position.**

3 Remove the bearing cap and shell and, using the Plastigage scale provided with the thread, read off the clearances. The maximum width will indicate the minimum clearance and the minimum width, the maximum clearance.

Reassembly:

Refitment of the pistons and connecting rods is the reverse of the removal sequence. Fitment of the gudgeon pins requires a press and the same tooling setup as for their removal (see **FIG 1:24**). Use guide bolts 605351, lubricate the piston rings, pistons and the cylinder bores

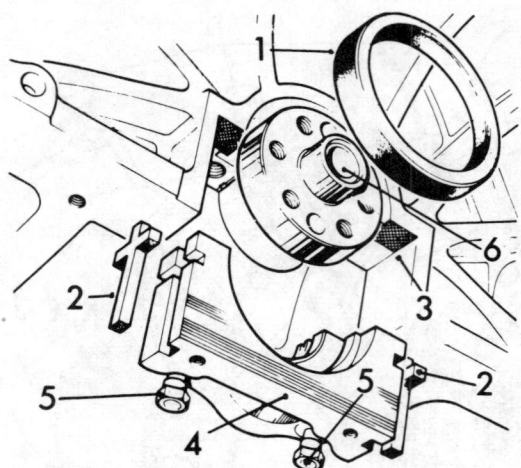

FIG 1:27 Crankshaft rear bearing cap and oil seal

Key to Fig 1:27   1 Rear seal   2 Cruciform face seal
3 Location for jointing compound   4 End piece and rear
main bearing cap   5 Rear cap retaining bolts   6 Crankshaft

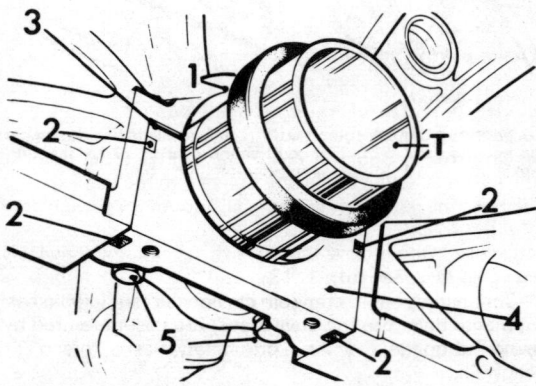

FIG 1:28 Fitting the rear oil seal

Key to Fig 1:28   1 Rear oil seal   2 Cruciform face seals
3 Location for jointing compound   4 End piece and rear
main bearing cap   5 Rear cap retaining bolts   T Guide tool
RO 1014

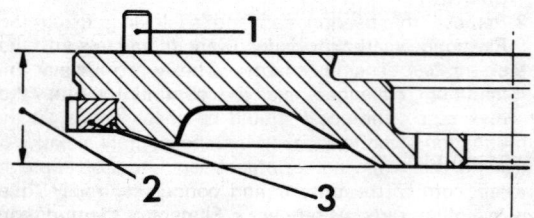

FIG 1:29 A part cross-section through the flywheel

Key to Fig 1:29   1 Dowel   2 Overall thickness   3 Ring
gear

with engine oil and use a piston ring compressing tool to
enter the piston into the bores. Check that the bossed
domes (see **FIG 1:22**) face each other on each crankpin
and that the caps are fitted the correct way round.
Lubricate the crankpins and big-ends. Torque tighten the
cap retaining nuts. The end float between the connecting
rod on each crankpin should be within 0.15 to 0.36mm
(0.006 to 0.014in).

Refer to the relevant chapter and sectional texts for the
remaining assembly operations which follow the reverse of
the dismantling sequence.

1:13 The crankshaft

Crankshaft removal:

1 Drain off the engine oil. Remove the engine and
gearbox unit as described in **Section 1:4**. Separate
the gearbox from the engine as described in **Chapter
6, Section 6:3** or **Chapter 7, Section 7:5**.

2 On manual transmission models, refer to **Chapter 5,
Section 5:4** and dismount the clutch. Remove the
flywheel or the drive plate as described in **Section
1:14**. Remove the camshaft and its drive as described
in **Section 1:8**. Remove the connecting rods and
pistons as described in **Section 1:12**.

3 Refer to **FIG 1:26**. Withdraw the main bearing cap
retaining bolts 5 and 12. Remove the main bearing caps
4 and 7. Keep them identified to their locations.
Withdraw seal 1. Lift out the crankshaft.

4 Withdraw the main bearing shells from the block. If the
original bearing shells are to be refitted, keep them
identified to their other halves.

Reject bearing shells which are scored or excessively
worn. If a bearing failure has occurred, inspect the journal
for transfer of metal and check that the oilways in the
crankshaft and in the block are clear and clean (this will
also apply if there has been a big-end failure). Note that the
centre bearing shells 8 are flanged. They control the axial
float of the crankshaft. The rear bearing cap and end-piece
4 are integral and the assembly carries cruciform side face
seals 2 (see also **FIG 1:27**) and the lower half of the rear
seal 1 location.

If cylinder bores have been honed either to deglaze their
surfaces for new piston rings or to resize to suit oversize
pistons, the block must be thoroughly cleaned and the
oilways flushed through with clean engine oil.

Main bearing to crankshaft journal clearances are best
measured by using Plastigage as described in **Section
1:12**. Crankpins and main journals may be reground to
suit the one non-standard big-end and main bearing size of
0.508mm (0.020in) undersize. Refer to the **Technical
Data** section of the **Appendix** for the acceptable range of
clearances.

Crankshaft refitment:

1 Locate the upper bearing shells in the block and check
that the oilways align. Lubricate the shells and shaft
journal with engine oil and lift the shaft into position.

2 Lubricate the lower bearing shells and fit all shells and
caps except that at the rear (4 in **FIG 1:26**). Fit the cap
retaining bolts but leave them slack. Align the thrust
faces of the centre bearing by tapping the crankshaft
with a mallet, forwards and rearwards. Torque tighten
the bearing retaining bolts for these caps.

3 Refer to **FIG 1 : 27**. Fit new cruciform side face seals 2. Do not cut them to length. They must protrude approximately 1.59mm (0.062in) beyond the cap parting line. Apply Hylomar PL 32m jointing compound to the rearmost half of the cap parting face or to the equivalent face of the cylinder block as shown at 3 in **FIGS 1 : 27** and **1 : 28**.

4 Lubricate and fit the rear cap 4. Fit bolts 5 but leave them slack. Check that the cap is fully home and squarely seated. Tension the cap bolts 5 equally by one quarter turn and then back each off by one full turn.

5 Lubricate the rear seal journal. Refer to **FIG 1 : 28** and use guide tool **T** (RO 1014) which must also be lubricated, to fit a new rear seal 1 without at any time handling the lip seal. Keep the outside diameter of the seal clean and dry. Push it home fully, withdraw the guide tool and torque tighten the rear cap retaining bolts.

6 Using a dial gauge against the rear of the crankshaft, check that the axial float is within 0.10 to 0.20mm (0.004 to 0.008in). The remaining sequence is the reverse of the removal operations 1 and 2. Refer to the relevant sectional and chapter texts.

Rear seal renewal:

The procedure for fitting a new seal is included in the crankshaft refitment sequence. A new seal may be fitted to an installed engine by carrying out operations 3 to 5 of that sequence after removal of the gearbox, flywheel or drive plate and the sump.

Pilot bearing:

This bearing is 6 in **FIG 1 : 27**. Withdraw the unserviceable pilot bearing and fit a new replacement flush with or to a maximum of 1.60mm (0.063in) below the crankshaft end face. Ream the bore to 19.060 +0.025mm (0.7504 +0.001 in).

1 : 14 The flywheel, the drive plate

Flywheel removal:

This procedure is applicable to manual transmission models only. The car must be on a ramp or over a pit.

Remove the gearbox as described in **Chapter 6, Section 6 : 3**. Remove the clutch as described in **Chapter 5, Section 5 : 4**. Remove the six bolts which retain the flywheel to the crankshaft and dismount the flywheel.

Inspection:

Refer to **FIG 1 : 29** and measure 2, the overall thickness. Fit a new flywheel if this is less than 29.33mm (1.155in). If the thickness is above this minimum, the rear face may, if necessary, be refaced by grinding after removing dowels 1. Recheck that the overall thickness has not been reduced below the minimum specified.

An unserviceable ring gear 3 may be removed by drilling through and breaking off (take precautions against flying fragments). Heat a new ring gear uniformly to 170° to 175°C (338° to 347°F) and, with the chamfered inner diameter towards the flywheel, fit it firmly and squarely. Allow the assembly to cool gradually.

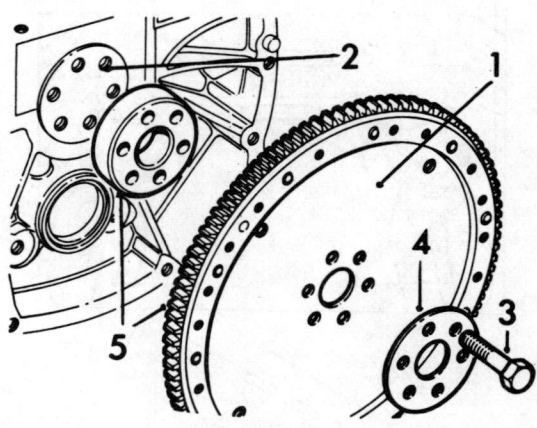

FIG 1 : 30 The drive plate

Key to Fig 1 : 30   1 Drive plate   2 Crankshaft
3 Retaining bolt   4 Reinforcing plate   5 Spacer

Flywheel refitment:

The bolt holes are not symmetrical. Work diagonally when gradually tightening the bolts. Finally torque tighten them. The remaining operations are the reverse of the dismantling sequence.

Drive plate removal:

This procedure is applicable to automatic transmission models only. The car must be on a ramp or over a pit.

Remove the gearbox and torque converter as described in **Chapter 7, Section 7 : 5**. Refer to **FIG 1 : 30**. Remove the six bolts 3 which retain the plate 1 to the crankshaft 2. Remove the reinforcing plate 4. Dismount the drive plate 1 and the spacer 5.

Ring gear renewal:

An unserviceable ring gear may be removed and a new ring gear bolted to the drive plate. Torque tighten the ten retaining bolts.

Drive plate fitment:

Follow the reverse of the removal sequence. The chamfers on spacer 5 and plate 4 must both face the drive plate 1. The bolt holes are not symmetrical. Work diagonally when gradually tightening the retaining bolts. Finally torque tighten them to the same figure as for the flywheel.

1 : 15 Reassembling the engine

Assembly instructions are given in the text of each relevant section and chapter. These are largely the dismantling procedures in reverse but, as they may not always be so, the point should be checked against the information given in the text. It is then simply a matter of tackling the work in the logical sequence, of applying normal automobile engineering practice, fitting only Rover replacement parts, using new gaskets and joint washers and, preferably, fitting new oil seals.

Adopt the reverse of the dismantling sequence which was followed when fully or partially dismantling the

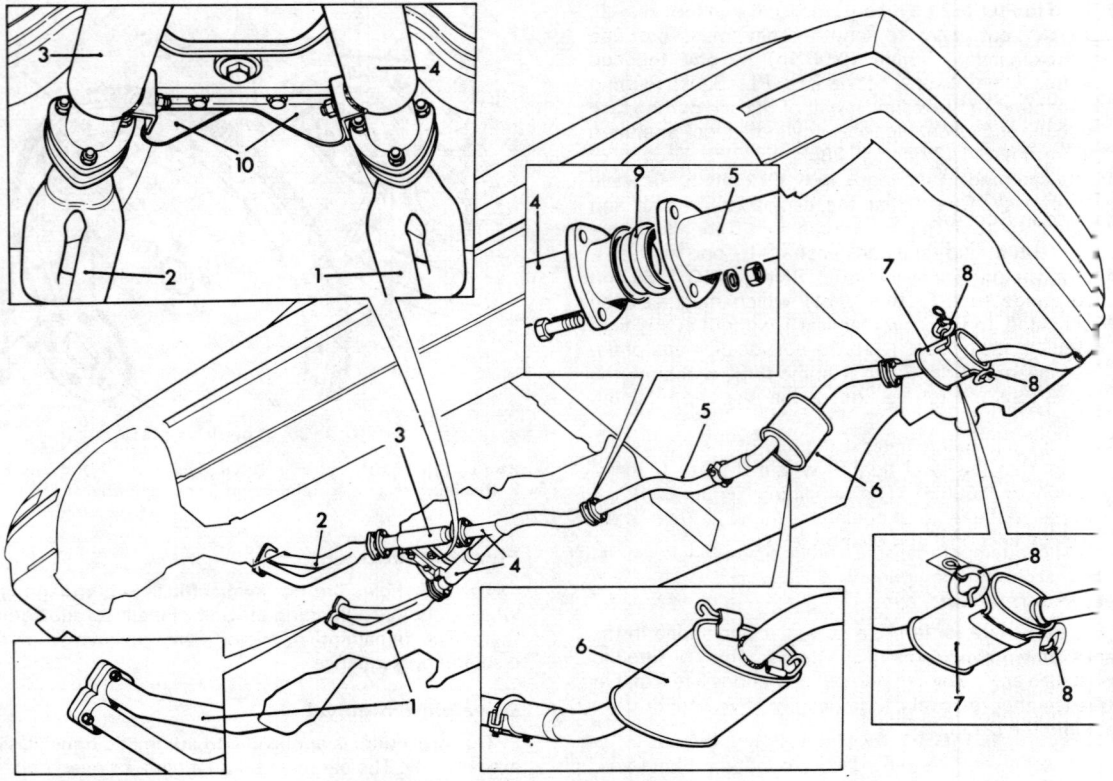

FIG 1:31   Layout of the exhaust system

Key to Fig 1:31   1 Front down pipe, righthand   2 Front down pipe, lefthand   3 Resonator, lefthand   4 Righthand resonator and branch pipe   5 Intermediate pipe   6 Intermediate silencer   7 Rear silencer   8 'O' ring   9 Olive   10 Cross-member bracket

engine but, to preclude the possibility of damage to the pistons and valve gear, **do not fit the rocker shafts until after the camshaft has been timed** by fitting its drive chain and chain wheels as described in **Section 1:8**.

Assemble working parts wetted with engine oil and use the specified (or equivalent) jointing compound where recommended in the text but assemble dry where indicated (the cylinder head gasket and the outside diameter of the crankshaft rear oil seal are examples). It is important to ensure that joints are well made as it may not be easily possible to rectify an oil leak which is not discovered until reassembly and installation of the engine and gearbox has been completed. For this reason also, scrutinise carefully the condition of oil seals and, even if their condition appears acceptable, recognise that it may be prudent to fit new.

At each stage of assembly check, where relevant, the free rotation of the assembly or component. Ensure that nuts and bolts are correctly tightened (refer to the **Technical Data** section of the **Appendix**) and, where applicable, properly locked. Recoupling pipes, hoses and electrical connections should not present any problem if they were properly identified before uncoupling. If identification has been lost, refer, in the case of electrical connections, to the wiring diagram **FIG 14:1** in the **Appendix**. Unidentified pipe connections will be more easily re-identified.

Have available the requisite quantities of lubricant(s) of the recommended type and of reputable brand. Capacities are listed in the **Appendix**.

1:16 The breather system

Refer to **Chapter 2, FIG 2:1**. Breather gases are drawn through the flame trap 3 on the righthand rocker cover and piped via hoses 4, 7 and 8 to be consumed by the engine. Filtered air is admitted to the rear of the lefthand rocker cover to maintain a balanced pressure. The breather system conforms to emission control requirements and, in countries where these requirements are mandatory, the system must be operational and correctly maintained

Filter renewal:

The filter is 1 in **Chapter 2, FIG 2:2**. Pull off the connecting hoses, discard the old filter and ensure that the new filter is fitted the correct way round with the end marked IN towards the rocker cover. The filter should be renewed every 12,000 miles (20,000km).

Flame trap:

Dismount the flame trap for cleaning by uncoupling the hose and unscrewing the unit from the rocker cover. Wash in petrol, dry thoroughly, refit and reconnect the hose. The flame trap should be cleaned every 12,000 miles (20,000km).

1:17 The exhaust system

Exhaust manifolds:

If a manifold has been separated from a cylinder head, use a new gasket on refitting. Fit new tab washers and torque tighten the retaining bolts. Do not bend up the tabs until the engine has been run up to operating temperature, allowed to cool and the retaining bolts retightened to the specified torque. Salvage of cylinder head threads is covered in **Section 1:6**.

Pipes and silencers:

The layout of the exhaust system is shown in **FIG 1:31**. If difficulty is experienced in dismantling, refer to 2 in **Hints on Maintenance and Overhaul** in the **Appendix**. Clean the olives. Discard spring washers which have lost their spring. Tighten joint flange nuts and bolts before tightening bracket nuts and bolts. Ensure that 'O' rings at body hooks are in good condition and renew those which may be of doubtful life. Check that the buffer (not shown in **FIG 1:31**) which is located on top of the rear silencer 7 is serviceable.

Do not attempt to salvage a holed pipe or silencer but fit a new section or component.

1:18 Mountings

The engine and gearbox as a unit is supported by two front mountings (see **FIG 1:32**) and a single bridge type mounting (see **FIGS 1:33** and **1:34**) at the rear of the gearbox. Flexibility is provided by bonded rubber parts.

Front mountings:

These are located forwards on each side of the engine. The bonded rubber unit 5 in **FIG 1:32** is bolted to engine bracket 7 and is connected with the chassis bracket 6 by two sets of bolts, washers and nuts 1, 2, 3 and 4. Removal of both bolts 1 on both sides allows the engine to be separated from the chassis. Removal of both bolts on one side only allows the engine to be tilted sufficiently to give clearance for the sump removal operations described in **Section 1:11**.

Rear mounting:

The components of the rear mounting are shown in **FIG 1:33**. To release the rear end of the gearbox from the mounting, loosen locknut 1 in **FIG 1:34** and back off bolt 2 until it becomes disengaged from the gearbox. Remove nuts and washers 3.

Bonded rubber components:

Renew rubber mounting components which show sign of bonding separation, cracking or perishing.

Refitment:

Reverse the separation sequence in each case. Note that a clearance of 5mm (0.2in) is required between the bridge and the centre rubber in **FIG 1:34**. Adjust, if necessary, by resetting the locknut 1.

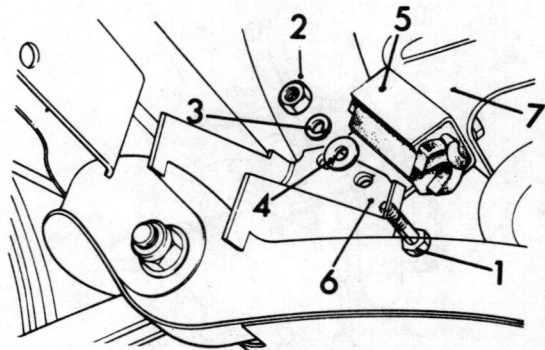

FIG 1:32   An engine front mounting

Key to Fig 1:32   1 Bolt   2 Nut   3 Spring washer
4 Washer   5 Bonded rubber mounting unit   6 Bracket
(chassis)   7 Bracket (engine)

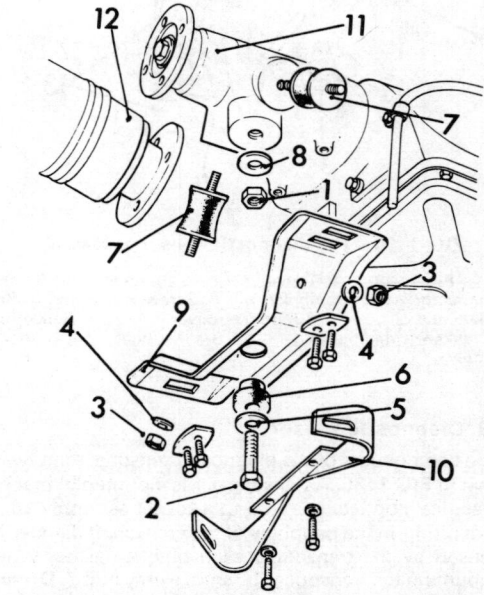

FIG 1:33   Components of the rear mounting

Key to Fig 1:33   1 Locknut   2 Bolt   3 Nut   4 Washer
5 Washer   6 Rubber buffer   7 Bonded rubber unit
8 Washer   9 Bridge bracket   10 Bracket   11 Gearbox
12 Propeller shaft

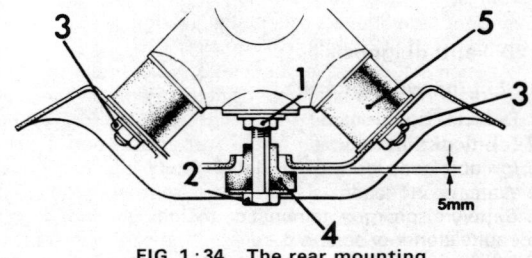

FIG 1:34   The rear mounting

Key to Fig 1:34   1 Locknut   2 Bolt   3 Nut   4 Rubber
buffer   5 Bonded rubber unit

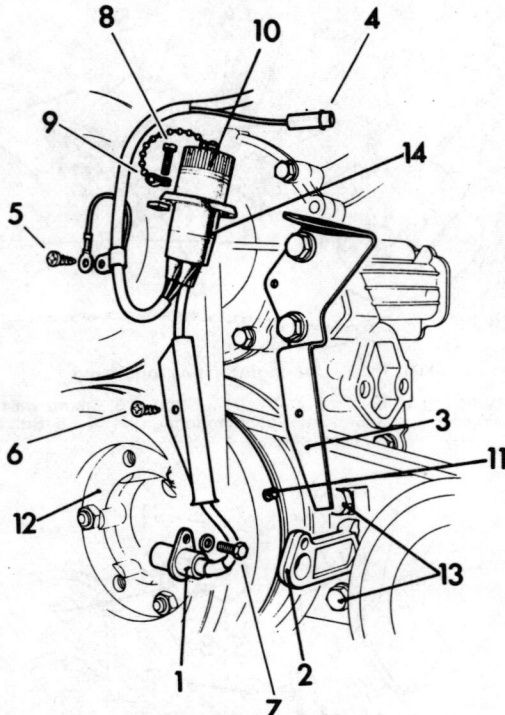

FIG 1:35   The diagnostic sensor assembly

Key to Fig 1:35   1 Transducer   2 Bracket   3 Bracket
4 Connector   5 Earthing screw   6 Screw   7 Bolt   8 Bolt
9 Chain and clip   10 Socket cover   11 Sensor pip
12 Crankshaft damper unit   13 Bracket bolts   14 Socket
assembly

1:19 Diagnostic sensor

The components of the diagnostic sensor assembly are
shown in **FIG 1:35**. A transducer 1 is mounted in bracket
2. Electrical connections lead to a socket assembly 14. A
sensor pip 11 in the periphery of the crankshaft damper 12
is sensed by the transducer each time it passes. When
dismounting the transducer 1, remove only bolt 7. **Do not
disturb the bracket bolts 13.**

Electronic diagnostic equipment may be plugged in to
socket 14. With the engine running, electronic information
from the transducer and from the distributor then indicates
precise ignition timing data and allows accurate
adjustment to be carried out (see **Chapter 3**).

1:20 Fault diagnosis

(a) Engine will not start

1 Defective ignition coil
2 Faulty distributor unit
3 Ignition leads loose or insulation faulty
4 Water on HT leads
5 Battery discharged, terminal corrosion
6 Faulty starter or solenoid
7 Sparking plug leads wrongly connected
8 Defective fuel pump
9 Defective carburetter choke

10 Blocked fuel filter
11 Blocked carburetter jet, seized needle piston
12 Valves leaking or sticking
13 Camshaft or ignition timing incorrect

(b) Engine stalls

1 Check 1, 2, 3, 4, 8, 10, 11 and 12 in (a)
2 Sparking plugs defective or gaps incorrect
3 Excessively retarded ignition
4 Mixture too weak
5 Water in fuel system
6 Fuel tank vent blocked
7 Seized tappet(s)

(c) Engine idles badly

1 Check 1 and 7 in (b)
2 Faulty carburetter/manifold joint
3 Carburetter adjustment incorrect
4 Mixture too rich
5 Worn piston rings
6 Worn valve stems or guides
7 Weak valve springs

(d) Engine misfires

1 Check 1, 2, 3, 4, 7, 8, 10, 11, 12, and 13 in (a)
2 Weak or broken valve springs

(e) Engine overheats (see **Chapter 4**)

(f) Compression pressure low

1 Check 12 in (a), 5 and 6 in (c) and 2 in (d)

(g) Engine lacks power

1 Check 3, 8, 11, 12 and 13 in (a), 2, 3, 4 and 7 in (b) 5
  and 6 in (c), 2 in (d) and check (f)
2 Leaking joint gasket
3 Dirty sparking plugs

(h) Burnt valves or seats

1 Check 12 in (a)
2 Excessive carbon deposits round valve seats

(j) Sticking valves

1 Check 7 in (b), 2 in (d)
2 Bent valve stem
3 Scored valve stem or guide

(k) Excessive cylinder wear

1 Check 9 in (a)
2 Lack of oil, dirty oil
3 Piston rings gummed up or broken
4 Connecting rod bent

(l) Excessive oil consumption

1 Check 5 and 6 in (c)
2 Oil level too high
3 External oil leaks

(m) Main or big-end bearing failure

1 Check 2 and 4 in (k)
2 Restricted oilways
3 Worn main journal or crankpin
4 Loose bearing cap(s)
5 Extremely low oil pressure

(n) Noise from hydraulic tappets

1 Oil too heavy for prevailing ambient temperature
2 Leakage at check ball
3 Worn tappet body or plunger
4 Worn camshaft

(o) Internal water leakage

1 Failed cylinder head gasket
2 Cracked cylinder head
3 Cracked cylinder block

(p) Poor coolant circulation (see **Chapter 4**)

(q) High fuel consumption (see **Chapter 2**)

(r) Engine vibration

1 Loose alternator or power steering pump
2 Engine mounting(s) loose or defective
3 Misfiring due to mixture, ignition or mechanical fault
4 Faulty crankshaft damper

NOTES

CHAPTER 2
THE FUEL SYSTEM

2:1 Description

An electrically operated pump is submerged in the fuel tank. It draws fuel through a gauze strainer. Pressure fuel is delivered to the carburetters via an in-line disposable filter mounted adjacent to the lefthand carburetter. The fuel tank contents gauge is operated electronically from a float and arm type transmitter in the tank.

Refer to **FIG 2:1**. Exhaust manifold heated air is ducted to the air temperature control valve 5 via duct 9. Cold air is ducted to the control valve via duct 10. Air of thermostatically controlled temperature is supplied to the centre of the air cleaner canister 16. Air flows left and right through individual cleaner elements and via duct elbows 2 to the lefthand and righthand carburetters 14 and 15 respectively.

The layout of the system with the air control valve and the air cleaner removed is shown in **FIG 2:2**. Each of the side-draught SU carburetters serves one bank of cylinders. It will be noted that the choke and throttle controls both of which are Bowden type cable controls are directly connected with the lefthand carburetter. The righthand carburetter is controlled by linkage rods from the lefthand unit.

Associated with the induction system are the breather pipes, float chamber vent pipes, brake servo and ignition distributor vacuum pipes. Note also that the illustration shows the location of the breather system air inlet filter 1.

The induction manifold is heated by the cooling system coolant and is connected with the radiator via 15 in **FIG 2:2** (the hose connection is 13 in **FIG 2:1**), with the car heater via pipes 14 and, via ports, with the cylinder heads. The induction manifold gasket encloses the cylinder block between the two banks of cylinders.

The SU HIF-6 carburetters are variable area choke units in which the choke area is formed by the carburetter body and a piston which rises and falls automatically depending upon the depression in the induction system as controlled by the throttle openings and the engine load. To maintain suitable fuel/air mixture in the varying volume of intake air, a tapered jet needle attached to the piston rises and falls in the orifice of the fuel jet. The smallest diameter of the needle is in the orifice when the piston is at the top of its travel and the jet 'size' is then a maximum. The smallest jet 'size' is when the piston is at the bottom of its travel. Rapid fluctuations of the piston are prevented by an oil filled hydraulic damper above the choke piston. When correctly

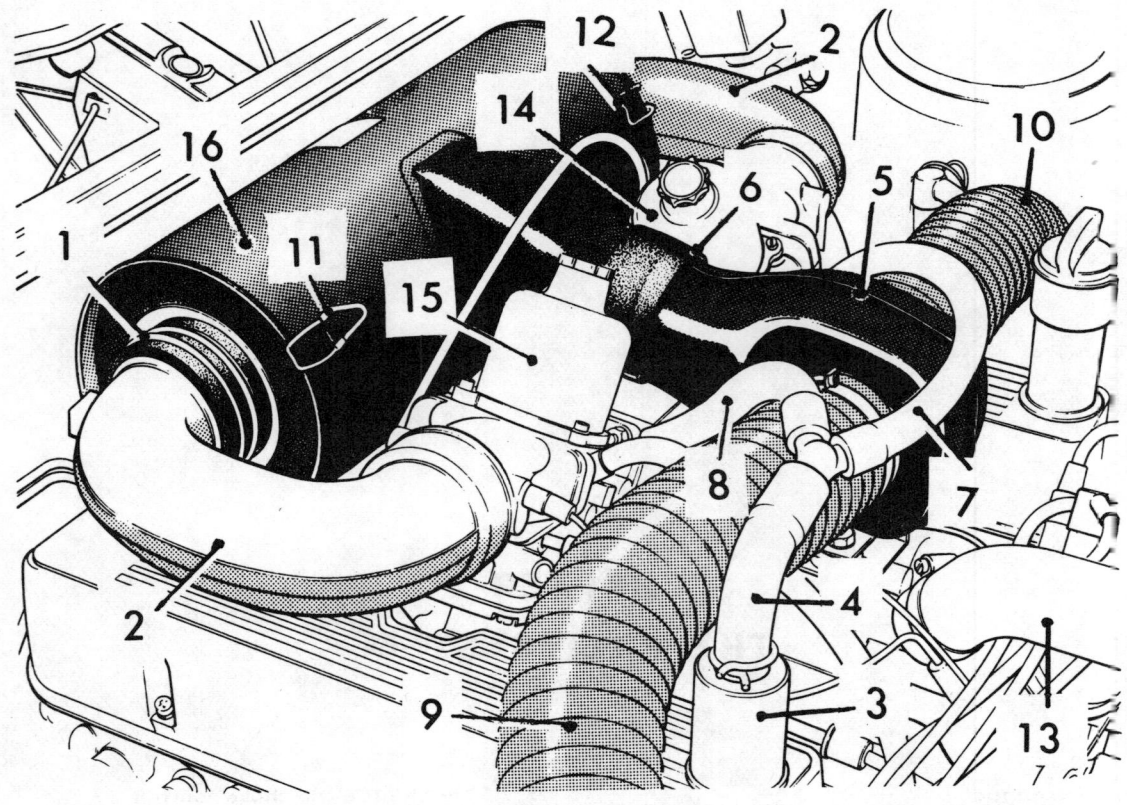

FIG 2:1 The induction system

Key to Fig 2:1 1 Elbow/cover joint sleeve   2 Cleaner/carburetter elbow   3 Breather system flame trap   4 Breather pipe   5 Air temperature control valve   6 Valve/cleaner joint sleeve   7 and 8 Breather pipes   9 Warm air duct   10 Cold air duct   11 Righthand clip   12 Lefthand clip   13 Manifold coolant hose   14 Lefthand carburetter   15 Righthand carburetter   16 Air cleaner canister

adjusted, the carburetters conform to emission control requirements. It should be noted in this connection that the basic setting of the position of the fuel jet is critical and, to preclude improper resetting, the adjuster is sealed off. Cold starting enrichment is selected manually.

The components of a righthand carburetter are shown in **FIG 2:3**.

2:2 Maintenance

Controls:

Lubricate the throttle control pivots (including those of the foot pedal) every 6000 miles (10,000km). Check the condition of the Bowden type cables at regular intervals and adjust if necessary as described in **Section 2:7**.

Carburetter piston dampers:

Every 6000 miles (10,000km), check the level of the oil in the dampers and top up if necessary. The procedure is as follows.

Refer to **FIG 2:3**. Unscrew the cap 1 on each carburetter. Lift the piston dampers to the top of their travel. Fill the retainer recess with SAE 20 oil and push the damper down until the cap touches the top of the suction chamber 3. Repeat this sequence as necessary until oil is just visible at the bottom of the retainer recess with the piston down as shown in **FIG 2:4**. If a retainer is inadvertently displaced it should be refitted by pressing fully into the piston rod. Finally screw down the caps firmly.

Air cleaner:

Every 12,000 miles (20,000km), renew the air cleaner elements as described in **Section 2:3**.

Fuel filter:

Every 12,000 miles (20,000km), renew the in-line fuel filter as described in **Section 2:5**.

2:3 The air cleaner

The air cleaner is 16 in **FIG 2:1**. Air from the temperature control valve 5 enters the cleaner canister via joint sleeve 6 and passes left and right through separate cleaner elements to elbows 2 which lead filtered air to the carburetters 14 and 15. An outlet at the rear of the canister supplies unfiltered air to the breather system air filter 1 in **FIG 2:2**.

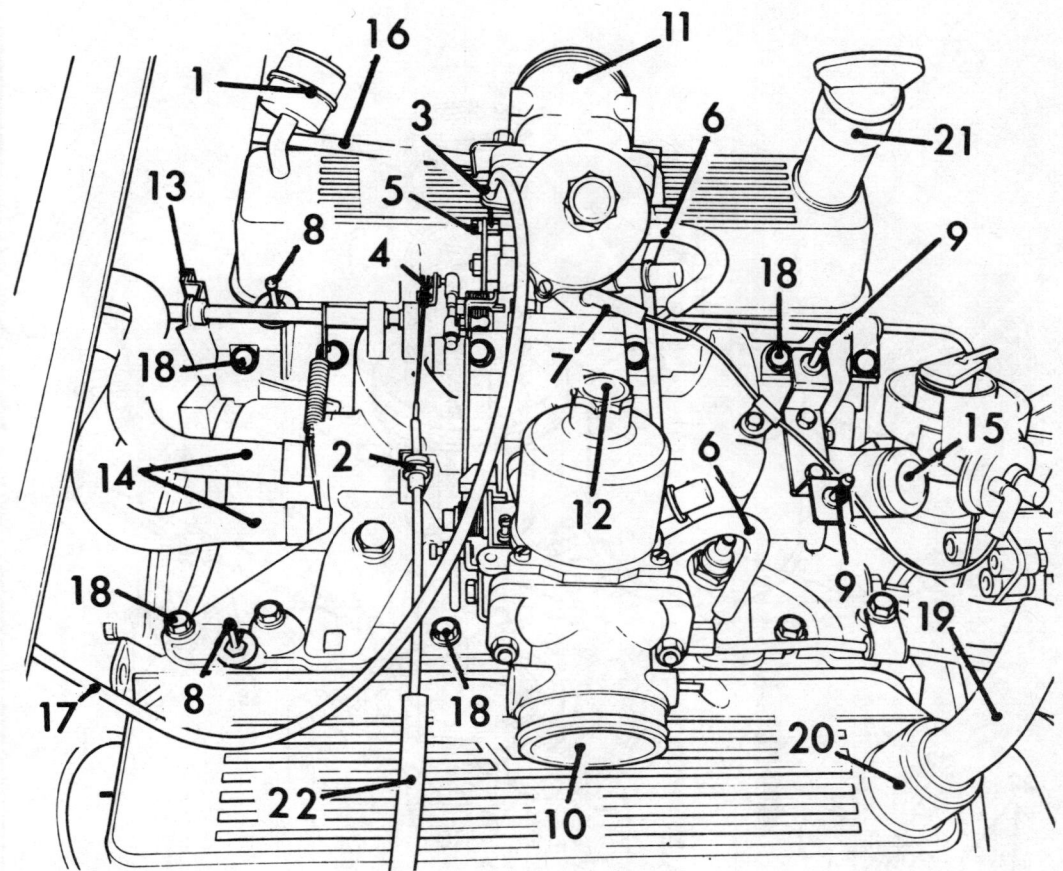

FIG 2:2   The manifold and carburetters

Key to Fig 2:2   1 Breather system air filter   2 Throttle control adjuster   3 Choke control anchor   4 Throttle control quadrant   5 Choke control adjuster   6 Vent pipe   7 Distributor vacuum pipe   8 Location peg   9 Location peg   10 Right-hand carburetter adaptor   11 Lefthand carburetter adaptor   12 Damper cap   13 Downshift bracket   14 Heater pipes   15 Coolant pipe   16 Fuel feed pipe   17 Choke control cable   18 Manifold retaining bolts   19 Breather pipe   20 Flame trap   21 Oil filler cap   22 Throttle control cable

Element renewal:

Both lefthand and righthand elements should be renewed every 12,000 miles (20,000km). The procedure is as follows.

1 Refer to **FIG 2:5**. Release clips 1 which retain the end covers 3. Remove the hose from the breather filter 1 in **FIG 2:2** on the lefthand side by disconnecting it from the filter and from the rear of the canister.

2 Withdraw the elbows 2 (see **FIG 2:5**) from the carburetters and remove them complete with the end covers 3 and elements 6.

3 Remove the element retaining screws 4, plates 5 and the elements. Discard the elements. Remove the sealing washers 7. Clean the end covers and the canister.

4 Using new elements, reverse operation 3 and assemble the elements to the end cover units. Check that the 'O' rings 9 are in good condition. Refit the end cover units to the carburetters and to the canister. Check that the covers are correctly seated. Fasten the clips.

Cleaner removal:

1 Carry out operations 1 and 2 of the element renewal procedure described earlier and dismount the end cover/elbow units.

2 Lift the air temperature control valve 5 in **FIG 2:1** off its location pegs (these are 9 in **FIG 2:2**) and move the valve forwards towards the radiator.

3 Move the valve sufficiently to allow the air cleaner to be lifted off its location pegs (these are 8 in **FIG 2:2**) and withdrawn from the control valve joint sleeve 6 in **FIG 2:1**.

Cleaner fitment:

Renew the elements as described earlier if they are at or are approaching their service life. Refer to **FIG 2:5** and check the condition of the 'O' rings 9. Check the condition of the joint sleeves 10 and that their clips are secure. Clean the canister and check that the cleaner to air valve joint sleeve 6 in **FIG 2:1** is in good condition.

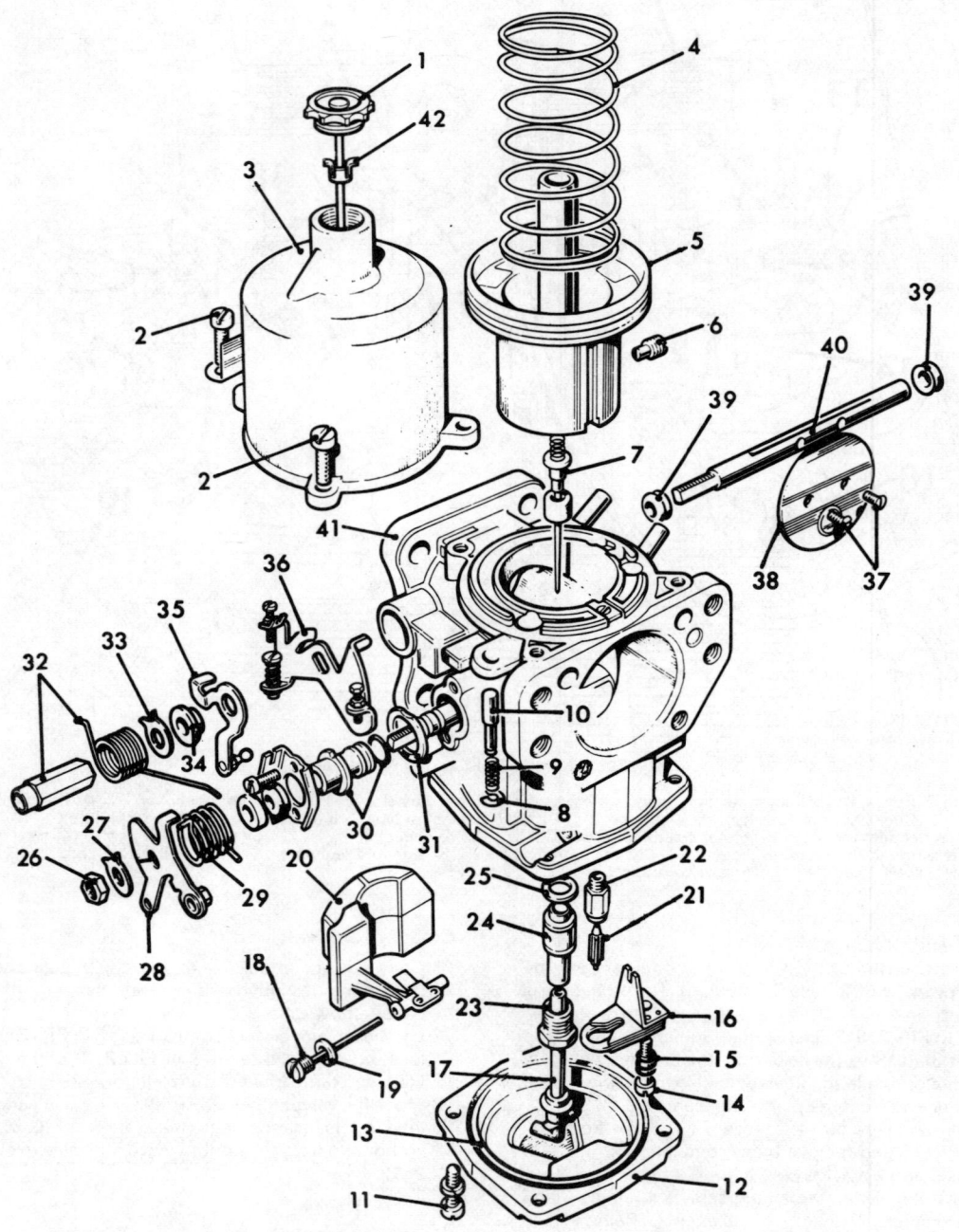

FIG 2:3   Components of an SU HIF-6 carburetter (righthand shown)

Key to Fig 2:3   1 Damper cap   2 Screw   3 Suction chamber   4 Spring   5 Piston   6 Needle locking screw   7 Needle assembly   8 Circlip   9 Spring   10 Piston lifting pin   11 Screw   12 Bottom cover plate   13 Sealing ring   14 Screw   15 Spring   16 Bi-metal blade   17 Jet   18 Float spindle   19 Sealing washer   20 Float   21 Needle valve   22 Valve seat   23 Jet bearing locking nut   24 Jet bearing   25 Sealing washer   26 Nut   27 Tab washer   28 Cam lever   29 Spring   30 Cold start valve and 'O' ring   31 Gasket   32 Nut and spring   33 Tab washer   34 Sleeve   35 Throttle lever   36 Stop lever   37 Screws   38 Butterfly valve   39 Seals   40 Throttle spindle   41 Body   42 Retainer

Refitment of the cleaner is now the reverse of the removal sequence. Do not omit to reconnect the pipe between the cleaner canister and the breather system air filter.

2:4 The air temperature control valve

The control valve is 5 in **FIG 2:1**. Cold air from a forward facing duct leads ambient air to the lefthand entry to the valve. The upper section of this duct is 10. Warm air which is heated by the righthand exhaust manifold is ducted to the righthand entry to the valve. The upper section of this duct is 9. The air temperature control valve thermostatically mixes cold and warm air from these ducts and delivers air of approximately constant temperature to the air cleaner canister 16 via valve outlet 6. Satisfactory control of the CO content of the exhaust gases is assisted by this substantially constant temperature air supply to the carburetters.

A cross-section through the control valve is shown in **FIG 2:6**. The valve shutter **E** can close off either the cold air entry **A** or the warm air entry **B** or can take up an intermediate position as dictated by the bi-metal control **F** which is directly in the flow of the air being delivered via exit **C** to the filter canister.

A defective control valve cannot be repaired by an owner and should be removed and a new unit fitted.

Function test:

1 Inspect the condition and security of the warm and cold inlet ducts. Disconnect the cold air entry duct **A** and check that the valve shutter is in the warm air position (entry **A** blanked off).
2 Reconnect the cold air entry duct. Start the engine and run until normal operating temperature is reached. Quickly disconnect the warm air entry duct **B** and check that the valve shutter is now blanked off.
3 If this is so, reconnect the warm air duct. If it is not, remove the control valve assembly as described later and fit a replacement unit.

Valve removal and fitment:

Uncouple the warm and cold ducts 9 and 10 in **FIG 2:1** from the valve and move them aside. Disconnect the breather pipes 7 and 8. Lift the control valve off its locating pegs (these are 9 in **FIG 2:2**), pull it forwards to disengage its outlet 6 in **FIG 2:1** from the air cleaner canister inlet and dismount the valve assembly.

Fitment is this sequence in reverse.

Warm air chamber:

The air heating chamber is shown in **FIG 2:7**. Ambient air is drawn across the exhaust manifold and passes via the space enclosed by the back plate 4 and the cover 3 to duct 1. This duct leads to the temperature control valve and is the lower section of 9 in **FIG 2:1**. To remove the chamber, refer to **FIG 2:7**, loosen clip 6, uncouple duct 1 from the cover 3, remove bolt 2 and dismount the cover. If necessary, dismount the back plate 4 after removing the retaining bolts 5.

Fitment is the reverse of this sequence.

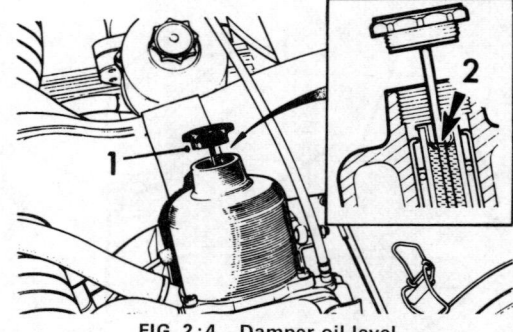

FIG 2:4 Damper oil level

Key to Fig 2:4   1 Cap   2 The oil level is arrowed

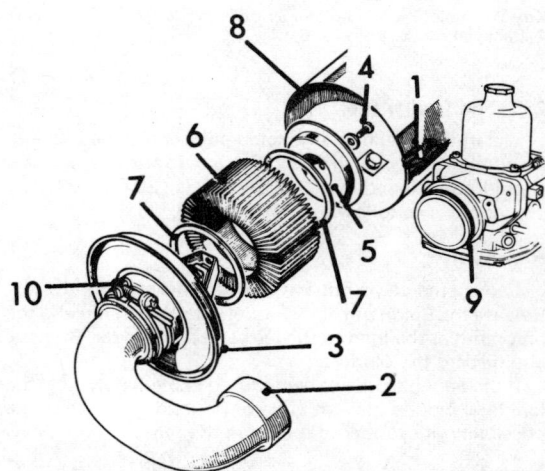

FIG 2:5 Renewing the air cleaner elements

Key to Fig 2:5   1 Clip   2 Elbow   3 Cover   4 Screw   5 Retaining plate   6 Element   7 Sealing washer   8 Canister   9 'O' ring   10 Clip and sleeve

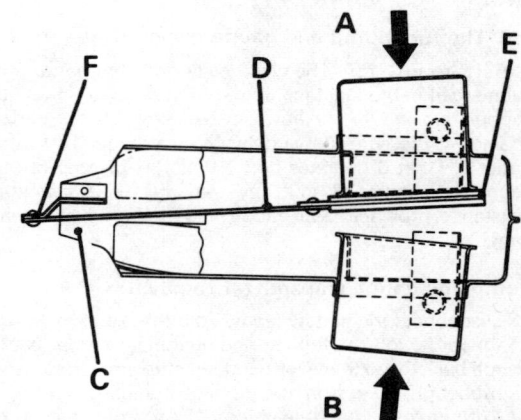

FIG 2:6 A cross-section through the air temperature control valve

Key to Fig 2:6   A Cold air entry   B Warm air entry   C Air exit to cleaner   D Arm   E Valve   F Bi-metal strip

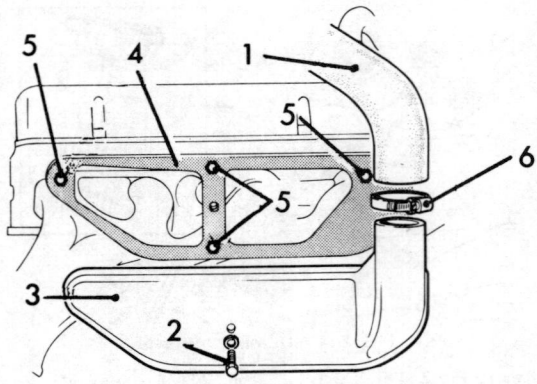

FIG 2:7   Air heater chamber

Key to Fig 2:7   1 Warm air duct   2 Bolt   3 Cover
4 Backplate   5 Bolts   6 Clip

2:5 The fuel filter

The in-line fuel filter is located adjacent to the lefthand carburetter as shown in **FIG 2:8**. It is a disposable type and should be renewed every 12,000 miles (20,000km). The procedure is as follows.

Removal:

Loosen the union nut 1 at the fuel inlet side of the filter. Release the union nut at the outlet side of the filter and the union nut at the inlet to the lefthand carburetter. Remove and discard the old filter.

If the new filter is not being fitted immediately, seal the fuel feed pipe to prevent entry of dirt and to preclude the possibility of syphoning fuel from the tank.

Refitting:

Reverse the removal sequence. Ensure that the filter is fitted the correct way round with the IN end towards the feed pipe from the tank (union nut 1). Run the engine and check that there are no leaks.

2:6 The fuel pump and gauge transmitter

Refer to **FIG 2:9**. The electrically operated pump 3 is submerged in the fuel tank. It is shown separated from its support bracket 11. It draws in fuel through the gauze strainer 4. Pressure fuel is delivered via elbow 13 to the outlet 2. Float 6 operates arm 7 which is pivoted at the gauge transmitter 8 and, by varying the transmitter resistance, provides a fuel gauge reading at the instrument panel.

Pump and gauge transmitter removal:

1 Disconnect the battery leads. Fold the rear seat squab forwards, roll the luggage compartment carpet back, roll back the extreme lefthand felt strip and remove the rubber grommet from the luggage compartment floor.
2 Withdraw the multi-lead connector from socket 1, uncouple the pipe outlet 2, remove the six screws which retain flange 5 to the fuel tank and withdraw the pump and gauge transmitter unit. Remove and discard gasket 10.

3 Release the pump 3 from the support bracket 11. Release the spring clip 12 and withdraw the pump from the elbow 13. Remove the terminal cover 14. Identify and disconnect the two electrical leads.

No procedures are prescribed for the repair or overhaul of a pump by an owner and a defective pump should be replaced by a new unit. Similarly, no procedures are prescribed for the repair of a gauge transmitter and, if the unit is defective, the whole assembly (less the fuel pump) must be renewed.

Pump and gauge transmitter refitment:

Refitment is the reverse of the removal sequence. The pump electrical leads must be correctly reconnected with black to negative(—) and red to positive (+). Clean the lower side of the flange 5 and its mating face on the tank. Fit a new gasket. On completion of refitment, check the operation noting the following points.

Electrical supply to the pump:

The electrical supply for the pump is taken from the starter motor solenoid or via the engine oil pressure switch (1 in **Chapter 1, FIG 1:17**). The pump will only operate while the engine is being turned by the starter motor or while the engine is running with sufficient oil pressure to close the oil pressure switch contacts. Check that there is voltage at the multi-lead connector under both conditions before suspecting that the pump is defective.

2:7 The throttle and choke controls

Both controls are Bowden type cable units. Both act directly on the lefthand carburetter with interconnecting linkages to the righthand carburetter.

Throttle cable adjustment:

A trunnion on the end of the inner cable engages with a slot in the extension to the foot pedal lever. A similar trunnion 11 in **FIG 2:10** engages with the carburetter control. Adjustment is made at adjuster 2. Access requires removal of the air cleaner as described in **Section 2:3**. Adjust as necessary to remove slackness of the inner cable 3 but avoid introducing tension.

Throttle control removal:

1 Remove the air cleaner as described in **Section 2:3**. Release the adjuster 2 from its bracket. Release the cable trunnion 11 from the quadrant.
2 Refer to **Chapter 13, Section 13:10** and remove the glovebox. Release the cable trunnion from the pedal arm extension. Pull the cable through the bulkhead into the engine bay. Remove the grommet from the bulkhead.

Throttle control fitment:

Fit the grommet to the bulkhead with the sleeve end into the engine bay. Grease the accessible ends of the inner cable. Feed the cable through from the engine bay (grease the outer cable to facilitate this) and couple the trunnion to the foot control arm. Couple the other trunnion to the quadrant and engage the adjuster with its bracket. Adjust the cable as described earlier. Refit the glovebox and the air cleaner.

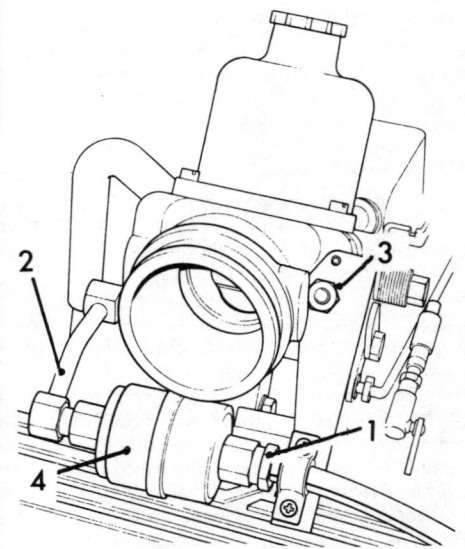

FIG 2:8   The in-line fuel filter

Key to Fig 2:8   1 Inlet union   **2** Delivery pipe   **3** Bracket
4 Filter

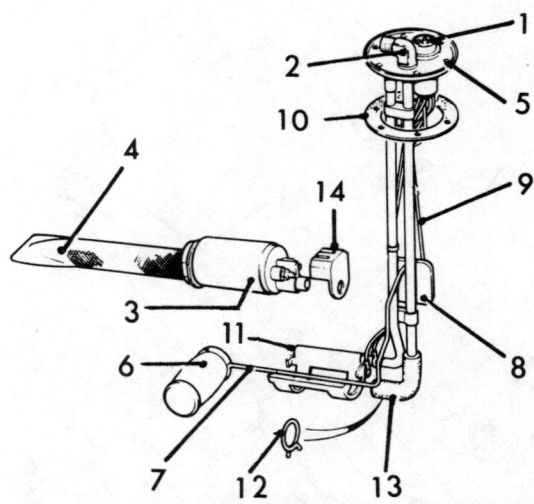

FIG 2:9   The fuel pump and gauge transmitter

Key to Fig 2:9   1 Multi-lead socket   **2** Fuel outlet
3 Pump   **4** Strainer   **5** Flange   **6** Float   **7** Float arm
8 Transmitter   **9** Transmitter leads   **10** Gasket   **11** Bracket
12 Clip   **13** Elbow   **14** Terminal cover

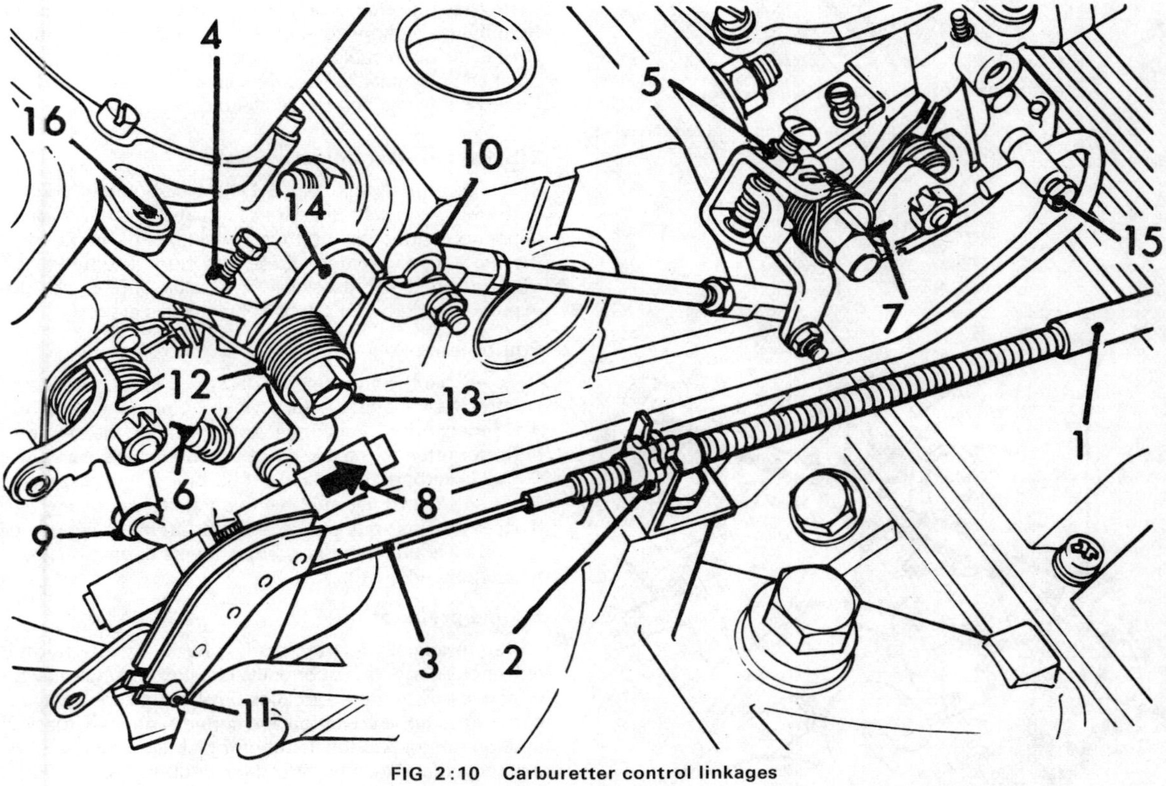

FIG 2:10   Carburetter control linkages

Key to Fig 2:10   1 Throttle control cable   **2** Throttle adjuster   **3** Throttle inner cable   **4** Idle adjusting screw   **5** Lost
motion adjusting screw   **6** Scribed mark (lefthand)   **7** Scribed mark (righthand)   **8** Countershaft link   **9** Choke connecting
rod   **10** Throttle link rod   **11** Throttle cable trunnion   **12** Throttle lever spring   **13** Retaining nut   **14** Throttle lever
15 Choke connecting rod bolt   **16** Choke anchor and connecting points (choke control removed)

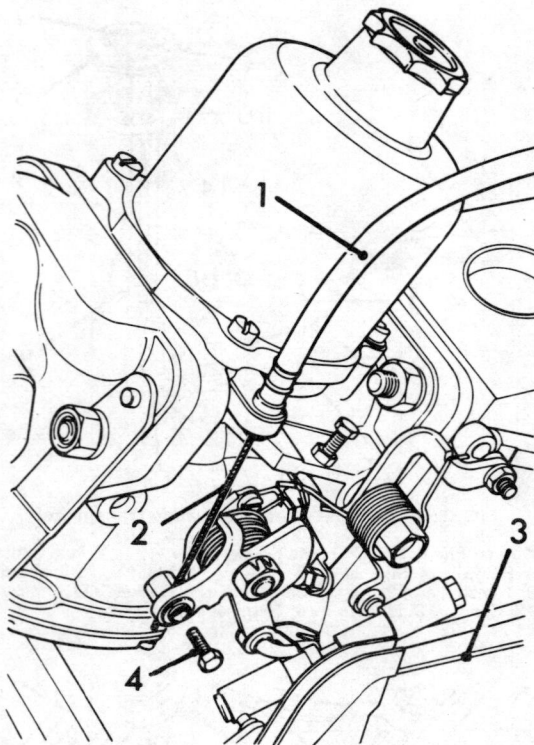

FIG 2:11 Choke control adjustment

Key to Fig 2:11 1 Control cable   2 Inner cable (choke)
3 Inner cable (throttle) 4 Bolt

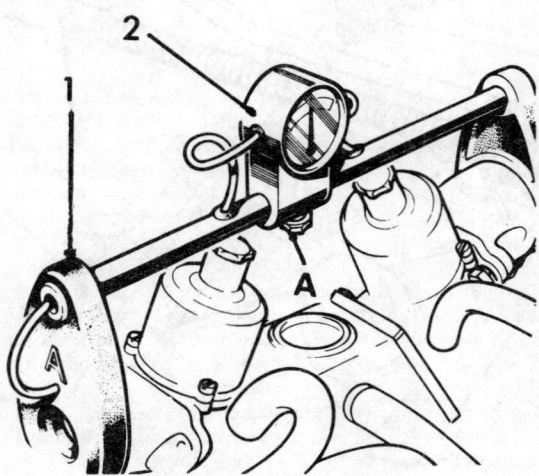

FIG 2:12 Balancer tool fitted to the carburetters

Key to Fig 2:12 1 Tool 605330   2 Gauge   A Gauge
zero adjuster

Choke control adjustment:

Adjustment is made by loosening bolt 4 in **FIG 2:11**, repositioning the inner cable 2 as necessary and retightening bolt 4. For access, carry out removal operations 1 and 2 as necessary.

Choke control removal:

1 Dismount the breather system filter 1 in **FIG 2:2** as described in **Chapter 1, Section 1:16**. Refer to **Section 2:3** and dismount the lefthand air cleaner to carburetter elbow 2 in **FIG 2:1**.
2 Remove the nut securing the fuel pipe to the lefthand carburetter and slide the bracket along the pipe to give access to the bolt 4 in **FIG 2:11**. Release this bolt. Remove the cable retaining clip.
3 Refer to **Chapter 13, Section 13:10** and remove the glovebox. Refer to **Chapter 6, FIG 6:11**, prise out panel 3 from the console 11, remove the screw which retains the choke control lever assembly and remove the clip 8 retaining the inner cable rod 10. Identify and disconnect the electrical leads 12.
4 Remove the console as described in **Chapter 13, Section 13:10**. Grease the outer cable to facilitate its passage through the bulkhead grommet and withdraw the cable assembly towards the inside of the car.

Choke control fitment:

Reverse the removal sequence. Separate the inner cable from the outer, apply grease to the inner and reassemble. Grease the outer cable to facilitate its passage through the bulkhead grommet. Adjust the cable as described earlier. Refit the console and the glovebox.

2:8 Carburetter adjustments

When correctly adjusted, SU HIF-6 carburetters comply with EEC exhaust emission regulation 15. To deter tampering with critical settings, sealing caps are fitted to the idle adjusting screws and sealing plugs are fitted to the mixture adjuster recesses. The seals fitted by the manufacturer are blue. Replacement seals are red.

Equipment:

To enable the adjustments described in this section to be effectively made, the following equipment is required. An independent, accurate tachometer (the rev min indicator fitted to the car is not suitable), special spanner 605927, carburetter balancer 605330, a non-dispersive infra-red exhaust gas analyser and a portable cooling fan. If access to this equipment cannot be arranged, an owner should have any necessary adjustments carried out by a fully equipped agent.

Engine preparation:

Before adjustments are made, check that the throttle and choke controls are correctly adjusted and that they do not have any tendency to stick. Ensure that the sparking plugs are in good condition and correctly gapped, that the ignition timing and the distributor pick-up air gap are set correctly, that the carburetter damper oil levels are topped up, that the engine has been warmed up to normal operating temperature and, on automatic transmission models, the downshift cable setting is correct (see **Chapter 7, Section 7:4**). The downshift cable setting must be rechecked after any adjustment has been made to the carburetter linkage. Remove the air cleaner as described in **Section 2:3**.

The ambient air temperature should, if possible, be between 15° and 26°C (60° and 80°F).

Idle speed adjustment:

With the engine warm and prepared as described earlier, refer to **FIG 2:10** and disconnect the countershaft link rod from the lefthand carburetter by sliding the sleeve 8 in the direction of the arrow. Loosen the lost motion adjusting locknut 5 on the righthand carburetter and turn the screw well clear of the spring-loaded pad. Using special spanner 605927, loosen the idle adjusting screw locknut 4 on both carburetters. Run the engine and adjust both idle screws by equal amounts to give an idle speed of 725 to 775 rev/min on the independent tachometer. Tighten both locknuts and recheck the idling speed. Proceed to the fast-idle adjustment procedure.

Fast-idle speed adjustment:

Operate the console choke control until the scribed mark 6 in **FIG 2:10** on the lefthand carburetter fast-idle cam is aligned with the centreline of the fast-idle adjusting screw as shown in the illustration. Check that the righthand scribed line 7 is also aligned with its fast-idle adjusting screw. If there is a misalignment, correct by loosening bolt 15 on the righthand carburetter and rotating the cam assembly until alignment is achieved. Retighten bolt 15. Using special spanner 605927, loosen the fast-idle adjustment screw locknut on both carburetters. Run the engine and adjust both screws by equal amounts to give a fast-idle speed of 1100 to 1200 rev/min on the independent tachometer. Tighten the locknuts and recheck the fast-idle speed. Close the choke control and proceed to the carburetter synchronisation procedure.

Synchronising the carburetters:

Fit the balancer 605330 as shown in **FIG 2:12** with the gauge facing forwards. If necessary, zero the gauge pointer by means of adjuster **A**. Run the engine at idle speed. If the gauge pointer is in the zero sector, no adjustment is required. If the pointer has moved to the right, decrease the air flow through the lefthand carburetter or increase the air flow through the righthand carburetter by means of the relevant idle speed screw. If the pointer has moved to the left, reverse the adjustment. Keep the idling speed within the range of 725 to 775 rev/min by appropriate adjustments to the idling screws. When correctly synchronised, the idle speed will be within the specified range and the gauge reading will be in the zero sector. Note that, on dismounting the balancer, the idle speed will alter by approximately ± 25 rev/min. Proceed now to reset the lost motion screw which was unlocked at the beginning of the idling speed adjustment sequence.

Relocking the lost motion screw:

Hold the lefthand carburetter lever firmly against its idling screw. Screw down the lost motion screw on the righthand carburetter until it just touches the spring-loaded pad. Tighten locknut 5 (see **FIG 2:10**). Proceed to measure the CO level in the exhaust gases.

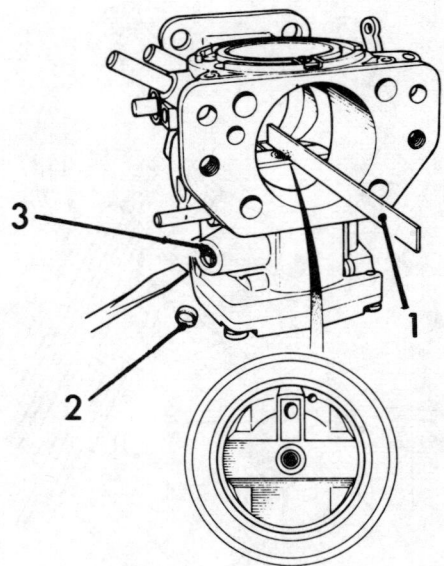

FIG 2:13 Setting the jet

Key to Fig 2:13   1 Straightedge   2 Blanking plug
3 Adjusting screw

CO level measurement:

Use a non-dispersive infra-red exhaust gas analyser with its probe inserted as far as possible up the tail pipe. Start the engine and allow a few minutes stablising period. Maintain the idle speed at 725 to 775 rev/min and, following the equipment manufacturer's instructions, record the CO content. This should be between 3 per cent and 4.5 per cent. If the CO content is outside this range, proceed to adjust the mixture setting.

Mixture adjustment:

A portable cooling fan in front of the car must, for effectively carrying out this procedure, maintain a reasonable air flow through the engine bay.

With the engine warm, remove the intake adaptors 10 and 11 in **FIG 2:2** from the carburetters. Refer to **FIG 2:13** and remove the mixture screw recess plugs 2. Mark the relationship of the suction chambers and the carburetter bodies (3 and 41 in **FIG 2:3**), remove the three retaining screws and, being careful not to tilt the chambers, lift them off complete with their piston/needle assemblies.

Set the mixture adjusting screws 3 in **FIG 2:13** by turning them anti-clockwise until the jets are level with the choke bridge as indicated by using a straightedge 1 as shown in the illustration. Align and refit the suction chamber/piston assemblies. Turn each mixture adjuster screw clockwise by two and one-half turns.

Measure the CO content as described earlier. If necessary, adjust each adjuster screw by equal amounts until the CO content is between 3 per cent and 4.5 per cent at an idling speed of between 725 and 775 rev/min.

Fit new sealing plugs to the adjuster recesses. Fit new caps to the idle adjustment screws. Refit the adaptors and the air cleaner.

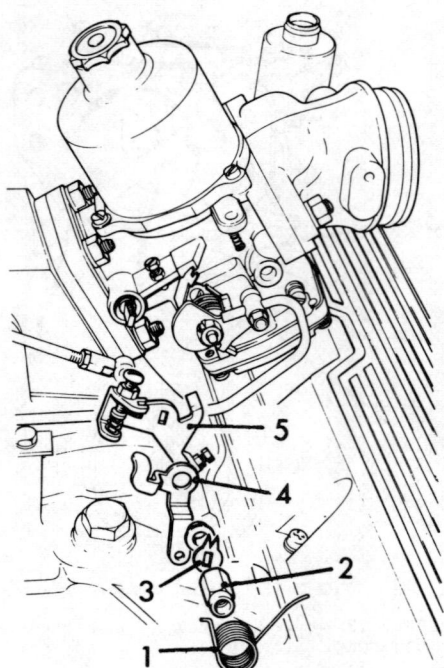

FIG 2:14   Throttle lever components

Key to Fig 2:14   1 Spring   2 Nut   3 Tabwasher
4 Throttle lever   5 Stop lever

Difficulties in adjustment:

Carburetters with worn pistons or suction chambers, worn butterfly valves, spindles and seals, worn linkage joints, weak springs or other damage cannot be correctly adjusted. Such carburetters should be overhauled as described in **Section 2:9** or new carburetters should be fitted.

2:9 The carburetters
Carburetter removal:

Since the throttle and choke controls operate directly on the lefthand carburetter with interconnecting links only to the righthand carburetter, the removal operations are not identical for lefthand and righthand units. When working to the following procedure it will be evident that some operations are relevant to the lefthand or to the righthand carburetter and some are common to both.

1 Remove the air cleaner and air temperature control valve as described in **Sections 2:3** and **2:4**. Refer to **FIG 2:2**. Disconnect the choke and throttle controls 3 and 4 from the lefthand carburetter. Uncouple the throttle and choke link rods with the righthand unit.

2 Remove the fuel feed pipe 16 from between the filter and the two carburetters. Disconnect the brake servo pipe. Pull off the vent pipe 6 and the distributor vacuum pipe 7. Refer now to **FIG 2:10** and disconnect the countershaft link by sliding the sleeve 8 in the direction of the arrow.

3 Access requires the following on a lefthand carburetter: remove the throttle lever spring 12, untab and remove the throttle lever retaining nut 13 and

withdraw the throttle lever 14. Access requires the following on a righthand carburetter: refer to **FIG 2:14** and remove spring 1. Untab 3 and remove nut 2, actuating lever 4 and stop lever 5.

4 Remove the four nuts and spring washers and withdraw the carburetter from its studs. Note their relative positions and remove the gaskets, liner and insulator.

Carburetter refitment:

Do not use jointing compound. Ensure that the liner lugs locate correctly. Follow the reverse of the removal sequence. Adjust the throttle and choke controls as described in **Section 2:7**. Top up the oil in the damper wells as described in **Section 2:2** and, in the case of automatic transmission models, refer to **Chapter 7, Section 7:4** and check the downshift cable setting. Subject to access to the necessary equipment, adjust and synchronise the carburetters as described in **Section 2:8**. If access to this equipment cannot be arranged, have the adjustments carried out by a fully equipped agent.

Carburetter dismantling:

Unless an owner has appropriate experience of carburetter work, the overhaul of the carburetters is best entrusted to a competent agent. The following notes will assist those who have the necessary experience.

Refer to **FIG 2:3** and dismantle by following the sequence in which the components are numbered. Mark the relationship of the suction chamber 3 and of the bottom cover plate 12 with the carburetter body 41 so that they may be refitted in their original positions. To preclude jamming with the piston 5, do not tilt the suction chamber 3 when removing it. Be careful not to bend the jet needle. **Do not disturb the mixture adjusting screw** (3 in **FIG 2:13** but not shown in **FIG 2:3**) **without referring to Section 2:8**. Discard old seals and gaskets.

Inspection:

Reject worn and damaged parts, weak springs and worn linkage parts. If the suction chamber and piston appear to be serviceable, check that all the balls are in both piston races (six balls in each). Fit the piston to the chamber without spring 4, hold it horizontally and check that the piston will spin freely. Renew a worn or bent needle 7. Renew the float needle valve 21 and needle valve seat 22 if there has been any suspicion of flooding. It will be prudent to renew the cold start 'O' ring 30 and, possibly, the sealing ring 13 also. Check the fit of the butterfly valve 38 in the carburetter body.

Reassembly:

Reverse the dismantling sequence. Use new seals and gaskets. Do not use jointing compound. After fitting the float 20, invert the assembly and, using a straightedge across the body face, check that the float ridge is 1.0 ± 0.5mm (0.04 ± 0.02in) below the face. If necessary, adjust by bending the hinge tab to achieve this dimension. The seals 39 should be 0.9mm (0.035in) below the level of the spindle housing flanges. Ensure that the cutouts in the cold start valve 30 and in the gasket 3 are aligned. Filling the damper wells with SAE 20 oil is best left until the carburetter has been refitted to the manifold. The procedure is given in **Section 2:2**.

2:10 The induction manifold

Removal:

1 Disconnect the battery leads. Drain the cooling system as described in **Chapter 4, Section 4:3**. Remove the air cleaner and temperature control valve as described in **Sections 2:3** and **2:4**. Remove the breather pipes 4, 7 and 8 in **FIG 2:1**.

2 Refer to **FIG 2:2**. Disconnect the feed pipe 16 to the in-line fuel filter. Refer to **Section 2:7** and disconnect the throttle and choke cables. In the case of automatic transmission models, remove the kick-down cable bracket 13. Pull off the vent pipes 6.

3 Disconnect the heater pipes 14. Disconnect the lead from the coolant temperature transmitter (2 in **Chapter 12, FIG 12:19**). Disconnect from the manifold: the heater return pipe to the pump, the thermostat by-pass hose, the brake servo vacuum pipe, the distributor vacuum hose 7 and the vent pipe to the radiator. Uncouple the sparking plug leads. Remove the distributor cap.

4 Remove the 12 manifold retaining bolts (18 in **FIG 2:2**), identify their different lengths and the positions from which they were removed and immediately clean their threads as described in operation 4 of the cylinder head removal procedure (**Chapter 1, Section 1:5**).

5 Lift off the induction manifold. Clean off coolant from the gasket 2 (see **FIG 2:15**). Remove the two bolts 4 and lift off the gasket clamps 3. Lift off and discard the gasket 2. Remove and discard the gasket seals 1.

Fitment:

1 Refer to **FIG 2:15**. Smear silicon grease on both sides of new seals 1 and position them with their ends engaged in the notches formed between the cylinder head and the block. Apply Hylomar PL 32/m jointing compound on the corners of the cylinder head, manifold gasket 2 and the manifold around the coolant passage joints.

2 Fit the manifold gasket 2 with FRONT forwards and the open bolt hole at the front righthand side. Fit the gasket clamps 3 but do not fully tighten the clamp bolts 4 at this stage. Position the manifold.

3 Coat the cleaned threads of the 12 retaining bolts with 3M EC776 sealant and fit them to their identified positions. Tighten them gradually and evenly working from the centre outwards. Finally torque tighten them. Torque tighten the gasket clamp bolts 4.

4 The remaining operations are the reverse of operations 1 to 3 the removal sequence. Adjust the throttle and choke controls as described in **Section 2:7**. On completion of the reassembly, refill the cooling system as described in **Chapter 4, Section 4:3**, run the engine and check for leaks.

2:11 Fault diagnosis

(a) No fuel supply to carburetters

1 Float valve needle stuck
2 Blocked filter or pipeline
3 Blocked fuel tank vent
4 Pump inoperative
5 Fuel tank empty

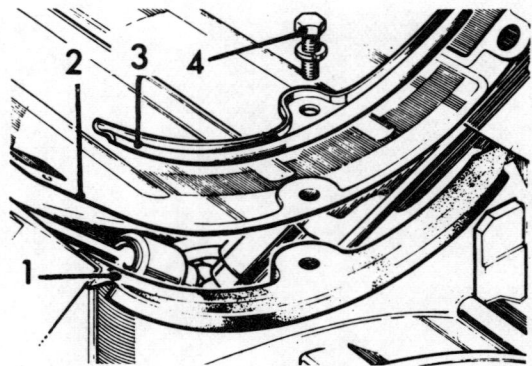

FIG 2:15 The induction manifold gasket, seals and clamps

Key to Fig 2:15   1 Seal   2 Gasket   3 Clamp
4 Clamp bolt

(b) Fuel pump not delivering

1 Check 2, 3, 4 and 5 in (a)
2 Wiring discontinuity
3 Defective oil pressure switch
4 Blocked gauze strainer

(c) Difficult cold starting

1 Check (a) and (b)
2 Choke control requires resetting
3 Fast-idling speed requires resetting
4 Incorrect fuel level in float chamber
5 Carburetter(s) flooding

(d) Difficult warm starting

1 Check (a) and (b), 2 and 4 in (c)
2 Blocked air filter element(s)
3 Defective air temperature control valve

(e) Stalling, erratic slow-idling

1 Float level incorrect
2 Mixture setting incorrect
3 Air leaks at throttle spindles
4 Air leaks at manifold joints
5 Damper oil too thick or level incorrect
6 Breather, vent, vacuum pipe(s) adrift

(f) Lack of engine power

1 Check 6 in (e)
2 Throttle control requires adjustment
3 Damper oil too thin or level incorrect
4 Carburetter piston(s) sticking
5 Water in fuel

(g) Excessive fuel consumption

1 Check 2 and 4 in (c), (d) and 2 in (e)
2 Carburetters incorrectly adjusted
3 Worn or bent jet needle
4 Incorrect needle type
5 Fuel leakage
6 Binding brakes
7 Tyres under-inflated
8 Engine running too hot
9 Car overloaded
10 Mechanical or ignition defects

NOTES

CHAPTER 3

THE IGNITION SYSTEM

3:1 Description

The Lucas 'Opus' electronic ignition system is fitted to vehicles covered by this manual. The system comprises an engine driven distributor, an ignition coil and a ballast resistor unit. Wiring diagram **FIG 14:1** in the **Appendix** includes these units (83, 84 and 85) and their interconnecting wiring.

The components of the distributor are shown in **FIG 3:1** and it will be noted that there are no 'make and break' contact breaker points. Ignition HT is triggered electronically by the impulse generated by ferrite rods 3 in the periphery of the timing rotor 2 passing a pick-up coil unit 1 (see **FIG 3:2**). The impulses are amplified by the electronic assembly 10 (see **FIG 3:1**) which is built into the distributor. The absence of a mechanical 'make and break' precludes the accurate static timing of the ignition and precise adjustment of the timing can only be carried out dynamically. These timing checks and adjustments can either be made using the diagnostic sensor which is fitted externally to the engine or by means of a stroboscopic light arranged to illuminate the timing scale shown in **FIG 3:3**.

The distributor is driven by gear 13 in **FIG 3:1** engaging with a gear keyed to a forward extension of the camshaft and is shown in **Chapter 1, FIG 1:14**. A dog on the lower end of the distributor shaft drives the oil pump. The distributor incorporates both vacuum and centrifugal automatic advance/retard mechanisms.

3:2 Maintenance

Distributor:

Every 6000 miles (10,000km), refer to **Section 3:5** and lubricate the distributor felt pad 4 in **FIG 3:1** with a few drops of engine oil.

Ignition timing:

Every 6000 miles (10,000km), check the ignition timing dynamically and adjust as necessary. The alternative procedures are described in **Section 3:6**.

Sparking plugs:

Every 6000 miles (10,000km), clean and regap the sparking plugs as described in **Section 3:7**.

Every 12,000 miles (20,000km), fit a new set of sparking plugs. Champion N12Y plugs are officially recommended.

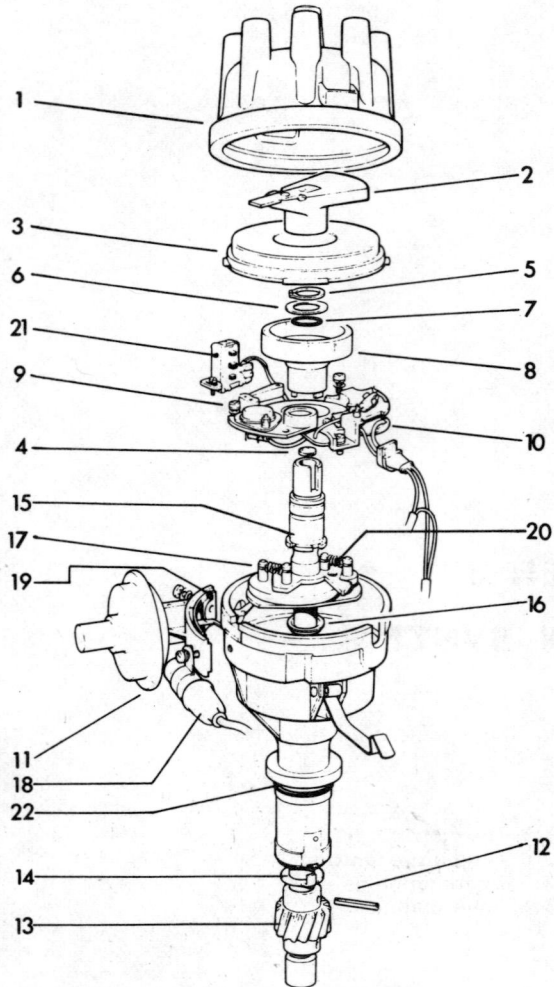

FIG 3:1   Components of the distributor

Key to Fig 3:1   1 Cover   2 Rotor   3 Anti-flash cover
4 Felt pad   5 Circlip   6 Washer   7 'O' ring   8 Timing
rotor   9 Pozidrive screws and washers   10 Grommet and
electronic assembly   11 Vacuum unit   12 Pin   13 Drive
gear   14 Thrust washer   15 Shaft assembly   16 Plastic
collar   17 Centrifugal unit   18 Capacitor   19 Gasket
20 Centrifugal springs   21 Pick-up   22 'O' ring

3:3 Ignition faults

If the engine runs unevenly, set it to idle at about
1000rev/min and disconnect and reconnect each high
tension cable from its sparking plug in turn. Doing this to a
plug which is firing properly will accentuate the uneven
running but it will make no difference if the plug is not
firing. Locate the faulty plug and, taking care not to touch
any metal part of the lead while the engine is running, push
back the insulator. With the engine running, hold this lead
so that the conductor is about 3mm (0.125in) away from
the cylinder head. A strong, regular spark will confirm that
the fault lies with the sparking plug which should be
cleaned or renewed. If, on the other hand, there is no spark,
suspect the cable or its connection at the distributor cover.

If the spark is weak and irregular, check the condition of
the HT cable and, if it is perished or cracked, renew it. If no
improvement results, check the distributor cover. It must
be clean and dry. Check that good contact is being made
between the centre carbon brush and the rotor arm and
that there is no 'tracking' which will show as a thin black
line between the electrodes or to a metal part in contact
with the cover. 'Tracking' cannot be rectified except by
fitting a new cover.

If there is no spark from any plug, refer to the wiring
diagram in the **Appendix** and check that there is voltage
throughout the LT circuit. Trace and correct the faulty
cable, loose connection or faulty ignition switch. If the
circuit is in order but the trouble persists, the coil, capacitor
or ballast resistor unit must be suspect. These are best
checked by individual substitution. The procedure for the
overhaul of a distributor is described in **Section 3:5**.

3:4 The coil and ballast resistor

No procedures are prescribed for the testing or repairing
of either of these units. A suspect unit should be removed
and a replacement unit fitted. Both are located on the
lefthand wing valance.

Coil removal and fitment:

Disconnect the leads from the battery. Pull off the HT
lead and disconnect the four Lucas connectors. Remove
two bolts, spring washers and plain washers. Collect the
four distance pieces and lift out the ignition coil.

Fitment is the reverse of this sequence. Note that the
cold air duct clip is retained by the forward of the two bolts.
Connect the Lucar connectors as follows: black/white/
green and black/red to the positive terminal and
white/white/black and the green to the negative
terminal.

Ballast resistor removal and fitment:

Disconnect the leads from the battery. Disconnect the
two harness plugs. Remove two bolts, spring and plain
washers. Collect two distance pieces and lift out the
ballast resistor.

Fitment is the reverse of this sequence. The harness
plugs are keyed and cannot be incorrectly connected.

3:5 The distributor

Pick-up air gap adjustment:

The pick-up air gap is shown between arrows in **FIG
3:2. Do not insert a feeler gauge into the gap when
the ignition is energised.** The gap should be checked
every 6000 miles (10,000km) and maintained between
0.35 and 0.40mm (0.014 and 0.016in). The checking and
adjustment procedures are as follows.

1 Disconnect the leads from the battery. Refer to **FIG
3:1**. Unclip the distributor cover 1, pull off the rotor 2
and remove the plastic anti-flash cover 3.

2 Using feeler gauges, check the gap dimension. If
adjustment is necessary, loosen screws 4 in **FIG 3:2**,
reposition the pick-up 1 and retighten the screws.

3 Recheck the gap as it may change substantially when
the screws are retightened. When the gap is correct,
reassemble the parts removed and reconnect the
battery leads.

Distributor removal:

Disconnect the leads from the battery. Remove the two straps which secure the distributor harness to the cantilever bracket. Disconnect the two Lucar connectors from the ignition coil and one harness plug from the ballast resistor. Pull off the pipe 7 in **Chapter 2, FIG 2:2** from the distributor vacuum unit. Pull off the HT lead from the coil. Release the four lefthand HT leads from their sparking plugs and from the rocker cover. Remove the distributor cover and rest it on the alternator bracket. Pull off the distributor rotor, remove the plastic anti-flash cover and refit the rotor.

Turn the crankshaft in the direction of engine rotation until No 1 cylinder is at TDC (see **FIG 3:3**) of its firing stroke (rotor approximately in position **B** in **FIG 3:4**). Refer to **FIG 3:5**. Withdraw bolt 1 and remove clamp 2. Lift the distributor out of the timing cover noting, as it is withdrawn from engagement with the driving gear, that the rotor moves from position **B** to position **A** (see **FIG 3:4**). Note also that the oil pump driving dog slot is in the position **C** shown in **FIG 3:6**.

Distributor refitment:

Using a large screwdriver, turn the oil pump shaft to the position shown in **FIG 3:6**. Turn the crankshaft in the direction of engine rotation until No 1 cylinder is at TDC (see **FIG 3:3**) of its firing stroke (both valves closed). Check the condition of the 'O' ring 22 in **FIG 3:1** and renew if necessary. Prepare the distributor by turning the rotor to position **A** in **FIG 3:4**. Insert the distributor into the timing gear cover. The drive gear will engage and turn the rotor towards the **B** position, the 'O' ring will engage and, finally, the oil pump driving dog will engage and the rotor will be in the **B** position. Refer to **FIG 3:5**. Position the clamp 2. Fit and tighten the bolt 1. Before fitting the cover, set the static ignition timing as described in **Section 3:6**. Refit the distributor cap and vacuum pipe. Reconnect the coil and ballast resistor wiring and the battery and sparking plug leads. Run the engine and dynamically check and adjust the ignition timing by either of the alternative procedures described in **Section 3:6**.

Distributor overhaul:

Remove the distributor as described earlier. Check the cover for any evidence of 'tracking' (see **Section 3:3**). Check that the HT leads and sparking plug connectors are free of any indication of perishing or cracking. Check that the carbon brush in the cover is not excessively worn and is not sticking.

Distributor dismantling:

Refer to **FIG 3:1** and dismantle by following the sequence in which the components are numbered. Note the following points. No procedures are prescribed for repairing the electronic assembly, the pick-up unit or the vacuum unit. Work on the centrifugal unit should be limited to renewing springs 20 if necessary. Renew parts or subassemblies as dictated by normal serviceability considerations.

Distributor reassembly:

Follow the reverse of the dismantling sequence. Note the following points. Use Rocol 'Moly pad' to lubricate the

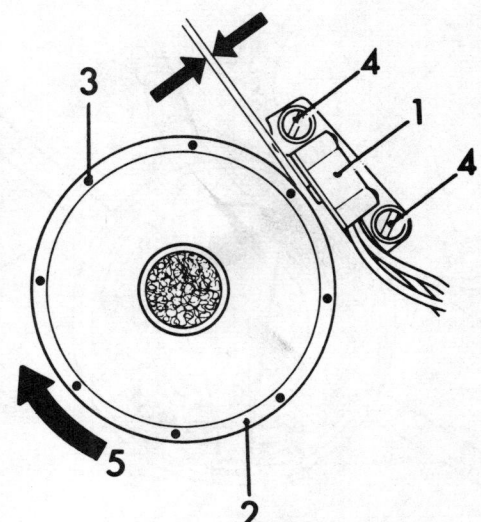

FIG 3:2   The pick-up air gap

Key to Fig 3:2   1 Pick-up   2 Timing rotor   3 Ferrite rods   4 Screws   5 Direction of rotation

working surfaces of centrifugal advance/retard assembly, the shaft and the pick-up moving plate pin. Take great care, when fitting the control springs 20, not to distort them. The plastic collar 16 is fitted with its concave surface upwards. Ensure that, when fitting the vacuum unit, the assembly seats correctly to the distributor body step. Ensure that the pick-up moving plate pin is carefully engaged into the vacuum unit link and that the electronic assembly plate and grommet are together carefully positioned. Ensure that the master projection on the timing rotor engages in the master slot. Lubricate the felt pad 4 with a few drops of engine oil. Set the pick-up air gap as described earlier. Check over the assembly for free rotation and proper movement of both the advance/retard mechanisms.

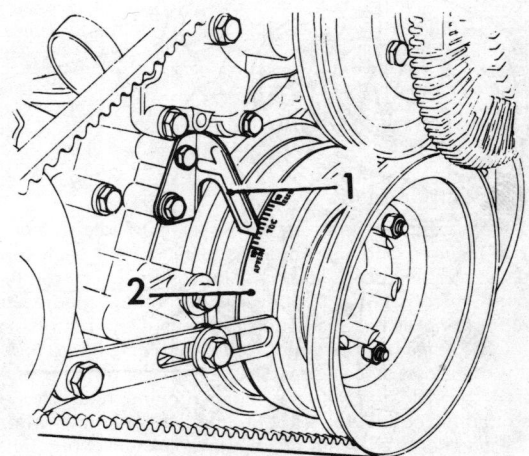

FIG 3:3   The timing marks

Key to Fig 3:3   1 Pointer   2 Crankshaft damper

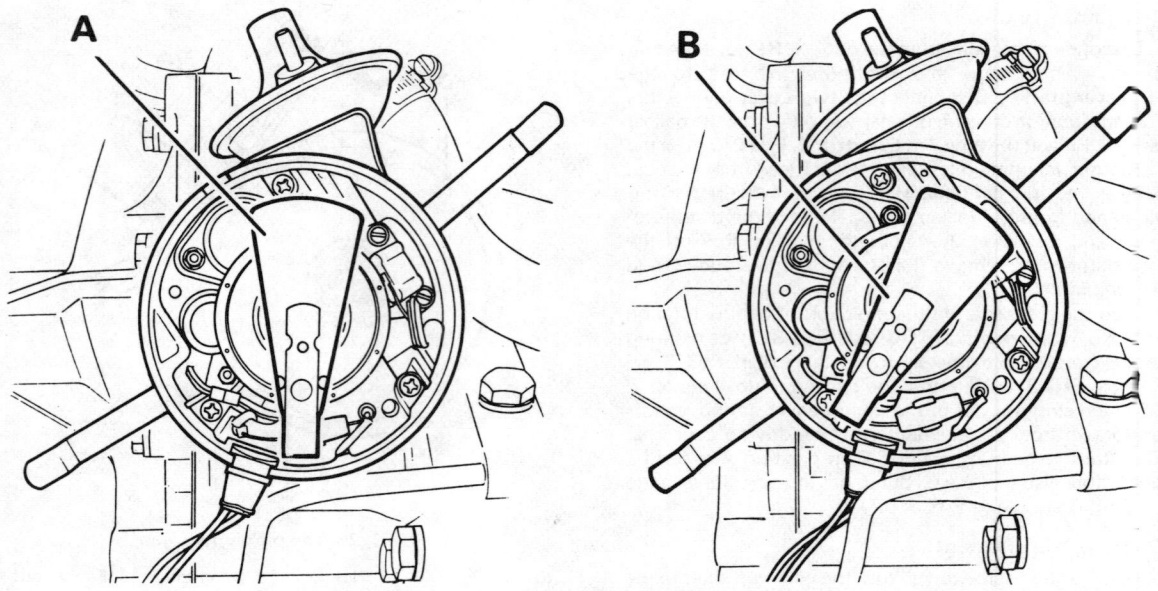

FIG 3:4   Distributor rotor positions

Key to Fig 3:4   A Before engaging the drive gear   B After engaging the drive gear

Distributor testing:

For complete testing of the centrifugal and vacuum advance/retard characteristics, distributor test bench facilities are required. These characteristics are tabulated in the **Technical Data** section of the **Appendix**. Note that this information is quoted against distributor rev/min. To convert to an engine speed datum, multiply rev/min and degrees by two.

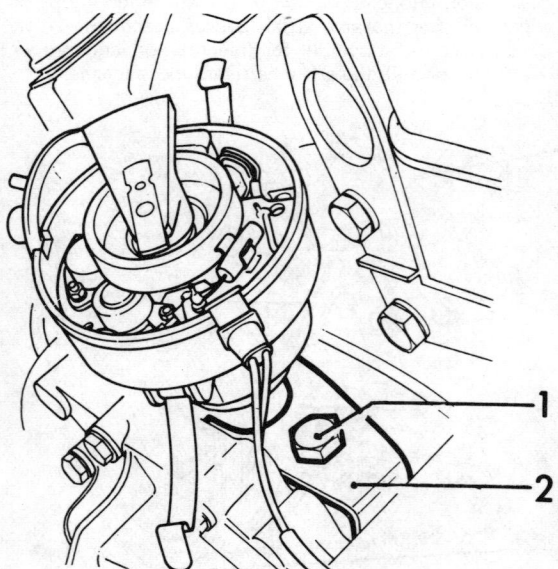

FIG 3:5   The distributor clamp

Key to Fig 3:5   1 Bolt   2 Clamp

3:6 Timing the ignition

The absence of a mechanical ignition timing point precludes the accurate static timing of the ignition and, following the imprecise setting of the timing statically, precise adjustment must be made dynamically by either of the alternative dynamic timing procedures described later in this section.

Static ignition timing:

Check and, if necessary, adjust the pick-up gap as described in **Section 3:5** but do not reassemble the distributor at this stage. Temporarily fit the rotor arm.

Refer to **FIG 3:3**. Turn the crankshaft in the direction of engine rotation to align the pointer 1 with the six degrees BTDC mark on the scale on the damper 2 on No 1 cylinder firing stroke. The rotor arm will now be in the **B** position in **FIG 3:4**. Remove the rotor arm and inspect the relationship of the pick-up sensor to the nearest ferrite rod. This should be just approaching the pick-up sensor as shown in **FIG 3:2**. If it is not, loosen bolt 1 in **FIG 3:5** and rotate the distributor body to achieve the position shown. Tighten the clamp bolt and reassemble the distributor

Run the engine, check and adjust the timing dynamically by either of the following procedures.

Dynamic timing procedures:

The engine is fitted with an electronic diagnostic socket (see **Chapter 1, Section 1:19, FIG 1:35**) and may be coupled to suitable diagnosis equipment. Alternatively, the timing may be checked under a stroboscopic light set to illuminate the crankshaft timing scale (see **FIG 3 3**) and, if possible, with an independent, accurate tachometer (the rev/min indicator fitted to the car is not altogether suitable) to record the engine speed. **In either case the vacuum advance/retard unit must be made** inoperative by pulling off the vacuum pipe 7 in Chapter 2, FIG 2:2 from the vacuum unit 11 in FIG 3:1.

Using diagnostic equipment:

Equipment designed to Leyland Cars specification 2007E will show engine rev/min and ignition timing on direct reading indicators.

1 **Disconnect the vacuum unit.** Connect the equipment to socket 14 in **Chapter 1, FIG 1:35**.
2 Run the engine. Hold the speed at each of the engine rev/min specified in the tabulation given later and note the ignition timing BTDC indicated.
3 If adjustment is required, stop the engine. Refer to **FIG 3:5**, loosen clamp bolt 1, rotate the distributor body slightly anti-clockwise to advance the timing or clockwise to retard the timing and retighten the clamp bolt.
4 Repeat operations 2 and 3 as necessary until the timing is correct.
5 Stop the engine. Disconnect the diagnostic lead and refit the socket cover. Refit the pipe to the vacuum unit.

Using a stroboscopic light:

1 Use an accurate, independent tachometer if possible. Connect up a stroboscopic light to No 1 cylinder (front lefthand bank). **Disconnect the vacuum unit.**
2 Carry out operations 2 to 4 of the procedure given earlier for checking and adjusting the timing when using diagnostic equipment. The timing will be the 'stationary' reading under the pointer on the crankshaft scale.
3 Stop the engine. Disconnect the stroboscopic light and uncouple the independent tachometer if one was used. Refit the pipe to the vacuum unit.

Dynamic timing:

When checking the timing dynamically, work to the following data which is inclusive of the six degree BTDC static setting.

Engine rev/min	Degrees BTDC (total)
1200	10.0
1800	17.5
2600	22.0

3:7 Sparking plugs

Champion N12Y sparking plugs are officially recommended and their gaps should be set at 0.8mm (0.032in).

Cleaning and testing:

At least every 6000 miles (10,000km) have the plugs cleaned on an abrasive-blasting machine and tested under pressure with the gaps correctly set. The gaps must always be adjusted by bending the earth electrode. **Do not attempt to bend the centre electrode or the insulation will be damaged.**

Plugs as a tuning guide:

Inspection of the deposits on the electrodes can be helpful when tuning. Normally, from mixed periods of high and low speed driving, the deposits should be powdery and range in colour from brown to greyish tan. There will

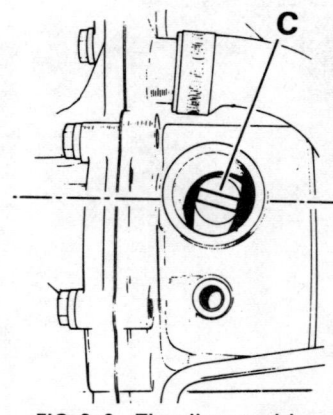

FIG 3:6   The oil pump drive

Key to Fig 3:6   C   See text

also be slight wear of the electrodes. Long periods of constant speed driving or low-speed city driving will give white or yellowish deposits. Dry, black fluffy deposits are due to incomplete combustion and indicate running with a rich mixture, excessive idling and possibly defective ignition. Overheated plugs have a white or light grey blistered look round the centre electrode and the electrodes will appear bluish and burnt. This may be due to weak mixture, poor cooling, incorrect ignition or sustained high speed running with heavy loads.

Black, wet deposits result from oil in the combustion chamber from worn pistons, rings, valve stems or guides or from worn or scored cylinder bores. Spark plugs which run hotter may alleviate this problem but the cure is in an engine overhaul.

3:8 Fault diagnosis

(a) Engine will not fire

1 Battery discharged
2 Pick-up air gap out of adjustment
3 Distributor cover dirty, cracked or 'tracking'
4 Carbon brush not touching rotor
5 Discontinuity in LT circuit
6 Rotor arm cracked
7 Defective coil
8 Defective ballast resistor
9 Defective distributor
10 Defective ignition switch

(b) Engine misfires

1 Check 2, 3, 5, 7 and 8 in (a)
2 Defective capacitor
3 HT cables cracked or perished
4 Sparking plug(s) loose
5 Sparking plug insulation cracked
6 Sparking plug gaps incorrectly set
7 Ignition timing incorrect
8 Fouled sparking plugs
9 HT cables incorrectly connected

(c) Engine fires but then stops

1 Check 2, 8 and 10 in (a)
2 Defective electronic assembly

NOTES

CHAPTER 4

THE COOLING SYSTEM

4:1 Description

The cooling system is pressurised and thermostatically controlled. The main assemblies of the system are shown in **FIG 4:1**. Coolant circulation is assisted by a centrifugal pump which, together with the alternator, is belt driven from a pulley on the crankshaft. A cooling fan is driven from the pump shaft through a variable slip viscous coupling.

The pump takes coolant from the bottom of the vertical-flow radiator and delivers it directly to the cylinder blocks where it rises to the heads and to the induction manifold. The thermostat is located in the manifold and, at normal operating temperatures, allows coolant to return to the top of the radiator. At lower coolant temperatures, the thermostat closes this return and provides a rapid warm-up of coolant both to the engine and to the car heater.

Expansion overflow from the radiator is piped to a separate tank from which, when the system cools and a partial vacuum is formed, coolant returns to the radiator.

4:2 Maintenance

General:

At least every 3000 miles (5000km), check over the cooling system for leaks. Renew any hoses which show signs of deterioration.

Coolant:

At least every 3000 miles (5000km), check the coolant level and top up as necessary. The procedure is included in **Section 4:3**.

Pump belt:

Every 3000 miles (5000km), check the tension of the drive belt. The belt also drives the alternator and the tensioning (and renewal) procedure is described in **Chapter 12, Section 12:5**.

4:3 The radiator

Draining:

Collect the coolant for re-use if its condition is serviceable (see **Section 4:7**).

Disconnect the leads from the battery. **When the coolant is cold**, set the car heater control in the HOT position. Refer to **FIG 4:1**. Remove the expansion tank cap 3 and the radiator filler plug 4. Open the radiator drain 5 and both cylinder block drains 6.

Filling:

Close the drains and fill the system through the radiator orifice 4. Fit the filler plug. Half fill the expansion tank and

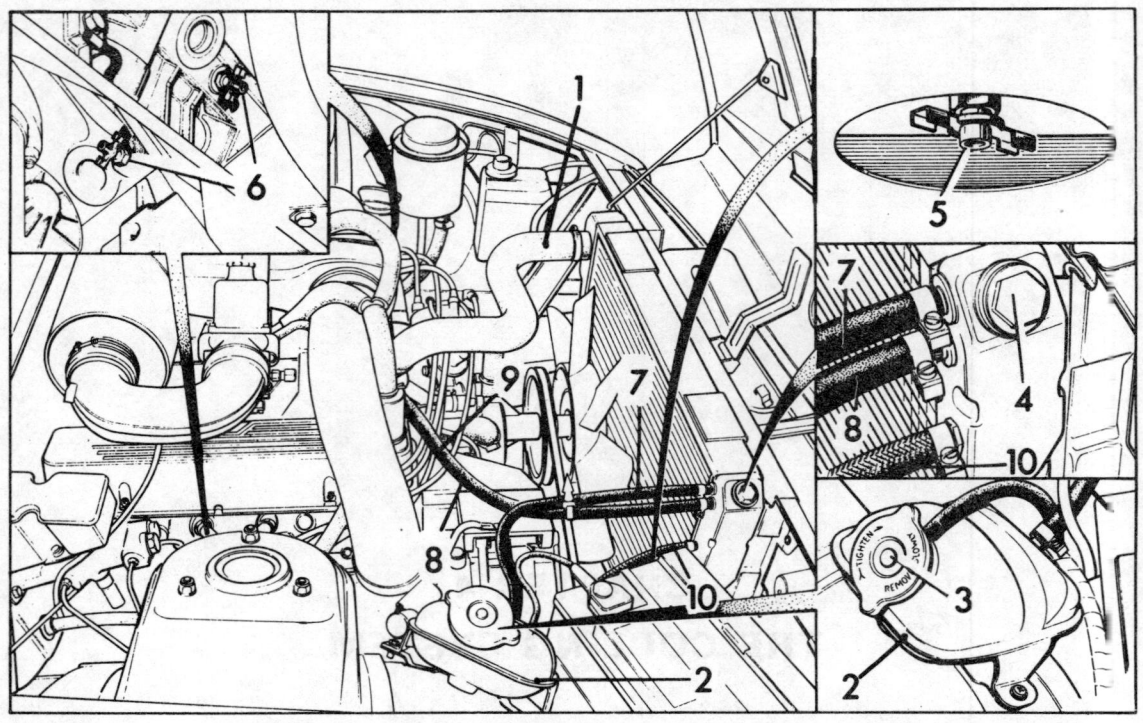

FIG 4:1   The cooling system

Key to Fig 4:1   1 Top hose   2 Expansion tank   3 Pressure cap   4 Filler plug   5 Radiator drain   6 Cylinder block drains   7 Hose   8 Vent pipe   9 Heater return pipe   10 Automatic gearbox fluid pipe (to REAR union)

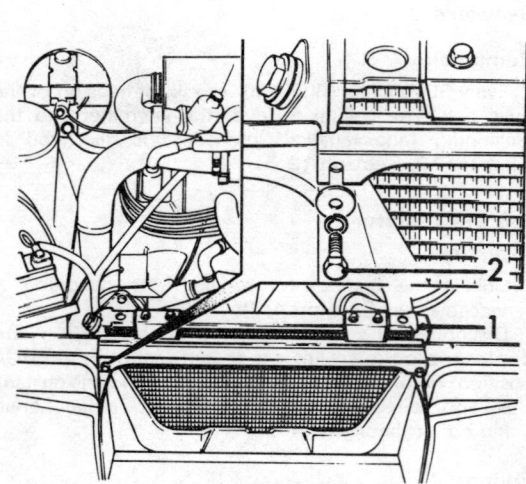

FIG 4:2   Removing the radiator

Key to Fig 4:2   1 Radiator   2 Retaining bolt

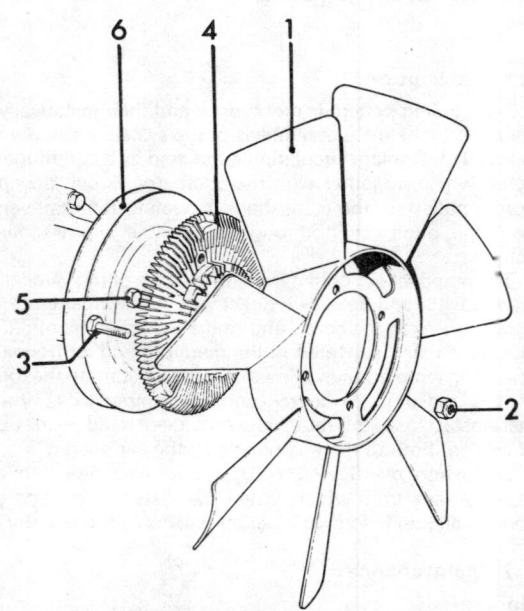

FIG 4:3   The cooling fan drive

Key to Fig 4:3   1 Fan   2 Nut   3 Bolt   4 Viscous coupling   5 Bolt   6 Pulley fit the pressure cap. Reconnect the battery and run the engine at 1200rev/min for three minutes. Stop the engine, remove plug 4, top up and refit the plug. Repeat the engine run and top up sequence until the system is full. If necessary, top up the expansion tank to the half full level.

Removal:

Disconnect the leads from the battery. Drain the system as described earlier. Refer to **FIG 4:1**. From the radiator, disconnect the top hose 1, the bottom hose, the expansion tank hose 7, the manifold vent pipe 8 and, in the case of automatic transmission models, the two fluid hoses (one, 10, is shown) from the righthand side of the radiator after identifying them upper and lower. Refer to **FIG 4:2**. Remove the two bolts 2 which retain the radiator 1 to the front panel and lift the radiator out vertically.

Fitment:

Locate the radiator bottom pegs into the two rubber grommets in the crossmember and continue by reversing the removal sequence. Refill the system as described earlier. In the case of automatic transmission models, top up the gearbox fluid level as described in **Chapter 7, Section 7:2**.

4:4 The fan and fan drive
The belt:

The belt drives the alternator and the coolant pump in addition to the fan. The procedures for tensioning, removal and refitment of the belt are described in **Chapter 12, Section 12:5**.

The viscous coupling:

No procedures are prescribed for the repair or overhaul of a coupling and a defective unit should be removed and a new replacement fitted.

Fan, coupling and pulley removal and refitment:

Disconnect the leads from the battery. Refer to **FIG 4:2** and remove the two bolts 2 which retain the radiator 1 to the front panel. Tilt the radiator forwards. Refer to **FIG 4:3**. Remove the four nuts and bolts 2 and 3 and dismount the fan 1 from the viscous coupling 4. Refer to **Chapter 1, FIG 1:13**. Remove nut 13 and its washer and dismount the coupling. Remove the drive belt. Remove the three bolts 5 in **FIG 4:3**, collect the spring washers and dismount the pulley 6 from the pump shaft flange.

Fitment is the reverse of this sequence.

4:5 The water pump
Pump removal:

Drain the system and remove the radiator as described in **Section 4:3**. Remove the fan, coupling and pulley as described in **Section 4:4**. Refer to **FIG 4:4**. Uncouple the heater return pipe 2 from the pump. Disconnect the diagnostic socket lead at the connector, remove bolts 9

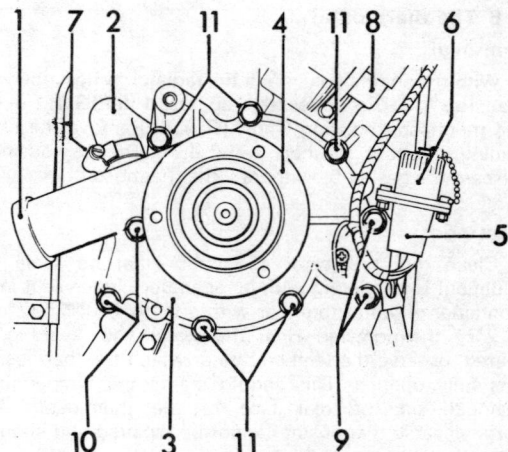

FIG 4:4 Removing the water pump

Key to Fig 4:4   1 Main pump inlet   2 Heater return pipe
3 Pump casing   4 Pulley   5 Diagnostic socket   6 Cover
7 Pipe clip   8 Distributor   9 Bolts (2)   10 Bolts (2)
11 Bolts (5)

and move the socket and bracket aside. Remove bolts 10 noting that the upper is longer. Remove the five bolts 11. Clean all bolt threads. Where thread sealant has been used see **Chapter 1, Section 1:5**. Withdraw the pump 3 and discard the gasket.

Pump fitment:

Clean the pump and timing cover mating faces. Lightly grease the faces of the new gasket. Apply sealant 3M EC776 to the threads of the long bolts. Work diagonally and torque tighten the bolts. The remaining operations are the reverse of the removal sequence.

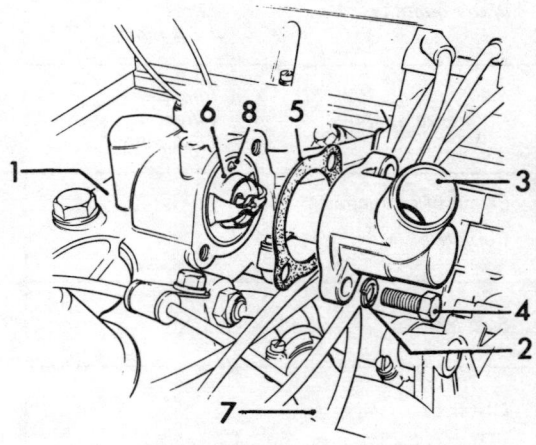

FIG 4:5 The thermostat

Key to Fig 4:5   1 Induction manifold   2 Spring washer
3 Thermostat housing   4 Bolt   5 Gasket   6 Thermostat
7 Heater return pipe   8 Jiggle pin

4:6 The thermostat

Removal:

With the engine cold, drain the radiator as described in **Section 4:3**. Disconnect the top hose 1 in **FIG 4:1** from the thermostat housing 3 in **FIG 4:5**. Remove the two retaining bolts 4, washers 2 and dismount the housing. Discard the gasket 5. Withdraw the thermostat 6.

Testing:

Clean the thermostat and check that no scale or sediment is interfering with its operation. Immerse it in a container of water together with a 0° to 100°C (32° to 212°F) thermometer. Heat the water and, keeping it stirred, observe the temperature at which the thermostat has fully opened. This should match the temperature stamped on the rear face of the thermostat. An unserviceable thermostat cannot be repaired and should be replaced by a new unit.

Fitment:

Fitment is the reverse of the removal sequence. Ensure that the jiggle pin 8 is uppermost.

4:7 The coolant

The use of antifreeze at all times is recommended since, apart from it providing protection from frost in relevant conditions, the correct solution will inhibit corrosion in the cooling system. The antifreeze must be a permanent type ethylene glycol base with a suitable inhibitor for aluminium engines. Approved fluids are Smith's Bluecol U or Shellsafe or antifreeze solutions meeting BSI 3150.

Frost protection:

The extent of frost protection provided by antifreeze in the coolant depends upon the concentration of fluid added to the water. Choose a concentration to match the ambient winter temperature conditions in which the car will operate and to suit the extent of protection which is required. The proportions of fluid and water for three extents of protection in a range of ambient temperatures are tabulated later. With proportions giving **Complete** protection, the car may be driven away immediately from cold. With **Safe Limit** protection the cold coolant will be in a mushy state and the car may be driven away after a short warm up period. With **Lower** protection the concentration prevents frost damage to the engine and radiator but thawing out will be required before the engine is started.

Preparing the coolant:

The chosen proportions of antifreeze and water should be measured into a separate container and the cooling system filled from this and not by adding the chemical directly to the radiator.

Renewing the coolant:

Unless an antifreeze solution is used for topping up the cooling system, the antifreeze concentration will gradually decrease and the specific gravity of the solution will drop. It will be prudent by checking the specific gravity at the start of each winter, to confirm the extent of the frost protection of the solution in the system and, if necessary to adjust or to renew the solution. It is normal to discard the coolant after two years and, after flushing the system, to refill with fresh solution.

Antifreeze solutions:

An indication of the meaning of **Complete, Safe Limit** and **Lower** extents of protection is given earlier in this Section.

Water quantity	Imp. pints	16.25	15.60	15.05	13.00
	Litres	9.23	8.86	8.45	7.38
	USA pints	19.50	18.70	18.00	15.60
Antifreeze quantity	Imp. pints	3.25	3.90	4.55	6.50
	Litres	1.85	2.23	2.59	3.70
	USA pints	3.90	4.68	5.46	7.80
Extent of protection Complete		−12°C 10°F	−16°C 3°F	−20°C −4°F	−36°C −33°F
Safe limit		−18°C 0°F	−22°C −8°F	-28°C −18°F	−41°C −42°F
Lower		−26°C −15°F	−32°C −26°F	−37°C −35°F	−47°C −53°F
Specific gravity of coolant at 15.5°C (60°F)		1.039	1.048	1.054	1.076

4:8 Fault diagnosis

(a) Internal coolant leakage

1 Cracked cylinder block
2 Loose cylinder head bolts
3 Cylinder head(s) cracked
4 Faulty head gasket(s)

(b) Poor circulation

1 Radiator matrix blocked
2 Coolant passages restricted
3 Low coolant level
4 Pump drive belt loose or broken
5 Defective coolant pump
6 Defective thermostat
7 Perished or collapsed hose(s)

(c) Corrosion

1 Impurities in the water
2 Incorrect type of antifreeze

(d) Overheating

1 Check (b)
2 Viscous coupling inoperative
3 Low oil level in sump
4 Tight engine
5 Incorrect ignition timing
6 Incorrect valve timing
7 Mixture too weak
8 Choked exhaust system
9 Binding brakes
10 Slipping clutch

NOTES

CHAPTER 5

THE CLUTCH

5:1 Description

The single dry-plate clutch assembly is shown in **FIG 5:1**. It is mounted on the flywheel 1 and the driven plate 4 operates directly on the rear face of the flywheel. The actuating force is provided to the pressure plate by a diaphragm spring 6.

When the clutch is engaged, the driven plate which is splined to the gearbox input shaft is nipped between the pressure plate and the flywheel, is caused to rotate with the flywheel and transmit torque to the manual transmission gearbox. The clutch is disengaged when the pressure plate is withdrawn from the driven plate by the clutch pedal being depressed. The clutch pedal operates the clutch release lever hydraulically by actuating the piston in the master cylinder and forcing fluid via a pipeline to actuate a piston in the slave cylinder which is mounted on the clutch housing.

Access to the clutch requires the gearbox to be dismounted as described in **Chapter 6, Section 6:3**.

5:2 Maintenance

Fluid level:

At least every 3000 miles (5000km), check the fluid level in the master cylinder reservoir 5 in **FIG 5:2** and top up as necessary. Use the same brand of fluid as that already in use. Approved fluids (they are the same as those approved for the braking system) are Castrol–Girling Universal Brake Fluid, Lockheed 329S Brake Fluid or Unipart 550 Brake Fluid. Where these brands of fluid are not available, use a fluid of reputable brand which meets specification SAE J1703d.

At this same mileage interval, check over the hydraulic piping and the slave and master cylinders for fluid leaks.

5:3 The hydraulic system

A cross-section through the master cylinder and the components of this unit are shown in **FIG 5:3**. The components of the slave cylinder are shown in **FIG 5:4**. The master cylinder pushrod 4 (see **FIG 5:3**) is coupled to the clutch foot pedal. A rigid pipe 7 (see **FIG 5:2**) in series with a flexible hose connects the slave and master cylinders. The slave cylinder pushrod 7 in **FIG 5:5** actuates the release lever 3.

Master cylinder removal and fitment:

Remove the splitpin, washer and clevis pin and uncouple the master cylinder pushrod 4 (see **FIG 5:3**) from the clutch pedal. Refer to **FIG 5:2**. Remove two nuts,

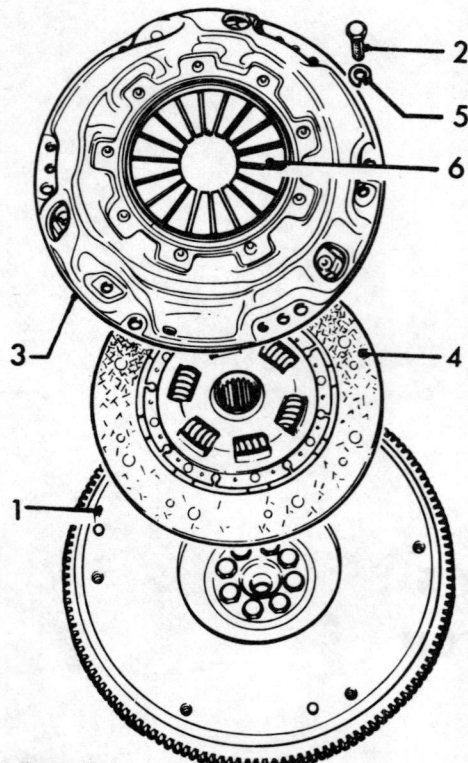

FIG 5:1   The clutch

Key to Fig 5:1   1 Flywheel (rear face)   2 Bolt   3 Clutch housing   4 Driven plate   5 Spring washer   6 Diaphragm spring

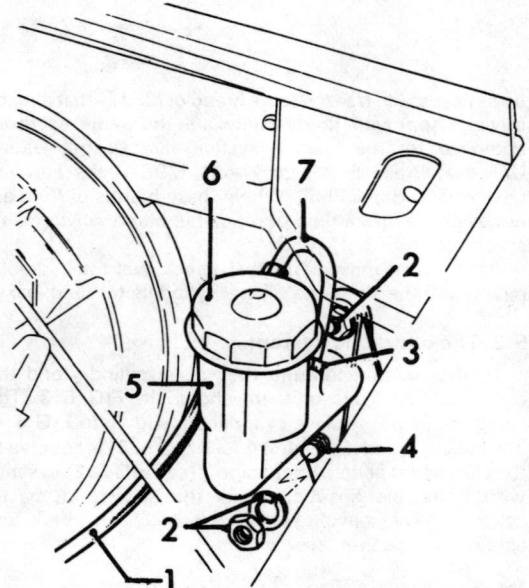

FIG 5:2   The master cylinder and fluid reservoir

Key to Fig 5:2   1 Hose   2 Nut and washer   3 Pipe connection   4 Mounting stud   5 Cylinder and reservoir unit   6 Cap   7 Rigid pipe

washers and bolts 2 and 4, release the pipe connection 3 and dismount the master cylinder unit 5. Collect the flange gasket.

Fitment is the reverse of the removal sequence and must be followed by bleeding the system as described later.

Master cylinder overhaul:

Use repair kit 8G8806. Dismantle by following the numerical sequence of the components in **FIG 5:3** noting that, to release piston 5, the tongue of the thimble 12 must be straightened and that the hole in the end of thimble is of keyhole shape. Discard the seals 6 and 9, the boot 1 and the circlip 2.

Use new fluid to to clean the internal parts. If the piston 5 and/or cylinder bore is scored or corroded, obtain new parts.

To assemble, reverse the dismantling sequence. Lubricate the internal parts with clean fluid. Smear the end of the cylinder and the inside of the new boot with rubber grease (supplied with the repair kit).

Slave cylinder removal and fitment:

With the car on a hoist, on stands or over a pit, the cylinder may be dismounted after removing the two retaining bolts. Take great care not to jerk the pushrod 7 in **FIG 5:5** in a forward direction as this could dislodge it and necessitate the removal of the gearbox and bellhousing to refit it. If the slave cylinder is to be separated from the hose, clean off around the union before disconnecting the hose.

Fitment is the reverse of the dismounting or removal sequence. If the hose was disconnected, bleed the system as described later.

Slave cylinder overhaul:

Dismantle by following the numerical sequence of the components in **FIG 5:4**. Discard the seal 3 and the boot 1. If the piston 2 and/or cylinder bore is scored or corroded, obtain new parts.

Assemble with the internal parts wetted with new fluid. Smear the end of the piston and the inside of the new boot with rubber grease.

Bleeding the system:

Two operators are required for this procedure.

Thoroughly clean round the reservoir cap 6 in **FIG 5:2** and round the bleed nipple 5 in **FIG 5:4**. Top up the reservoir. Attach one end of a bleed tube to the bleed nipple. Immerse the other end in a transparent container partially filled with fluid. Open the bleed nipple by approximately three-quarters of a turn. Depress and release the clutch pedal pausing briefly at each down stroke until fluid which is free of air issues from the bleed tube. throughout this procedure keep the reservoir fluid level at not less than half full. Finally, with the pedal depressed, close the bleed nipple.

5:4 Removing and refitting the clutch

Removal:

Dismount the gearbox as described in **Chapter 6, Section 6:3**. If the same clutch housing is to be refitted, mark the housing and the flywheel to identify their relative position.

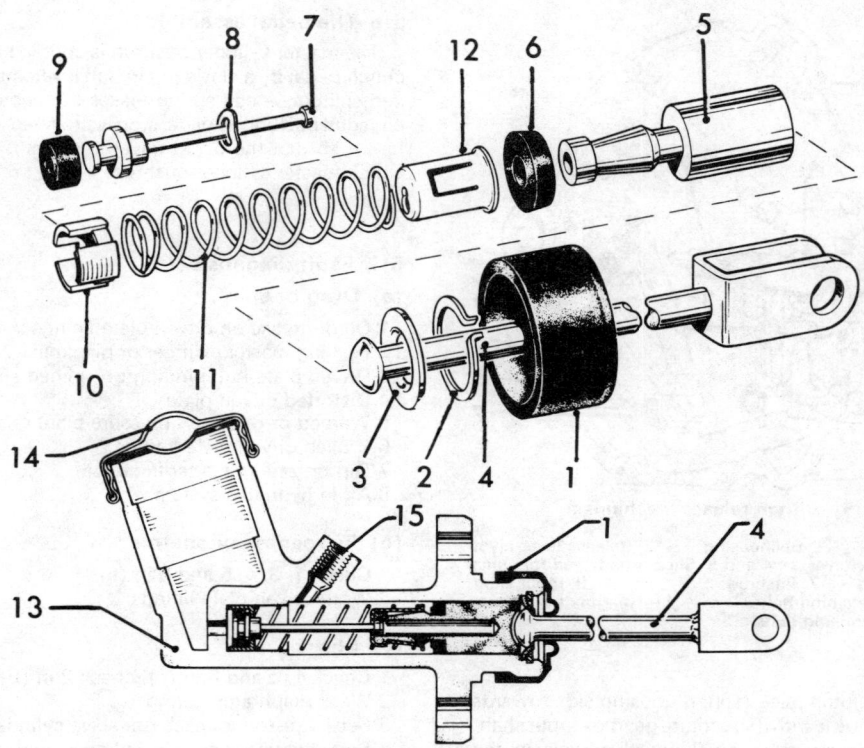

FIG 5:3   Components of the master cylinder

Key to Fig 5:3   1 Boot   2 Circlip   3 Dished washer   4 Pushrod   5 Piston   6 Seal   7 Valve stem   8 Wave washer
9 Seal   10 Seal spacer   11 Spring   12 Thimble   13 Cross-section through assembly   14 Cap   15 Pipeline orifice

Refer to **FIG 5:1**. Working diagonally and evenly, remove the housing retaining bolts 2 and washers 5. Dismount the clutch housing 3 and driven plate 4.

Inspection:

A polished surface on the plate linings is normal but a highly glazed or a resinous surface results from burned or partially burned-off oil. This condition cannot be rectified. Excessive wear of the linings or of the hub splines will also dictate the fitment of a new plate. Check that the fingers of the diaphragm spring 6 are not either cracked or broken. Check that the plate hub springs are intact and that all rivets are secure. Clean the surface of the pressure plate. If the surface is excessively worn or scored, a new assembly will be required. An assembly with loose or broken rivets should be renewed.

Check that the flywheel rear face is serviceable (see **Chapter 1, Section 1:14**).

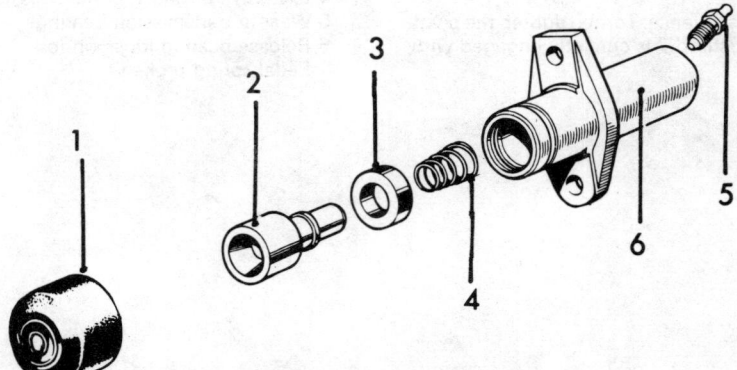

FIG 5:4   Components of the slave cylinder

Key to Fig 5:4   1 Boot   2 Piston   3 Seal   4 Spring   5 Bleed nipple   6 Cylinder

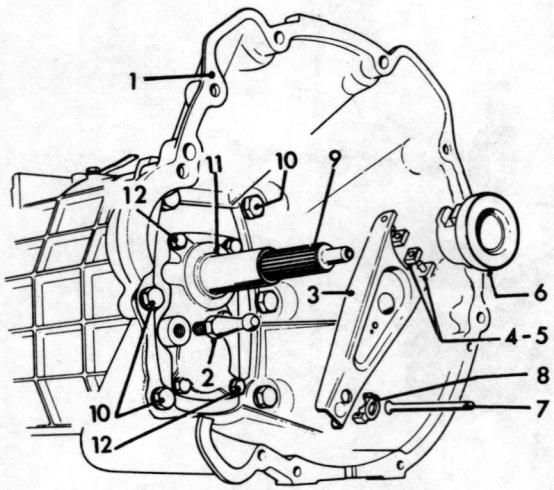

FIG 5:5 Clutch release mechanism

Key to Fig 5:5   1 Bellhousing   2 Release lever pivot
bolt   3 Release lever   4 and 5 Slipper pads and fork pins
6 Release bearing   7 Pushrod   8 Clip   9 Input shaft
10 Bellhousing retaining bolts   11 Gearbox front cover
12 Front cover retaining bolts

Fitment:

Position the clutch plate (spring housing side towards
the rear) and centre it with a substitute gearbox input shaft.
Engage the housing onto the flywheel dowels in the
marked position. Fit the six retaining bolts and washers.
Working diagonally and evenly, tighten the bolts. Finally
torque tighten them and withdraw the substitute shaft.
Refit the gearbox.

5:5 The release bearing
Removal:

Dismount the gearbox and bellhousing as described in
Chapter 6, Section 6:3. Refer to **FIG 5:5**. Using tool
ST1136, unscrew the lever pivot bolt 2, withdraw the
release lever 3 complete with the pivot bolt and the release
bearing 6. Detach the release bearing from the slipper pads
4 of the release lever fork pins 5.

Fitment:

Reverse the removal sequence. Torque tighten the pivot
bolt. Ensure that the pushrod 7 is correctly engaged with
the clip 8.

5:6 The pedal assembly

The master cylinder pushrod is coupled to the pendant
clutch pedal by a clevis pin which is retained by a washer
and splitpin. A coil spring biases the pedal in the clutch
engaged position. A pedal stop is provided and this should
be set so that the pedal travel matches the travel of the
clutch master cylinder pushrod.

5:7 Fault diagnosis
(a) Drag or spin

1 Oil or grease on driven plate linings
2 Leaking master cylinder or pipeline
3 Driven plate hub binding on splined shaft
4 Distorted driven plate
5 Warped or damaged pressure plate or housing
6 Broken driven plate linings
7 Dirt or foreign matter in clutch
8 Air in hydraulic system

(b) Fierceness or snatch

1 Check 1, 3, 4, 5 and 6 in (a)
2 Worn driven plate linings

(c) Slip

1 Check 1, 3 and 8 in (a), check 2 in (b)
2 Weak diaphragm spring
3 Seized piston in master or slave cylinder
4 Port between master cylinder and fluid reservoir
  choked
5 Pedal bearing seized
6 Loose slave cylinder

(d) Judder

1 Check 1, 3, 4, 5 and 6 in (a)
2 Bent or worn input shaft
3 Badly worn splines in driven plate hub
4 Buckled driven plate

(e) Rattle

1 Check 5 and 6 in (c)
2 Broken springs in driven plate hub
3 Worn release mechanism
4 Excessive backlash in transmission
5 Wear in transmission bearings
6 Release bearing loose on fork
7 Pedal spring broken

CHAPTER 6

MANUAL TRANSMISSION

6:1 Description

A longitudinal cross-section through the gearbox is shown in **FIG 6:1**. The box has five forward speeds and reverse and is provided with a remote gearchange control. Synchromesh engagement is provided for all forward speeds. Gear ratios are quoted in the **Technical Data** section of the **Appendix**.

Individual gears may be identified from **FIG 6:1**. Note that the layshaft gears are all fixed and that the mainshaft gears (except reverse) are free running. Fourth speed is a direct drive (with the third/fourth synchro sleeve forwards). Reverse gears have straight teeth. The reverse driven gear is integral with the first/second synchro sleeve and is engaged when the reverse idler gear is engaged with the layshaft reverse driving gear and this driven gear. Fifth speed gears give an overdrive ratio and are located rearwards of the gearbox centre plate. The speedometer drive gear is located at the rear of the mainshaft adjacent to the output flange.

Lubrication of the gear teeth is by splash oil. Pressure oil is supplied to the bore of the mainshaft from an epicyclic type gear pump driven from the layshaft. The forward oil seal runs on the input shaft; the rear oil seal runs on the gearbox output flange.

The gearbox and engine form a unit but the gearbox can be removed leaving the engine in the car. If necessary, the gearbox rear extension casing which carries the pump, the speedometer drive and the rear oil seal can be removed without dismounting the complete gearbox.

The switch which operates the reversing lights is automatically closed when reverse gear is engaged.

6:2 Maintenance

At least every 3000 miles (5000km), check over the gearbox for joint, plugs and oil seal leaks.

Oil level:

At least every 6000 miles (10,000km), check the level of the oil in the gearbox and top up as necessary. The filler plug is in the lefthand wall of the gearbox extension casing 3 in **FIG 6:1**. The level is correct when the oil is just up to the bottom of the plug orifice. For preference, use the same brand of Hypoid 75W oil as that already in use. Torque tighten the filler plug.

Oil draining and refilling:

The drain plug is in the lower righthand wall of the gearbox casing. The plug carries a magnet and it is normal

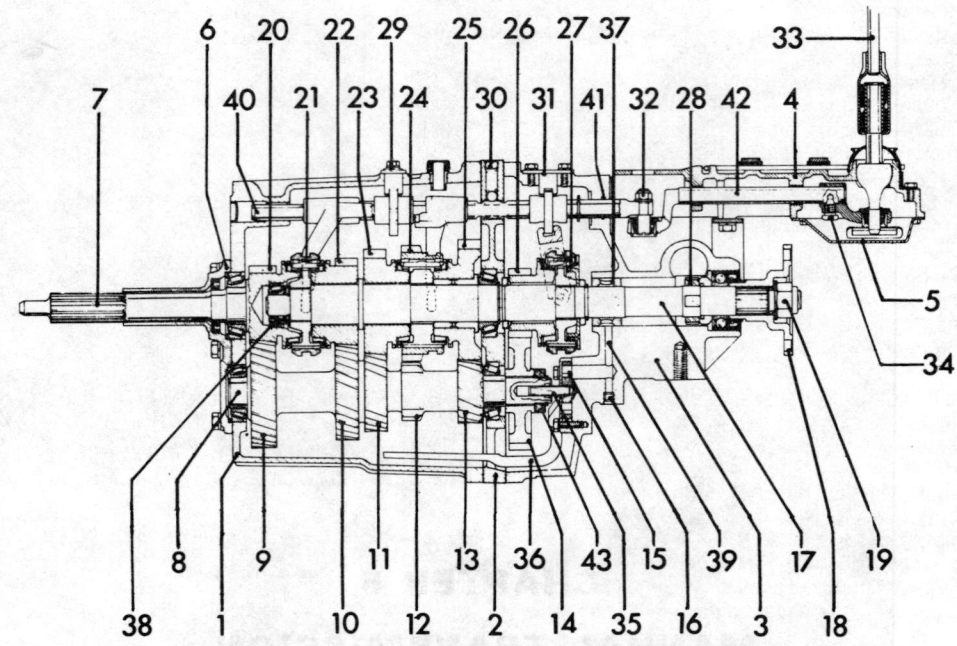

FIG 6:1 Longitudinal cross-section through the gearbox

Key to Fig 6:1   1 Gearbox casing   2 Centre plate   3 Extension casing   4 Gearchange casing   5 Cover   6 Front cover   7 Input shaft   8 Layshaft   9 Layshaft driven gear   10 Third speed driving gear   11 Second speed driving gear   12 Reverse driving gear   13 First speed driving gear   14 Fifth speed driving gear   15 Oil pump   16 Plug   17 Mainshaft   18 Flange   19 Flange nut   20 Layshaft driving gear   21 Third/fourth speed synchro unit   22 Third speed driven gear   23 Second speed driven gear   24 First/second synchro unit and reverse driven gear   25 First speed driven gear   26 Fifth speed driven gear   27 Fifth speed synchro unit   28 Speedometer drive gear   29 Front spool locating boss   30 Plug, centre spring and ball   31 Fifth gear spool locating boss   32 Nut and pin   33 Gearchange lever   34 Pinch bolt   35 Pump drive shaft   36 Pump intake tube   37 Oil transfer sleeve   38 Pilot bearing   39 Oil delivery passage   40 Selector shaft   41 'O' ing   42 Selector arm   43 Spacer

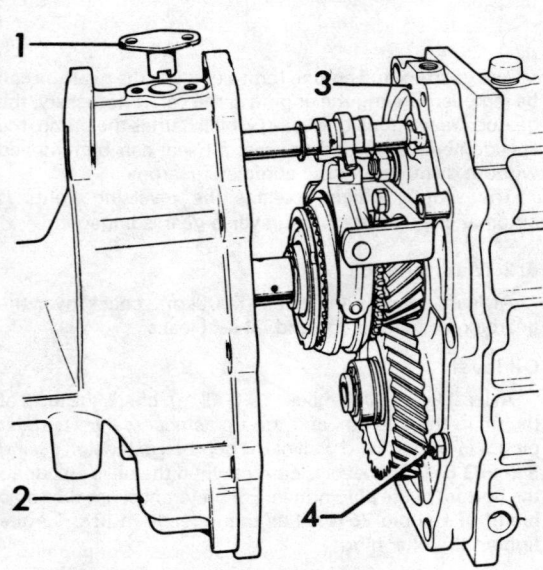

FIG 6:2   Removing the extension casing

Key to Fig 6:2   1 Spool locating boss   2 Extension casing   3 Centre plate   4 Slave bolt

to find small steel particles adhering to it. If large particles are found, investigate their source.

Refill up to the bottom of the filler orifice with a Hypoid 75W oil of reputable brand. Torque tighten the drain and the filler plugs.

6:3 Removing and refitting the gearbox

The procedures for the removal of the gearbox and for the removal of the extension casing only, leaving the engine in the car in both cases are described in this Section. The procedure for the removal of the engine and the gearbox as a unit is described in **Chapter 1, Section 1:4** and, if this course has been adopted, separate the gearbox from the engine as described in operations 6 to 8 of the following procedure.

Gearbox removal and refitment:

1 With the car on a hoist or over a pit, remove the gearchange lever assembly as described in **Section 6:7**. Refer to **Chapter 1, Section 1:17** and remove the front section of the exhaust system (items 3 and 4 in **FIG 1:31**). Refer to **Chapter 8, Section 8:3** and uncouple the propeller shaft from the gearbox flange 18 in **FIG 6:1**.

2 Position a jack under the engine sump (interpose a piece of wood) and raise the jack to support the engine.

Remove the bolts and spring washers and dismount the two plates which secure the bridge of the rear mounting to the chassis.

3 Lower the jack and, as the engine and gearbox unit tilt, take care that the air cleaner assembly does not foul the engine bulkhead. Lower only as far as is necessary to allow removal of the bellhousing retaining bolts.

4 Remove the speedometer drive cable. Identify and disconnect the leads from the reverse light switch at the two snap connectors and bend back the tab to release the harness from the gearbox.

5 Refer to **Chapter 5, Section 5:3**, remove the two bolts which secure the clutch slave cylinder to the bellhousing, carefully withdraw the cylinder and secure it to one side.

6 Remove the two bolts and washers which secure the sump stiffener plate to the gearbox. Remove the four bolts which retain the flywheel cover plate to the bellhousing. Support the gearbox.

7 Remove the eight bolts which secure the bellhousing to the engine. Note the different lengths of these bolts and identify them to the positions from which they were removed.

8 Taking great care not to strain the gearbox input shaft as it is withdrawn from the crankshaft pilot bearing and the clutch driven plate, separate the gearbox from the engine.

Refitment of the gearbox unit to the engine and reassembly of the installation is the reverse of the separation and removal sequence but note the following points.

Ensure that the clutch slave cylinder pushrod is correctly clipped to the clutch release lever (see **Chapter 5, Section 5:3**). Engage first gear. Ensure that the input shaft is not strained while it is being engaged with the splines of the driven plate and entered into the crankshaft pilot bearing. If necessary, turn the output drive flange to align the input shaft and driven plate splines. Ensure that the eight bolts are fitted to their identified positions. First gear may now be disengaged. Torque tighten the bolts. Refer as necessary to the relevant section and chapter texts and complete the installation.

Extension casing removal and fitment:

Drain the oil from the gearbox. Carry out operations 1 to 5 of the gearbox removal procedure described earlier. Remove the output drive flange as described in **Section 6:4**. Refer to **Section 6:7** and remove the gearbox remote control assembly. Refer to **Section 6:4** and to **FIG 6:2** and withdraw the extension casing 2 and its gasket. Ensure that the centre plate 3 is not disturbed. Fit temporary slave bolts 4 to retain the centre plate to the gearbox casing.

Fitment is as described in **Section 6:6**.

6:4 Dismantling the gearbox

Drain off the oil if this was not done earlier.

Drive flange removal:

Refer to **FIG 6:1**. Hold the drive flange 18 from turning (RG421 or 18G 1205 are the official tools) and remove the retaining nut 19. Withdraw the flange. Collect the washer.

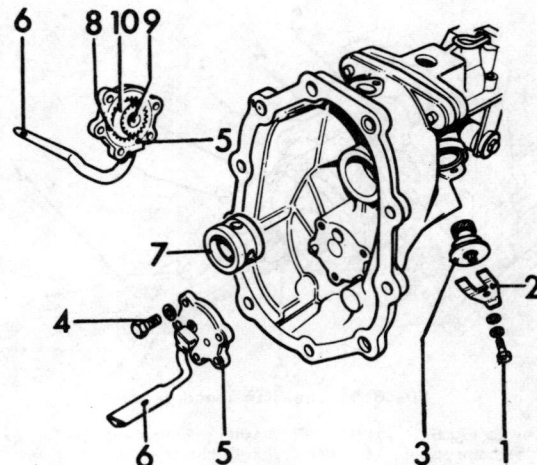

FIG 6:3 Dismantling the extension casing

Key to Fig 6:3 1 Bolt 2 Plate 3 Speedometer driven gear unit 4 Bolt 5 Pump 6 Oil intake tube 7 Transfer sleeve 8 Driven gear 9 Driving gear 10 Crescent filler piece

Bellhousing removal:

Refer to **Chapter 5, Section 5:5** and remove the release lever pivot, release lever and release bearing. Refer to **FIG 5:5** and remove the retaining bolts 10. Remove the bellhousing.

Extension casing removal and dismantling:

Refer to **Section 6:7** and remove the gearchange remote control assembly. Refer to **FIG 6:2**. Remove the two retaining bolts and spring washers and withdraw the fifth gear spool locating boss 1. Refer to **FIG 6:3**. Remove the speedometer drive retaining bolt 1 and its washers, the plate 2 and the driven gear unit 3. Remove the bolts and

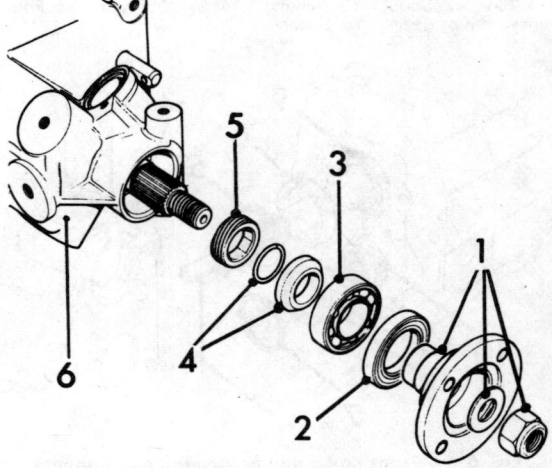

FIG 6:4 Drive flange and associated components

Key to Fig 6:4 1 Drive flange, nut and washer 2 Oil seal 3 Ballbearing 4 Circlip and sleeve 5 Speedometer drive gear 6 Extension casing

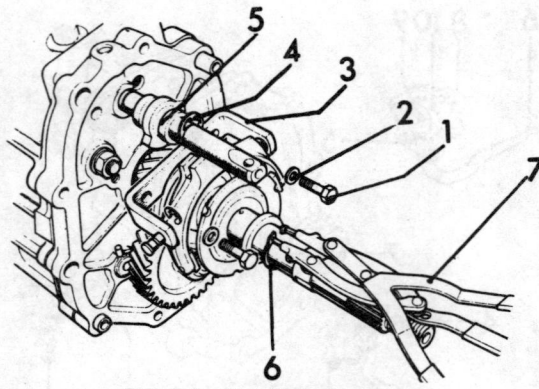

FIG 6:5   The fifth speed gears

Key to Fig 6:5   1 Bolt   2 Washer   3 Bracket   4 Circlip
5 Selector spool   6 Circlip   7 Circlip pliers

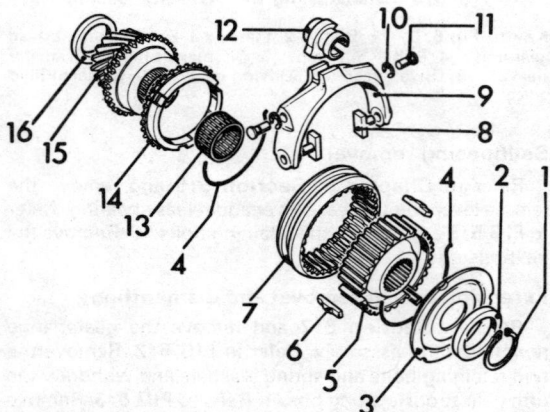

FIG 6:6   Components of the fifth speed synchro unit

Key to Fig 6:6   1 Circlip   2 Spacer   3 Cover   4 Spring
5 Hub   6 Key   7 Sleeve   8 Slipper   9 Fork   10 Circlip
11 Pin   12 Spool   13 Bearing   14 Synchro ring   15 Fifth
speed driven gear   16 Spacer

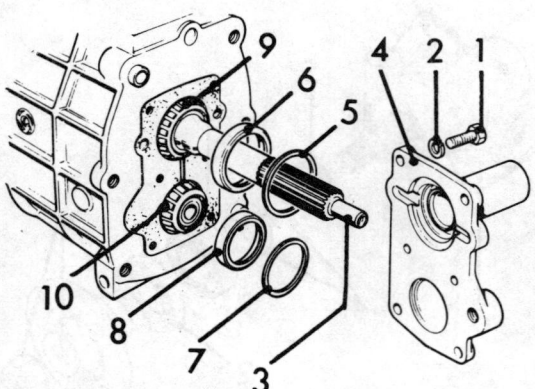

FIG 6:7   Front cover and associated components

Key to Fig 6:7   1 Bolt   2 Spring washer   3 Input shaft
4 Front cover   5 Shim washer   6 Bearing outer race
7 Shim washer   8 Bearing outer race   9 Input shaft
bearing   10 Layshaft bearing

washers which secure the casing to the gearbox. Withdraw the casing. Collect the oil pump drive shaft 35 in FIG 6:1). Refer to Section 6:5 and remove the oil pump. Refer to FIG 6:4. Remove and discard the oil seal 2. Remove bearing 3, spacer and circlip 4 and the speedometer drive gear 5.

Removing the fifth speed gears:

Refer to FIG 6:5. Remove the two bolts 1 and spring washers 2 and dismount the fifth gear selector fork 3. Remove the circlip 4 from the selector shaft. Withdraw the selector spool 5 noting that the longer cam is fitted downwards. Remove circlip 6 and withdraw the synchro assembly, fifth speed driven gear and the spacer. These components are shown dismantled in FIG 6:6.

Front cover removal:

Refer to FIG 6:7. Remove the retaining bolts 1 and spring washers 2 and withdraw the front cover 4. Identify and remove the shim washers 5 and 7 and the bearing outer races 6 and 8. Do not get them mixed. Remove the oil seal from the front cover. Remove the joint gasket.

Gearbox casing removal:

Refer to FIG 6:1. Remove the two bolts and spring washers and withdraw the selector shaft front spool locating boss 29. Remove the selector plug 30, spring and ball from the centre plate. Supporting the assembly on the centre plate as shown in FIG 6:8, withdraw the gearbox casing. Remove the input shaft and fourth speed synchro ring.

Layshaft removal:

Refer to FIG 6:9. Remove circlip 1. Using tool 18G 705 and adaptors 18G 705-1, withdraw the spacer 2 and the fifth speed driving gear 3 from the layshaft. Withdraw the layshaft 4 from the centre plate.

Mainshaft assembly removal:

Support the centre plate in a vice with protected jaws. Refer to FIG 6:9. Remove the reverse gear pivot pin circlip and pivot pin 5. Remove the reverse lever 6 and slipper pad. Slide the reverse shaft rearwards and withdraw the reverse gear, spacer, mainshaft assembly 9, selector shaft 8, selector shaft fork and spool in a forward direction out of the centre plate. Withdraw the selector fork and spool noting that the shorter cam of the spool is fitted downwards. If the pivot shaft 10 is to be removed, remove the retaining nut and washers. Remove the centre plate from the vice and, if the dowels are to be renewed, extract them from the plate.

Removing the bearings and bearing races:

Use tool RTR 47-23 to remove the bearing 9 in FIG 6:7 from the input shaft. Use extractor tools 18G 284 AAH and 284 to withdraw the outer race of the pilot bearing 38 in FIG 6:1. Use a suitable puller to remove the bearing and spacer. Use tool LC 370-2 to remove the layshaft bearings (the forward bearing is 10 in FIG 6:7).

Mainshaft dismantling:

Refer to **FIG 6:10**. Components 5 to 8 were removed from the mainshaft earlier but are included in this illustration for reference purposes. Remove the third/fourth speed synchro hub and sleeve assembly 1. Withdraw the third speed gear 2. Remove the circlip 3 which retains the mainshaft bearing. Withdraw components 4 (the bearing, the first speed gear and bush, the first/second speed hub, sleeve and synchro rings and the second speed gear).

Replacement parts:

Discard the old oil seals and circlips. Thoroughly clean and examine all other components. Discard worn, damaged and unserviceable parts. Brush clean gearbox oil over all steel components to inhibit rusting. Obtain replacement parts as necessary.

6:5 The oil pump

The oil pump 15 in **FIG 6:1** (5 in **FIG 6:3**) is driven from the rear end of the gearbox layshaft by the square-section drive shaft 35. Oil is drawn from forward of the centre plate via intake pipe 36 (6 in **FIG 6:3**), delivered to passage 39 and transferred to the bore of the mainshaft via transfer sleeve 37 (7 in **FIG 6:3**).

Testing:

If the operation of the pump is suspect, check the oil level in the gearbox as described in **Section 6:2** and, with the engine running at idling speed, remove plug 16 in **FIG 6:1**. A steady flow of oil should be expelled. Switch off the engine. Prime the threads of the plug with 'Locquic Primer Grade T' then, immediately before fitting, apply 'Loctite 270'. Torque tighten the plug. Top up the gearbox oil level.

If the oil flow from the plug orifice is negligible or intermittent, remove the pump for examination.

Removal and fitment:

Access to the pump requires removal of the extension casing from the gearbox either as described in **Section 6:3** or, if the complete gearbox has been removed, as described in **Section 6:4**.

Refer to **FIG 6:3**. Remove the retaining bolts 4 and their washers. Dismount the pump casing 5 complete with the intake pipe 6. Remove the internally and externally toothed gears 8 and 9. Worn or damaged gears, a scored casing 5 or crescent piece 10 must be renewed. Check that the oil delivery passage is clean and clear.

Fitment is the reverse of the removal sequence. Torque tighten the retaining bolts 4. Refit the extension casing as described in **Section 6:6**.

6:6 Reassembling the gearbox

Assemble with all internal components wetted with clean gearbox oil.

Synchro assemblies:

After fitting any new parts which may have been required, make the following check on each synchro assembly. With the outer sleeve held, a push-through load applied to the outer face of the hub should register 8.2 to 10.0kg (18 to 22lb) to overcome spring detent in either direction.

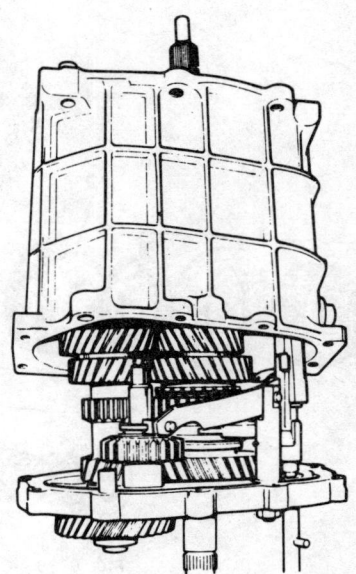

FIG 6:8 Removing and fitting the gearbox casing

First speed bush end float:

Temporarily fit the second speed gear, the first/second speed synchro hub and the first speed gear bush to the mainshaft. Manufacture a spacer to the following dimensions: OD, 50.0 ± 0.10mm (1.970 ± 0.004in); ID, 31.80 + 0.05mm (1.252 + 0.002in); width, 16.82 + 0.05mm (0.662 + 0.002in). Slide this spacer onto the shaft. Using an old circlip and feeler gauges, measure the clearance between the spacer and the circlip. This should be within the range of 0.015 to 0.055mm (0.0006 to 0.0022in). If necessary, select a new first speed bush **X** in **FIG 6:10** of appropriate collar thickness to achieve a clearance within this range. Dismantle this temporary assembly.

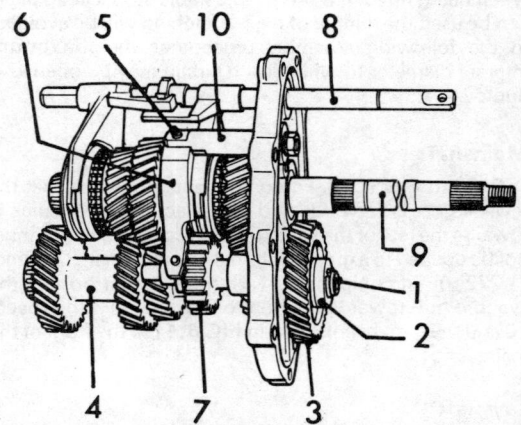

FIG 6:9 Removing and fitting the layshaft and mainshaft

Key to Fig 6:9 1 Circlip 2 Spacer 3 Fifth speed driving gear 4 Layshaft 5 Pivot pin 6 Reverse lever 7 Reverse idler gear 8 Selector shaft 9 Mainshaft 10 Pivot shaft

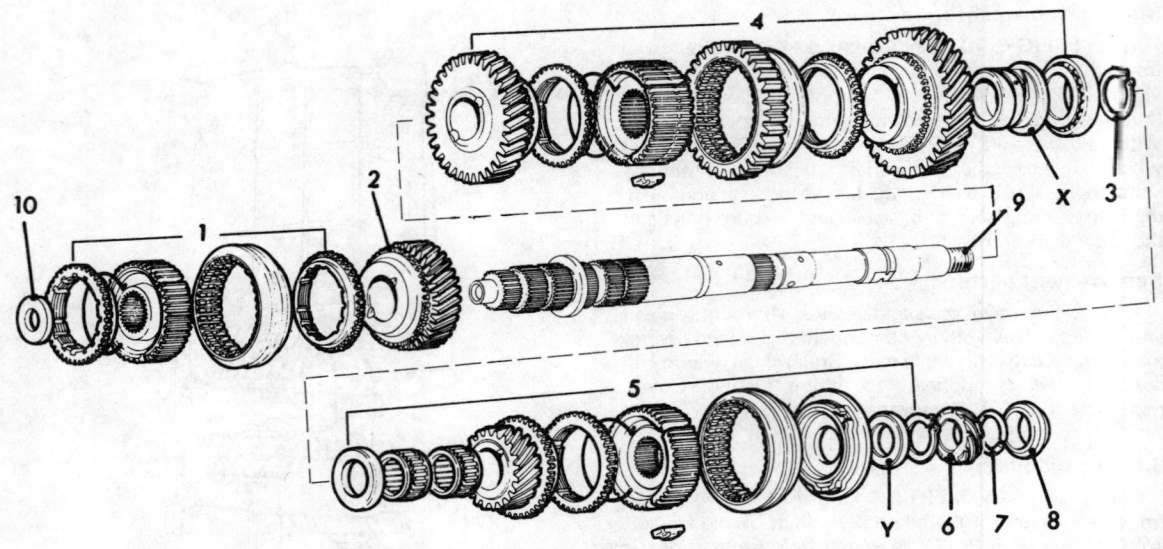

FIG 6:10   Components of the mainshaft assembly

Key to Fig 6:10   1 Third/fourth synchro unit   2 Third speed driven gear   3 Circlip   4 First/second synchro unit with integral driven reverse gear   5 Fifth speed gear and synchro unit   6 Speedometer driving gear   7 Circlip   8 Spacer 9 Mainshaft   10 Spacer   **X and Y** See text

Fifth gear end float:

Temporarily fit the fifth gear assembly (components 5 in **FIG 6:10**) to the mainshaft using an old circlip. Using feeler gauges, measure the end float. This should be within the range of 0.015 to 0.055mm (0.0006 to 0.0022in). If necessary, select a rear spacer **Y** in **FIG 6:10** of appropriate thickness to achieve an end float within this range. Dismantle this temporary assembly.

Fitting new circlips:

It is important that new circlips are not over-stretched when being fitted. If a set of 'adjustable stop' circlip pliers can be used the danger of over-stretching will be avoided. In the following assembly procedures the **maximum** internal diameter to which each circlip may be opened is quoted.

Mainshaft:

Refer to **FIG 6:10**. Fit components 4. Ensure that the reverse gear is forwards and the selector fork annulus is towards the rear of the shaft. Fit a new circlip 3 which must not be opened to a greater internal diameter than 32.30mm (1.272in). Fit components 1 with the longer boss of the synchro hub towards the front of the shaft. Fit the spacer 10 and the pilot bearing (38 in **FIG 6:1**) to the front of the mainshaft.

Layshaft:

Fit the bearings to the layshaft. Fit the layshaft bearing outer race to the centre plate. Fit the layshaft to the centre plate. Refer to **FIG 6:9**. Fit the fifth gear 3, spacer 2 and a new circlip 1 which must not be opened to a greater internal diameter than 22.50mm (0.886in).

Centre plate:

Fit the mainshaft bearing outer race to the centre plate. Hold the centre plate in a protected jaw vice. Take the selector shaft complete with the first/second fork, front spool and third/fourth fork and engage both forks in their respective synchro sleeves on the mainshaft assembly. Simultaneously engage the selector shaft and the mainshaft assemblies into the centre plate. Refer to **FIG 6:6**. Fit the fifth gear components in their correct order. Fit a new circlip 1 which must not be opened to a greater internal diameter than 27.63mm (1.088in).

Reverse idler gear:

Refer to **FIG 6:9**. Fit the reverse gear (lip for the slipper pad forwards), spacers and reverse shaft. Fit the reverse lever 6, slipper pad, pivot pin 5 and its retaining circlip. If a new pivot shaft 10 is being fitted, ensure that its radial disposition is consistent with the slipper pad engagement. This disposition is determined on assembly by checking the movement of the lever and engagement of the slipper pad after securing the new pivot shaft. Readjust the radial position as may be necessary.

Gearbox casing:

Hold the centre plate as shown in **FIG 6:8**. Ensure that the reverse shaft does not slide out of position. Fit the centre plate front gasket. Fit the forward main bearing and the pilot bearing outer race to the input shaft and fit the input shaft to the gearbox casing. Carefully slide the gearbox casing and input shaft into position over the mainshaft, layshaft and centre plate assembly. **Do not use force.** Ensure that the centre plate dowels and the forward end of the selector shaft engage in their respective locations. Refer to **FIG 6:7**. Fit the bearing outer races 6

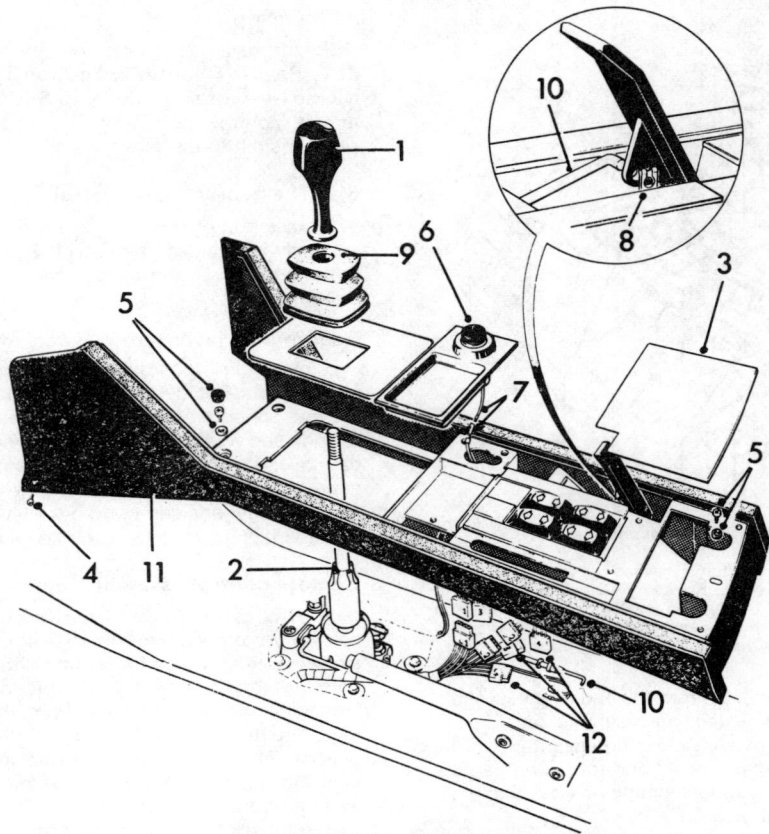

FIG 6:11   The gearchange lever and console

Key to Fig 6:11   1 Knob   2 Gearchange lever   3 Rear cover panel   4 Heater bracket screws   5 Screws   6 Cigar lighter   7 Snap connectors   8 Clip   9 Boot   10 Choke control   11 Console   12 Harness connectors

and 8. Refer to **FIG 6:2**. Using plain washers and seven slave bolts 4, draw the gearbox casing evenly into position on the centre plate.

Layshaft end float:

Fit the original layshaft shim washer 7 in **FIG 6:7**, the front cover gasket and the front cover 4 **without its oil seal**. Fit and torque tighten the cover retaining bolts. Using a dial gauge, measure the layshaft end float. This should be within the range of 0.015 to 0.055mm (0.0006 to 0.0022in). If the end float is outside this range, select a thicker or thinner shim washer to bring the end float within the specified range. Fit the new shim washer and confirm that the float is now within limits.

Input shaft/mainshaft end float:

Support the assembly with the input shaft upwards and a bearing ball in the centre of the shaft. Mount a dial gauge on the gearbox casing with its stylus resting on the bearing ball. Measure the combined end float of the mainshaft and the input shaft. If difficulty is experienced in differentiating between the end float and side movement, remove the front cover and wrap the plain portion of the input shaft below the splines with six turns of masking tape. After

refitting the front cover, check that the tape is not restricting the vertical movement of the input shaft.

Having measured the end float, select a thickness of shim washer 5 in **FIG 6:7** which will limit the end float to within the range of 0.015 to 0.055mm (0.0006 to 0.0022in). Fit the selected shim washer and recheck the end float. Remove the front cover. Remove the masking tape (if used).

Front cover:

Fit a new seal to the front cover (lip facing rearwards) and lubricate the lip. Mask the input shaft splines, fit the front cover and torque tighten the retaining bolts. Remove the masking from the splines.

Extension casing:

Remove the slave bolts and washers from the centre plate. Refer to **FIG 6:5**. Fit the fifth speed gear spool 5 (longer cam towards the bottom of the box) and circlip 4 to the selector shaft. Fit the fork and bracket and torque tighten the bracket retaining bolts. Refer to **FIG 6:1** and fit a new selector shaft 'O' ring 41. Fit the oil transfer sleeve 37. Fit the gasket to the rear face of the centre plate and

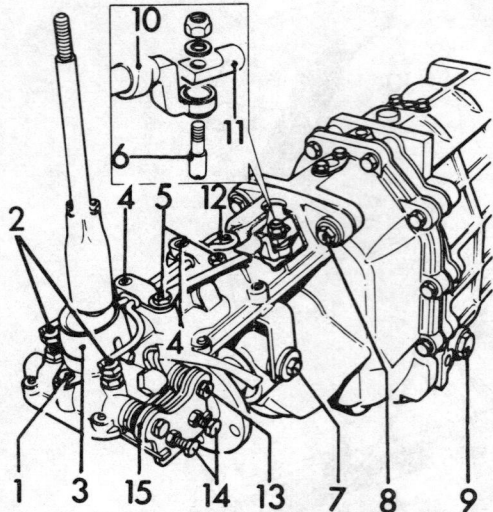

FIG 6:12 The remote gearchange control

Key to Fig 6:12 1 Bolt and washer 2 Adjuster bolts
3 Ball cover 4 Screws 5 Bolts 6 Coupling nut and pin
7 Bolt and washer 8 Bolt and washer 9 Drain plug
10 Selector arm elbow 11 Selector shaft 12 Bias spring
13 Bolts 14 Adjuster bolts 15 Backing plate

engage the pump drive shaft into the end of the layshaft.
Fit the oil pump to the extension casing as described in
Section 6:5. Fit the extension casing ensuring that the
drive shaft engages the pump. Fit and torque tighten the
assembly bolts. Fit both spool locating bosses 29 and 31.
Fit the ball, spring and plug 30.

Rear bearing, oil seal, drive flange:

Refer to **FIG 6:4**. Fit the speedometer drive gear 5 and
check that it is correctly engaged on the mainshaft flats. Fit
the circlip and sleeve 4, the ball bearing 3 and the oil seal 2.
Lubricate the lip of the oil seal and fit the drive flange, the
washer and the retaining nut 1. Torque tighten the
retaining nut. Fit the speedometer cable drive assembly 1,
2 and 3 in **FIG 6:3**.

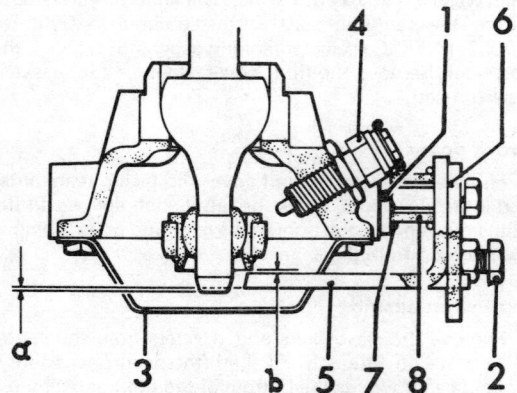

FIG 6:13 Reverse baulk/switch adjustments

Key to Fig 6:13 1 Shims 2 Adjuster bolts 3 Cover
4 Reverse light switch 5 Baulk plate 6 Backing plate
7 Spring 8 Spacer a and b See text

Bellhousing:

Fit the bellhousing and torque tighten the retaining
bolts. Refer to **Chapter 5, Section 5:5** and fit the clutch
release lever assembly. Refer to **Section 6:7** and fit the
remote control gearchange housing. Connect up the
selector shaft to the selector arm.

6:7 The gearchange control

A cross-section through the remote gearchange control
assembly is included in **FIG 6:1**. The arrangement of the
gearchange lever and central console is shown in **FIG
6:11**.

Gearchange lever removal and fitment:

Remove the knob from the lever. Remove the two lever
rubber boots. Remove the bolt and setscrew which secure
the bias spring bracket to the remote extension. Remove
the bolt and washer 1 in **FIG 6:12** which retains the lever
ball cover 3. Prise the bias spring over the bolt heads 2 and
remove the lever and ball cover. Take care not to lose the
nylon plunger and spring from the lever.

Fitment is the reverse of this sequence.

Remote control assembly removal and fitment:

With the car on a hoist or over a pit, refer to **Section 6:3**
and carry out operations 1 and 2 of the gearbox removal
sequence. Identify and disconnect the two leads to the
reverse switch at the snap connectors. Refer to **FIG 6:12**.
Uncouple the selector shaft from the selector arm by
removing the nut, washer and pin 6. Remove the bolts and
washers 7 and 8, engage the selector arm in the fifth speed
gate and carefully manoeuvre the remote control assembly
away from the gearbox.

Refitment is the reverse of this sequence. Torque tighten
the selector arm/shaft coupling pin nut.

Remote control assembly overhaul:

Remove the assembly as described earlier. Remove the
eight rubber mounting bushes noting the relationship of
the stepped bushes. Refer to **FIG 6:12**. Remove the
screws 4 and the bolts 5. Remove the bridge plates, liners
and the bias spring 12. Remove the adjuster bolts 2.
Remove the two bolts 13, the washers, reverse baulk plate,
springs and spacers. Refer to **FIG 6:13**. Remove the cover
3 and the reverse switch 4. Remove the square-headed
pinch bolt (34 in **FIG 6:1**), remove the selector arm elbow
and withdraw the selector arm. If necessary, press out the
selector arm bushes. If necessary, remove the circlips
which secure the pivot balls and bushes in the selector arm
elbows and press out the bushes and pivot balls. Discard
the circlips.

Renew bushes, pivot balls, mounting bushes and other
parts as necessary and reassemble by following the reverse
of the dismantling sequence. Adjust the reverse baulk the
stop gate, the bias spring and the reverse light switch after
the remote control has been refitted to the gearbox and
after the gearchange lever has also been refitted
(temporarily if necessary).

Reverse baulk plate adjustment:

Refer to **FIG 6:13**. Remove the cover 3. Locate the lever
vertically in neutral. Loosen the locknuts and bolts 2 until
the baulk plate 5 is in contact with the backing plate 6.

Tighten the bolts 2 **equally** until they just start to move the baulk plate out of contact with the backing plate. Using a straightedge and feeler gauges, move the bolts 2 **equally** until the clearance **a** between the lower face of the gearchange lever and the underside of the baulk plate is 1.27 to 1.52mm (0.050 to 0.060in). Tighten the locknuts. The clearance **b** between the upper face of the baulk plate and the lower edge of the gearchange lever bush must be a minimum of 0.25mm (0.010in).

First/second gate stop adjustment:

After adjusting the reverse baulk plate, engage first gear. By adding or removing shims 1 adjust the clearance between the side of the gearchange lever and the edge of the baulk plate to within the range of 0.10 to 0.30mm (0.004 to 0.012in). Check the clearance with the second gear engaged. Fit the cover 3.

Bias spring adjustment:

With the unit completely reassembled, engage third gear. Refer to **FIG 6:12** and adjust both bolts 2 until both legs of the spring are 0.50mm (0.02in) clear of the crosspin. Apply light load to the gearchange lever towards the left to take up play. Adjust the righthand bolt 2 downwards until the spring leg just contacts the crosspin. Repeat this adjustment towards the right (adjusting the lefthand bolt). Rock the lever across the gate several times. The lever should return to the third/fourth gate. Tighten the nuts which lock the bolts 2.

Reverse light switch adjustment:

Select reverse gear. Refer to **FIG 6:13**. With the switch locknut backed off and the ignition switched on, screw the switch 4 inwards or outwards until the reversing lights just come on. Screw the switch inwards by a further half turn. Hold the switch and tighten the locknut. Select other gears. The reversing lights should now be off.

6:8 Fault diagnosis

(a) Jumping out of gear

1 Gearchange control requires adjustment
2 Gearchange control worn
3 Selector parts worn
4 Detent spring broken
5 Synchro unit fork groove(s) worn
6 Excessive end play in gearbox shafts
7 Excessively worn synchro unit(s)

(b) Noisy gearbox

1 Check (a)
2 Worn or damaged bearings or gears
3 Insufficient oil
4 Worn or damaged pump
5 Worn splines

(c) Difficulty in engaging gear

1 Check 1, 2, 3 and 7 in (a)
2 Defective clutch release action (see Chapter 5)
3 Defective clutch (see Chapter 5)

(d) No drive when gear is engaged

1 Check 3 in (c)
2 Stripped input shaft or mainshaft splines
3 Stripped gear teeth
4 Broken input shaft, mainshaft or layshaft

(e) Oil leaks

1 Defective oil seal
2 Defective gasket, damaged joint face(s)
3 Oil level too high
4 Loose drain or filler plug
5 Cracked casing

NOTES

CHAPTER 7

THE AUTOMATIC TRANSMISSION

7:1 Description

The automatic transmission is a Borg Warner type 65. It comprises a three-element fluid torque converter and a three forward speed and reverse gearbox.

A cross-section through the transmission is shown in **FIG 7:1**. The torque converter 1 is coupled to the drive plate (see **Chapter 1, Section 1:14**) which, on automatic transmission models is provided instead of a flywheel. The action of the torque converter is as follows. The impeller 2 transmits torque by means of the transmission fluid to the turbine 3 which drives the gearbox input shaft 4. The stator element 5 redirects the flow of fluid as it leaves the turbine so that it re-enters the impeller at the most effective angle. The maximum torque multiplication through the converter is 2.08 and this occurs at maximum slip when the turbine is stationary (car moving off from standing start). As the turbine picks up speed and the slip between it and the impeller reduces, the torque multiplication reduces progressively until, when their speeds become substantially equal, the converter acts as a fluid coupling. The stator element is now no longer required to redirect the flow and its one-way clutch hub 6 permits it to rotate in the same direction as the impeller and turbine.

The three forward speeds and reverse are provided by a combination of epicyclic gearing, multiplate clutches, band clutches and a one-way clutch. Gear ratios are quoted in the **Technical Data** section of the **Appendix**. A fluid cooler is incorporated in the engine cooling system radiator and is connected with the gearbox by fluid feed and return pipes.

The transmission has a **P, R, N, D, 2, 1** selector arrangement. With **P** selected, no torque is transmitted, the car is 'parked' and held from rolling in either direction. With **R** selected, reverse drive is engaged; with **N**, no torque is transmitted but the car can roll in either direction; with **D**, forward drive is engaged with automatic upward and downward gearchanges; with **2**, forward drive is engaged with automatic upward and downward gearchanges between low (first) and intermediate (second) but not with top (third). With **1** selected, forward drive is engaged but no upward gearchanges will occur. Full throttle kick-down from third speed into second speed or, at lower speeds, into first speed provides immediate downshift for maximum acceleration.

As a safety measure, a starter inhibitor switch prevents the starter motor from operating except when either **P** or **N** is selected. A reversing light switch closes when **R** is selected.

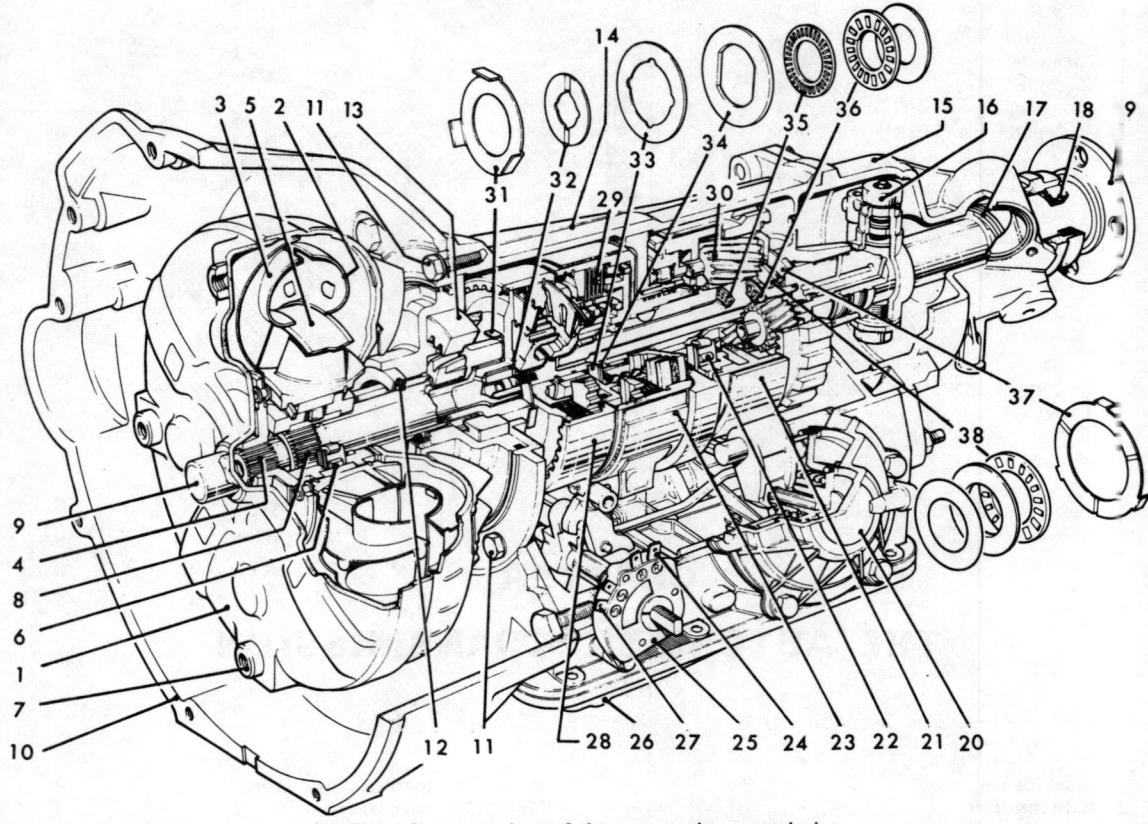

FIG 7:1   Cutaway view of the automatic transmission

Key to Fig 7:1   1 Torque converter   2 Impeller   3 Turbine   4 Input shaft   5 Stator   6 One-way clutch hub   7 Drive plate attachment points   8 Stator support   9 Boss (crankshaft spigot)   10 Bellhousing   11 Bolt   12 Oil seal   13 Pump   14 Gearbox casing   15 Extension casing   16 Governor   17 Speedometer drive gear   18 Oil seal   19 Output flange   20 Rear servo   21 Rear band clutch   22 One-way clutch   23 Front band clutch   24 Reversing light terminals   25 Starter inhibitor/reversing light switch   26 Sump   27 Starter inhibitor terminals   28 Front clutch   29 Rear clutch   30 Epicyclic gearing   31 to 38 Thrust washers, kit RTC 140

7:2 Maintenance

At least every 3000 miles (5000km), check over the gearbox, radiator and pipelines for joint, seal or connection leaks.

Fluid level:

At least every 6000 miles (10,000km), check the level of the fluid in the gearbox and top up as necessary. The dipstick/filler tube is on the lefthand side at the rear of the engine and the fluid level may be checked and topped up with the gearbox hot or cold.

With the car on level ground, run the engine for about two minutes and pass the selector lever through all positions to fully prime the transmission. Select **P** and allow the engine to idle. Withdraw the dipstick, wipe it dry on lint free cloth, re-insert and check the fluid level using the CHECK COLD side of the blade if the engine was started up from cold or the CHECK HOT side if the transmission is at normal operating temperature (after, say, a 20 mile (30km) run). Top up to the high hot or high cold mark as appropriate. **Do not overfill.** Use an AFT type F

fluid of reputable brand and, preferably, of the same brand as that already in the transmission.

Selector linkage:

Every 6000 miles (10,000km), lubricate the exposed pivots of the selector linkage with a few drops of oil

Fluid draining and refilling:

To drain the gearbox (the torque converter cannot be drained), refer to **FIG 7:2**, uncouple the dipstick/filler tube 1 from the sump and allow the fluid to drain off. Refit the tube and refill not higher than the high mark on the CHECK COLD side of the dipstick blade. Run the engine and check the fluid level as described earlier.

7:3 Tests

Starter inhibitor/reversing light switch:

This two-section switch is 3 in **FIG 7:2**. The starter motor should only operate when **P** or **N** is selected. If, with a correctly adjusted selector, the starter motor will operate when **R**, **D**, **2** or **1** is selected, the switch is defective and should be renewed. With the ignition switched on, the reversing lights should only come on when **R** is selected. If either section of the switch does not operate, check with a battery and test lamp that the switch is in fact defective before suspecting a wiring discontinuity.

Test conditions:

The carburetters and ignition timing must be correctly adjusted, the transmission fluid topped up and the engine and transmission at normal operating temperature before carrying out the following tests.

Stall test:

The stall speed is the maximum rev/min (recorded on an independent, accurate tachometer—see **Chapter 2, Section 2:8**) at which the engine can drive the converter impeller while the turbine is held stationary. Stall speed provides indications of both engine and transmission performance and efficiency.

Position the car with the front bumper (suitably protected) against a wall, select **D** and allow the engine to idle for approximately one minute. Depress the accelerator pedal to full throttle **but not to kick-down** and note the maximum tachometer reading. Do not run at stall conditions for more than 10 seconds before releasing the throttle.

The stall speed of an engine and transmission in good order should be between 1900 and 2100rev/min. If the stall speed is below 1900rev/min, refer to **Chapter 1, Section 1:5** and check the cylinder compression pressures. If the engine is in good condition but the stall speed is below 1300rev/min, renew the torque converter. If the stall speed is in excess of 2300rev/min, suspect clutch or brake band slip. Adjustment of the bands as described in **Section 7:4** should then be carried out and the stall test repeated.

Gear engagement:

With the engine idling and the brakes applied, select **N** to **D**, **N** to **2**, **N** to **1** and **N** to **R**. Engagement should be felt in each position selected.

Converter one-way clutch:

Inability to start on steep gradients combined with poor acceleration from rest and a stall speed of the order of 1300rev/min indicates that the converter one-way clutch is slipping. Poor acceleration in third gear above 30 miles/hr (50km/hr) indicates that the one-way clutch has seized. This condition will also be indicated by excessive overheating of the transmission fluid but will not be accompanied by an abnormal stall speed.

Cut-back pressure:

Using pressure gauge 601284 and piping CBW 1C-2 connected to the pressure take-off point at the rear of the gearbox, commence from a standing start with **D** selected and the accelerator pedal **at kick-down position**. The pressure should rise to 15.8 to 18.5kg/sq cm (225 to 265lb/sq in) and then cut-back to 6.8 to 8.6kg/sq cm (97 to 123lb/sq in) before second gear engages. If the pressure does not cut-back, the modulator or the governor valves are sticking.

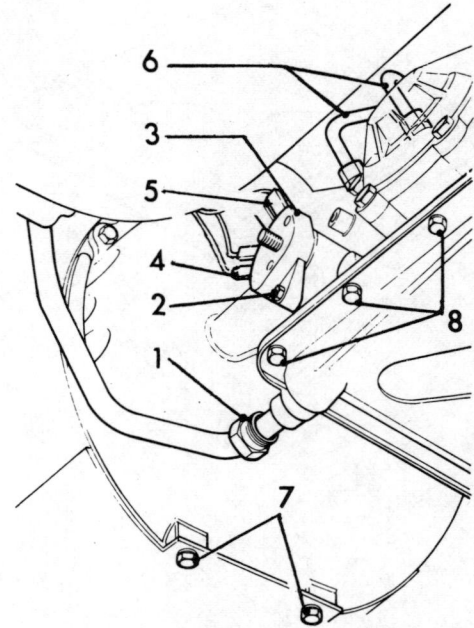

FIG 7:2   **Transmission fluid drain**

Key to Fig 7:2   1 Dipstick/filler tube union   2 Bolt
3 Starter inhibitor/reversing light switch   4 Starter
inhibitor terminals   5 Reversing light terminals   6 Cooler
feed and return pipes   7 Bolts   8 Bolts

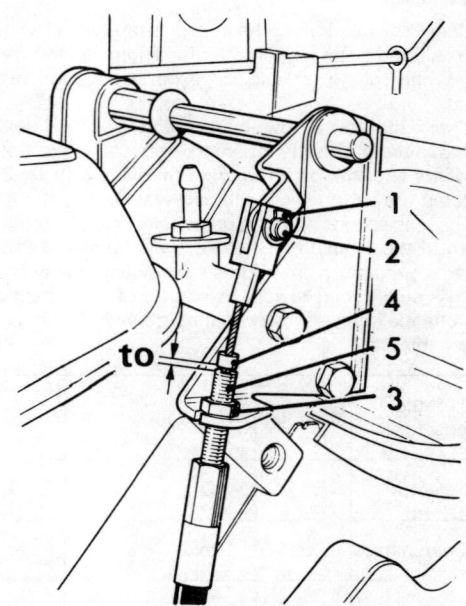

FIG 7:3   **The kick-down cable adjuster**

Key to Fig 7:3   1 Clip   2 Pin   3 Locknut   4 Crimped
stop   5 Adjuster

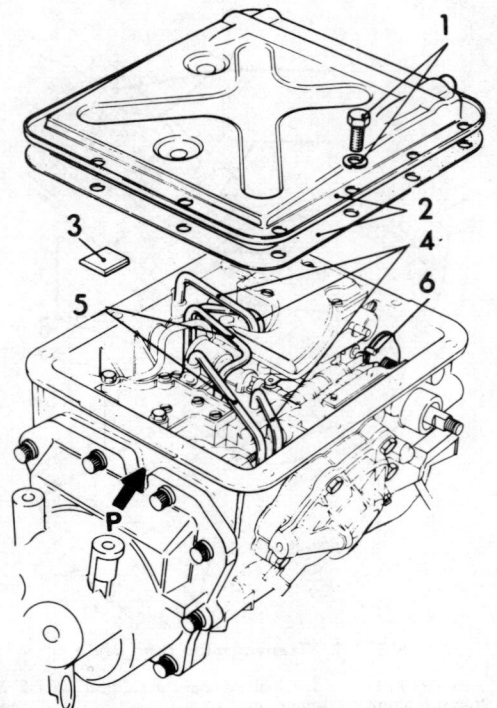

FIG 7:4   Removing the sump and oil pipes

Key to Fig 7:4   1 Bolt and spring washer   2 Sump and gasket   3 Magnet   4 Pipes   5 Pipes   6 Downshift inner cable and cam   **P** Pressure take-off point

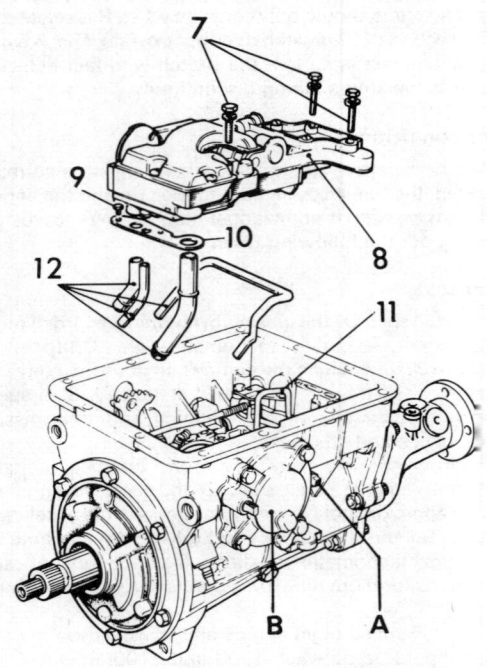

FIG 7:5   Removing the valve block and pipes

Key to Fig 7:5   7 Screws   8 Valve block   9 Screw   10 Plate   11 Pipe   12 Pipes (note 'O' ring)   **A** Adjuster   **B** Front servo

Road tests:

Check the freedom of the transmission with **N** selected. There should be no tendency for the engine to drive the car nor, when rolling, should there be any engine braking effect.

Check that, on a downward gradient with **R** selected and minimum throttle opening, the car does not roll forwards and that on an upward gradient with **D, 2** or **1** selected the car does not roll backwards.

The road speeds at which gearchanges should occur are given in the tabulation. If the actual gearchange speeds differ significantly from those tabulated, have the car professionally road tested. In addition to comparing the gearchange speeds, note the quality of the gear engagements.

7:4 Adjustments
Downshift cable removal, fitment and adjustment:

Drain off the transmission fluid as described in **Section 7:2**. Dismount the air cleaner as described in **Chapter 2, Section 2:3**. Refer to **FIG 7:3**. Remove the clip 1 and the clevis pin 2. Loosen locknut 3. Remove the gearbox sump as described in **Section 7:7** (see **FIG 7:4**) and uncouple the inner cable from the cam (6 in **FIG 7:4**). Using special boxspanner CBW 62, remove the outer cable from the gearbox casing. Withdraw the cable assembly.

Fit the cable assembly by reversing this sequence. Check the setting as follows. With the carburetters, idling speed and ignition timing correctly adjusted as described in **Chapters 2** and **3**, run the engine in **P** until it attains

Throttle position	Minimum	Light		Kick-down						
Selector	1	D	D	D	D	D	1	D	2	2
Gearchange	2 to 1	1 to 2	2 to 3	1 to 2	2 to 3	3 to 2	2 to 1	3 to 1	1 to 2	2 to 1
Road speed Miles/hr Km/hr	16 to 26 25 to 41	9 to 15 15 to 24	14 to 19 22 to 30	40 to 50 64 to 80	73 to 80 117 to 128	51 to 64 82 to 102	28 to 40 45 to 64	28 to 40 45 to 64	40 to 50 64 to 80	28 to 40 45 to 64

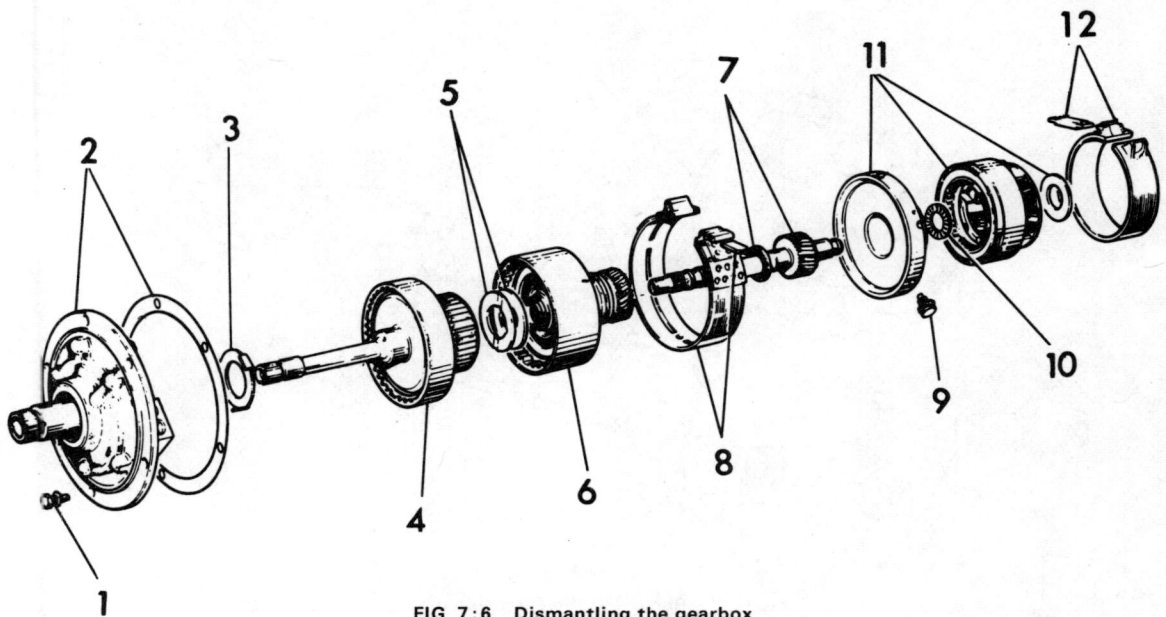

FIG 7:6 Dismantling the gearbox

Key to Fig 7:6 1 Bolt and washer 2 Pump and gasket 3 Washer (selective) 4 Front clutch assembly 5 Thrust washers 6 Rear clutch 7 Forward sun gear 8 Front band and strut 9 Bolts 10 Thrust washer 11 Centre support, planet gear and thrust washer 12 Rear band and strut

normal operating temperature. With the engine idling, actuate the throttle coupling shaft until the idling speed just starts to rise. Hold this condition and check the gap between the crimped stop 4 and the end of the adjuster 5. This gap should be between 0.25 and 0.5mm (0.010 and 0.020in).

If a new cable assembly has been fitted, reset the gap at the screwed adaptor and proceed to the pressure check described later. If the original cable assembly has been refitted and the gap is outside the specified range, check that the throttle linkage is free of distortion and correctly set before adjusting the gap and proceeding to the pressure check operations.

The purpose of the pressure measurement operations is to check the gearbox operating pressure relative to the correct downshift cable setting in order to diagnose a maladjusted cable or an internal gearbox fault which would be suspected if the results of the cable adjustment checks were not satisfactory.

With the carburetters, idling speed, ignition timing and transmission fluid level correct and the engine at normal operating temperature, remove the take-off plug (its location is arrowed in **FIG 7:4**) and connect piping CBW 1C-2 and pressure gauge 601284 to the pressure take-off point. With the foot and handbrakes firmly applied, run the engine and select **D**. At idling speed the pressure must be between 3.86 and 4.92kg/sq cm (55 and 70lb/sq in) and at 1250rev/min, 5.62kg/sq cm (80lb/sq in). There must be a rise of at least 1.05kg/sq cm (15lb/sq in) between the pressures recorded at these two engine speeds. If, with the gap within the specified limits, the pressure measurements do not align, an internal fault in the gearbox must be suspected.

Front and rear brake bands:

The rear brake band adjuster is shown **A** in **FIG 7:5**. The front brake band adjuster is on the opposite side of the gearbox casing. The adjustment procedure is the same for both.

With the handbrake applied, select **N**. Loosen the adjuster locknut, tighten the adjuster to a torque of 0.7kgm (5lb ft) and then back it off by three-quarters of a turn. Tighten the locknut to a torque of 4.8kgm (35lb ft).

7:5 Removing and refitting the transmission

The procedures for the removal of the complete automatic transmission and for the removal of the extension casing only, leaving the engine in the car in both cases are described in this Section. The procedure for the removal of the engine and transmission as a unit is described in **Chapter 1, Section 1:4** and, if this course has been adopted, separate the transmission from the engine as described in operation 9 of the following procedure.

Transmission removal and refitment:

1 With the car on a hoist or over a pit, select **N** and chock the wheels firmly. Disconnect the cables from the battery.
2 Dismount the air cleaner as described in **Chapter 2, Section 2:3**. Disconnect the downshift cable from the cylinder head bracket and throttle linkage as described in **Section 7:4**.
3 Disconnect the dipstick/filler tube and the transmission breather pipe from the cylinder head. Drain off the transmission fluid as described in **Section 7:2**.

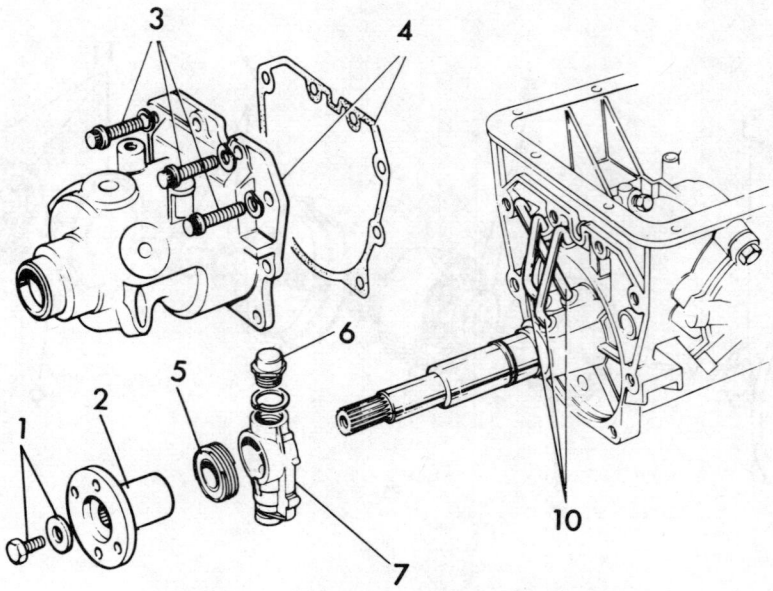

FIG 7:7 Removing the extension casing

Key to Fig 7:7   1 Bolt and plain washer   2 Output flange   3 Bolts   4 Extension casing and gasket   5 Speedometer drive gear   6 Counterweight and spring washer   7 Governor assembly   10 Pipes

4 Refer to **Chapter 1, Section 1:17** and remove the front section of the exhaust system (items 3 and 4 in **FIG 1:31**). Refer to **Chapter 8, Section 8:3** and uncouple the propeller shaft from the gearbox flange. Refer to **Section 7:8** and remove the selector rod.

5 Remove the righthand bolt from the rear of the engine sump flange. Remove the torque converter access plate (six bolts and spring washers). Remove the four bolts and thick plain washers which secure the torque converter to the drive plate. Remove the two bolts 7 in **FIG 7:2**.

6 Position a jack under the transmission (interpose a piece of wood) and raise the jack to support the transmission. Remove the bolts and spring washers and dismount the two plates which secure the bridge of the rear mounting to the chassis. Disconnect the speedometer drive cable.

7 Lower the jack only as far as is necessary to allow access to the bellhousing bolts and (after identifying them) the removal of the pipes 6 in **FIG 7:2**.

8 Identify and disconnect the leads 4 and 5 in **FIG 7:2**. Position a jack under the engine sump (interpose a piece of wood) and support the weight of the engine.

9 Remove the bellhousing bolts and washers and note the position of the harness clip bracket. Support and withdraw the transmission unit until it is clear of the crankshaft spigot and can be lowered away. **Do not allow the torque converter to slide out.**

Refitment of the gearbox unit to the engine and reassembly of the installation is the reverse of the separation and removal sequences but note the following points. Be careful not to damage the front pump oil seal and ensure that the driving dogs on the converter are engaged in the pump. Carefully align the transmission and engine to enable the torque converter to engage with the crankshaft spigot. On completion of the installation, check the downshift cable setting as described in **Section 7:4**. Refill the transmission with fluid as described in **Section 7:2**. Road test the car as described in **Section 7:3**.

Extension casing removal and fitment:

Carry out operations 1, 3, 4 and 6 of the transmission removal procedure described earlier. Remove the output drive flange 19 in **FIG 7:1** as described in **Section 7:7**. Lower the support jack only as far as necessary to allow access to the extension casing bolts. Withdraw the casing and discard the gasket.

Fitment is the reverse of this sequence. Refer to **Section 7:7** for relevant torque tightening figures.

7:6 The torque converter

The operation of the torque converter has been briefly described in **Section 7:1**. It is a sealed unit and cannot be repaired by an owner. A defective converter must be removed and a new assembly installed.

Removal:

Remove the transmission or, if the engine and transmission were removed as a unit, separate the transmission from the engine. The procedures are described in **Section 7:5**.

Withdraw the converter from the bellhousing.

Fitment:

Reverse the removal procedure. Be careful not to damage the front pump oil seal and ensure that the driving dogs on the converter are engaged in the pump.

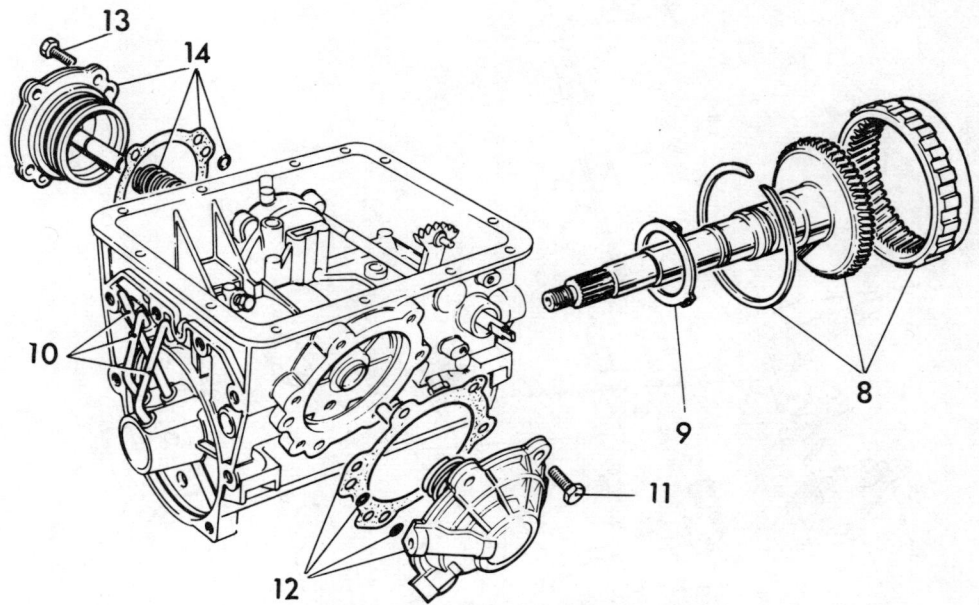

FIG 7:8 Removing the output shaft and servos

Key to Fig 7:8   8 Output shaft assembly   9 Thrust washer   10 Pipes   11 Bolt   12 Front servo, 'O' rings and gasket
13 Bolt   14 Rear servo, spring, gasket and 'O' ring

7:7 Gearbox overhaul

The procedures described in this section are intended to assist an owner who already has experience of overhauling automatic transmissions and can arrange access to the special tools which are required. Reference should also be made to **Hints on Maintenance and Overhaul** in the **Appendix**.

Note that, in addition to the replacement of worn or damaged parts as may be found necessary, the following repair kits will be required: thrust washers, kit RTC 140; valve body springs, kit RTC 146; piston rings and seals, kit RTC 139; rubber rings and oil seals, kit AAU 1052; gaskets, kit RTC 138; parking pawl torsion spring, kit RTC 31 and parking rod lever torsion spring, kit RTC 33.

Dismantling:

Withdraw the torque converter from the bellhousing. Clean off the exterior of the unit using petrol or paraffin. Remove bolts 11 in **FIG 7:1** and separate the gearbox from the bellhousing. Position the gearbox inverted in a suitable cradle (the official fixture is CBW 60). Remove the switch 3 in **FIG 7:2**.

Sump and valve block:

Refer to **FIGS 7:4** and **7:5**. Remove the components by following their numerical order. Keep the tubes identified and note that there is an 'O' ring on the pump suction tube. Dismantling of the valve block is covered later.

Pump, clutches, input shaft, gear assemblies:

Refer to **FIG 7:6**. Remove the bolts 1 and withdraw the pump and joint washer 2. Continue by withdrawing the

components in the order in which they are numbered and ensure that the location of the various thrust washers which will be renewed from kit RTC 140 are carefully identified. Squeeze together the ends of the brake bands and remove them together with their struts. Dismantling of the pump and clutches is covered later.

Rear extension casing, governor, output shaft, servos:

Refer to **FIGS 7:7** and **7:8**. Use tool 18G 1205 to hold flange 2 and remove the bolt and washer 1. Proceed by removing the components in the order in which they are numbered. Remove the retaining nut and dismount the selector lever. Dismantling of the governor is covered later.

Gearbox casing components:

Refer to **FIG 7:9** and remove the components in the order in which they are numbered. Remove the downshaft cable as described in **Section 7:4** after removing torsion spring 16.

Dismantling the front clutch:

To dismantle, proceed in the order in which the components are numbered in **FIG 7:10**. Note which way round the dished washers are fitted. To remove the piston it may be necessary to blank off the bores of the clutch drum and apply compressed air to the piston valve hole.

Assembly is the reverse of the dismantling sequence. Ensure that the dished washers are fitted the correct way round.

Dismantling the rear clutch:

To dismantle, proceed in the order in which the components are numbered in **FIG 7:11**. Spring 6 must be

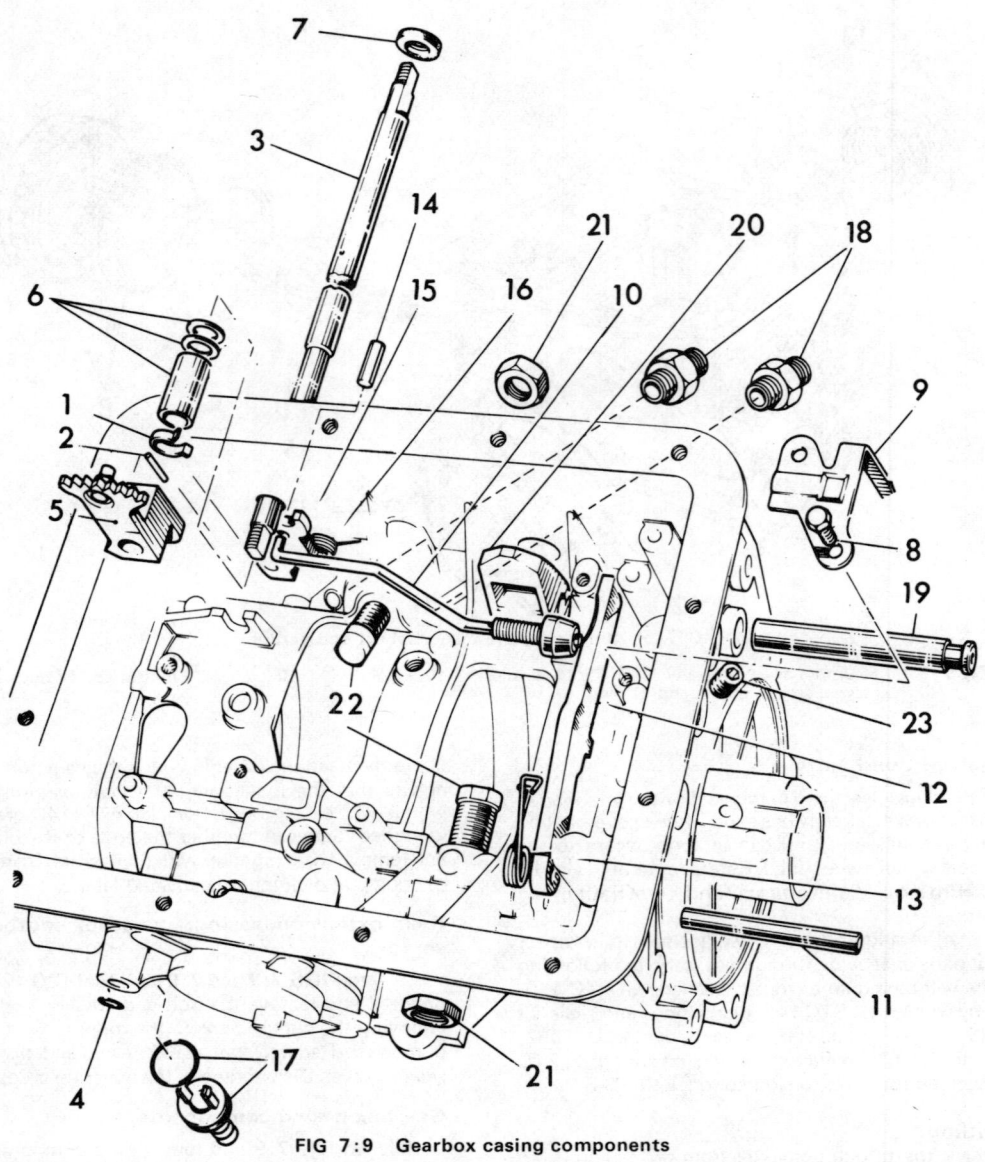

FIG 7:9 Gearbox casing components

Key to Fig 7:9   1 Spring clip   2 Pin   3 Cross-shaft   4 'O' ring   5 Detent lever   6 Collar, washers and 'O' ring
7 Oil seal   8 Screws   9 Cam plate   10 Parking pawl rod assembly   11 Pin   12 Parking pawl   13 Spring   14 Pin
15 Relay lever   16 Spring   17 Breather adaptor   18 Unions   19 Servo lever pivot pin   20 Rear servo lever   21 Locknuts
22 Adjusting screws   23 Pressure take-off plug

compressed using tool CBW 37A before circlip 4 and seat 5 can be removed.

Assembly is the reverse of the removal sequence. Use tool CBW 41A to fit the piston 7 and seal 8 assembly. Compress spring 6 with tool CBW 37A to fit the seat 5 and the circlip 4.

Dismantling the one-way clutch and planet gear assembly:

To dismantle the one-way clutch, refer to **FIG 7:12** and separate the centre support 1 from the planet gear assembly 5, withdraw the clutch 2, remove circlip 3 and withdraw the clutch outer race 4 from the planet gear assembly. The planet gear assembly cannot be dismantled by an owner.

Assembly is the reverse of this sequence.

Dismantling the governor:

To dismantle the governor, refer to **FIG 7:13** and follow the sequence in which the components are numbered noting that the counterweight and washers 1 and 2 were removed earlier.

Assembly is the reverse of the dismantling sequence.

74

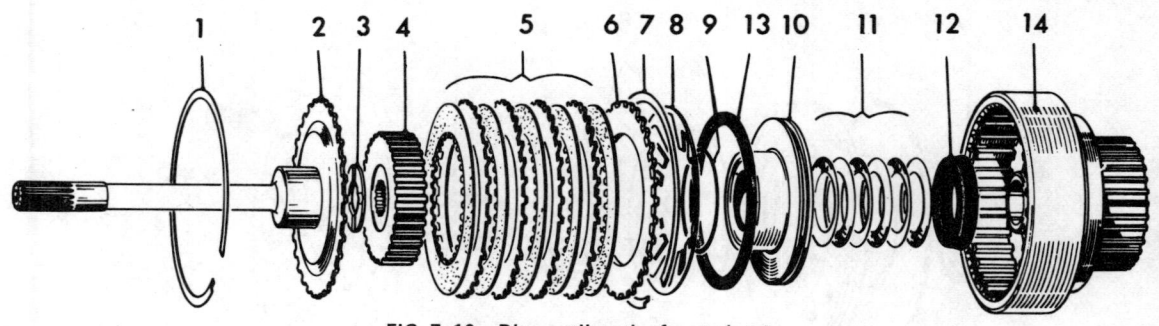

FIG 7:10   Dismantling the front clutch

Key to Fig 7:10   1 Circlip   2 Input shaft   3 Thrust washer   4 Hub   5 Inner and outer friction plates   6 Pressure plate   7 Circlip   8 Spring   9 Spring bearing   10 Piston   11 Six dished washers   12 Seal   13 Seal   14 Drum

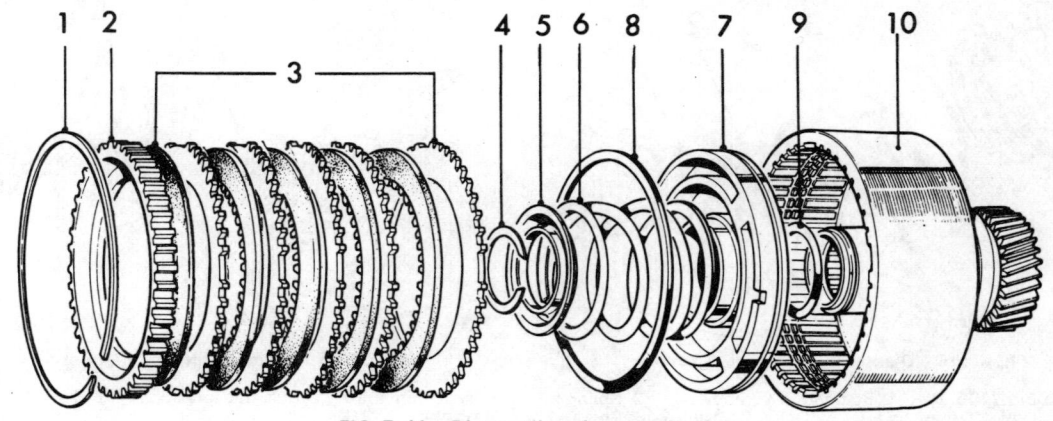

FIG 7:11   Dismantling the rear clutch

Key to Fig 7:11   1 Circlip   2 Pressure plate   3 Inner and outer friction plates   4 Circlip   5 Spring seat   6 Spring   7 Piston   8 Sealing ring   9 'O' ring   10 Drum

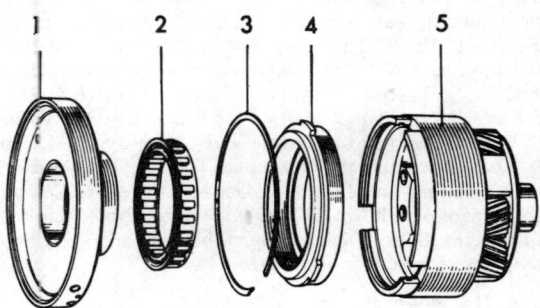

FIG 7:12   Dismantling the one-way clutch

Key to Fig 7:12   1 Centre support   2 One-way clutch   3 Clip   4 Clutch outer race   5 Epicyclic gear assembly

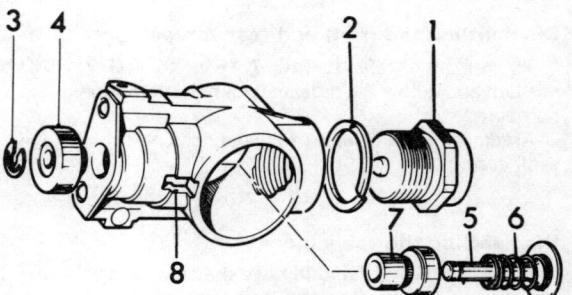

FIG 7:13   Dismantling the governor

Key to Fig 7:13   1 Counterweight   2 Spring washer   3 Clip   4 Weight   5 Stem   6 Spring   7 Valve   8 Casing

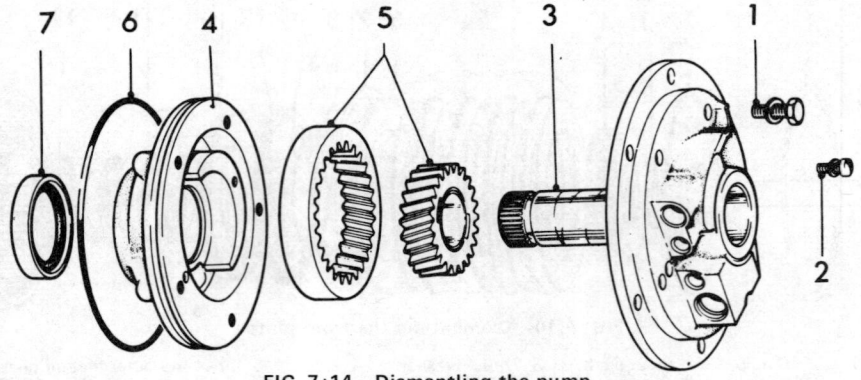

FIG 7:14 Dismantling the pump

Key to Fig 7:14   1 Bolt and washer   2 Bolt and washer   3 Stator support   4 Pump body   5 Gears   6 'O' ring
7 Seal

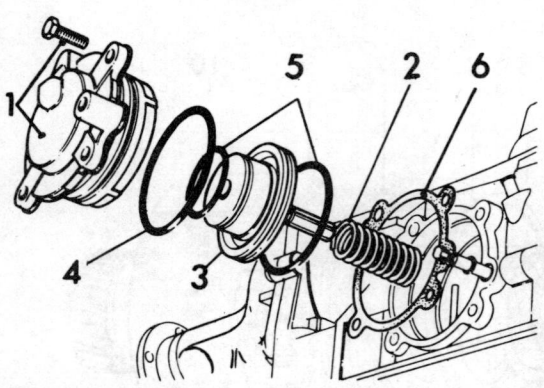

FIG 7:15   Dismantling the front servo

Key to Fig 7:15   1 Bolt and servo body   2 Spring
3 Piston   4 'O' ring (body)   5 'O' rings (piston)   6 Gasket

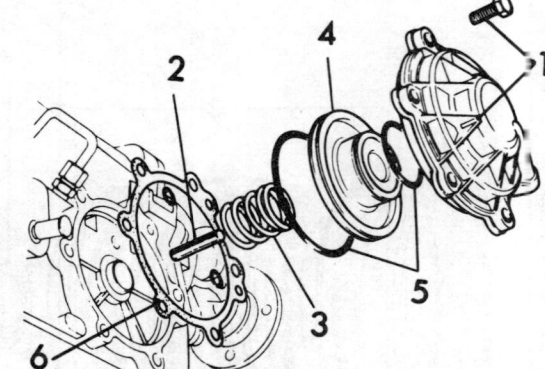

FIG 7:16   Dismantling the rear servo

Key to Fig 7:16   1 Bolt and servo body   2 Rod   3 Spring
4 Piston   5 'O' rings   6 Gasket

Dismantling the pump:

Refer to **FIG 7:14** and dismantle by following the order in which the components are numbered. To facilitate reassembly, pencil mark the outside faces of mating gear teeth.

Assembly is the reverse of the dismantling sequence.

Dismantling the front and rear servos:

To dismantle, refer to **FIG 7:15** or to **FIG 7:16** as relevant and follow the order in which the components are numbered.

Assembly is the reverse of the dismantling sequence in each case.

Dismantling the valve block:

Refer to **FIG 7:17** and remove the components in the order in which they are numbered.

Assembly is the reverse of the dismantling sequence. Use a torque screwdriver set to 0.22 to 0.35kgm (1.6 to 2.5lb ft) and tighten all valve block screws to this torque.

Gearbox assembly:

Reverse the dismantling sequences. Use petroleum jelly to 'hold' loose shims, thrust washers, thrust races etc in position while refitting. The gear train end float should be within the range of 0.25 to 0.75mm (0.010 to 0.030in) and is adjusted by selecting a thrust washer 3 in **FIG 7:6** of suitable thickness. Note the following bolt torque tightening figures: 8 in **FIG 7:9**, 0.62 to 0.80kgm (4.5 to 5.8lb ft); 11 and 13 in **FIG 7:8**, 1.8 to 3.4kgm (13 to 25lb ft); 1 in **FIG 7:6**, 1.8 to 3.4kgm (13 to 25lb ft); 7 and 9 in **FIG 7:5**, 0.22 to 0.35kgm (1.6 to 2.5lb ft); 1 in **FIG 7:4**, 0.6 to 0.9kgm (4.5 to 7.0lb ft); 11 in **FIG 7:1**, 10mm dia. to 2.7 to 4.1kgm (20 to 30lb ft) and 12mm dia. to 4.1 to 6.9kgm (30 to 50lb ft). Assemble all internal parts wetted with clean transmission fluid. Use 'Loctite grade CV' on the threads of bolt 1 in **FIG 7:7** and torque tighten it to 4.8 to 6.9kgm (35 to 50lb ft). Adjust the front and rear band clutches as described in **Section 7:4**.

7:8 The selector control

The lever assembly is shown in **FIG 7:18** and the rod assembly in **FIG 7:19**. The console is included in **Chapter 6, FIG 6:11**.

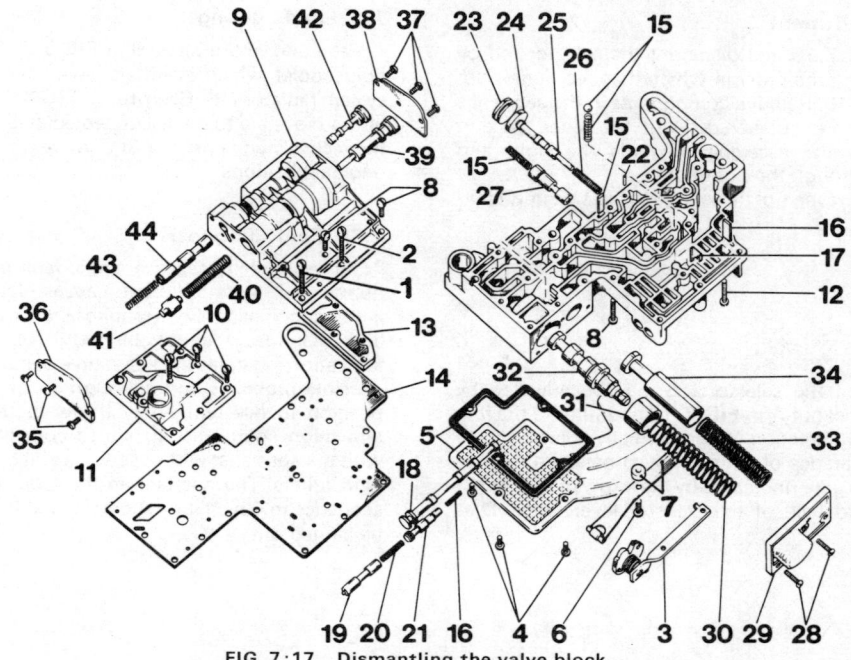

FIG 7:17   Dismantling the valve block

Key to Fig 7:17   1 and 2 Screws   3 Downshift cam assembly   4 Screws   5 Oil strainer and gasket   6 Screw   7 Detent spring and spacer   8 Screws   9 Upper valve body   10 Screws   11 Oil tube collector   12 Screws   13 Governor line plate   14 Separating plate   15 Check valve ball and spring   16 Throttle valve stop, return spring, servo orifice control valve spring and stop   17 Throttle valve plate   18 Manual control valve   19 Downshift valve   20 Throttle valve spring   21 Throttle valve   22 Dowel pin   23 Modulator plug   24 Modulator valve   25 Valve spacer   26 Valve spring   27 Servo orifice control valve   28 Screws   29 End plate   30 Spring   31 Sleeve   32 Primary regulator valve   33 Spring   34 Secondary regulator valve   35 Screws   36 Front end plate   37 Screws   38 Rear end plate   39 2- to 3-shift valve   40 Spring 41 Plunger   42 1- to 2-shift valve   43 Spring   44 Plunger

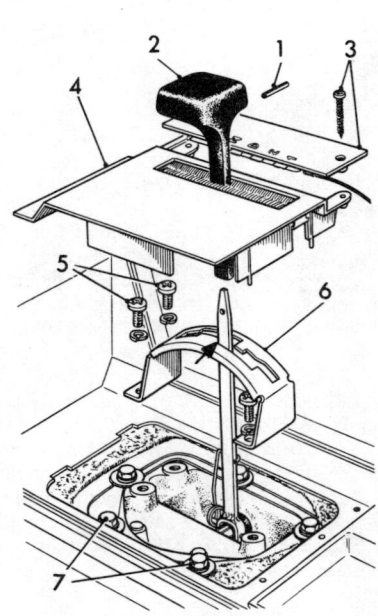

FIG 7:18   The selector lever

Key to Fig 7:18   1 Pin   2 Knob   3 Screw and panel 4 Cover   5 Screws   6 Gate plate   7 Bolts

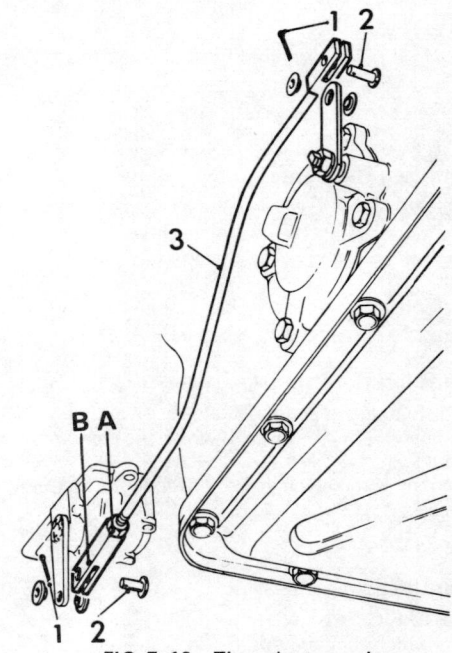

FIG 7:19   The selector rod

Key to Fig 7:19   1 Splitpin   2 Pin   3 Rod   **A** Locknut **B** Fork

Removal and fitment:

Refer to **FIG 7:19** and dismount the selector rod by removing parts in the order in which they are numbered. Refer to **FIG 7:18**. Remove components in the sequence in which they are numbered. With the lever back in position 1, tilt the assembly towards the right and manoeuvre it through the floor panel.

Fitment is the reverse of these sequences. Use new split-pins 1 in **FIG 7:19**.

Adjustment:

The length of the selector rod may be adjusted by loosening the locknut **A** in **FIG 7:19** and turning the fork **B** in the relevant direction. When correctly adjusted there should be a clearance of 3mm (0.12in) between the rear face of the drive gate (indicated by the arrow in **FIG 7:18**) and the forward face of the selector lever when **D** is selected.

7:9 Fluid cooling

Feed and return pipes 6 in **FIG 7:2** connect with the fluid cooler which is integral with the engine cooling system radiator (see **Chapter 4, FIG 4:1**). If the feed and return pipes are to be disconnected at either end, identify them clearly and ensure that they are reconnected to their original positions.

7:10 Fault diagnosis

Since, in many cases, a single fault may result from a number of quite different causes, fault diagnosis of automatic transmissions requires considerable experience and diagnosis cannot be very easily defined. The tabulation indicates the alternative diagnosis of a range of possible problems and although an owner may be in a position to deal with only a few of them himself, the tabulation should assist him to consult knowledgeably with the specialist whose services will be required to deal with others. The numbers in the tabulation indicate the sequence in which it is recommended that checks should be carried out.

Fault diagnosis chart

Diagnosis	Engagement of 1, 2, D or R — Bumpy	Delayed	None	Take off — None forward	None reverse	Seizure reverse	No neutral	Squawk	Slip	Upshifts — No 1 to 2	No 2 to 3	Above normal speed	Below normal speed	Upshift Quality — Slip 1 to 2	Slip 2 to 3	Rough 1 to 2	Rough 2 to 3	Seizure 1 to 2	Seizure 2 to 3	Downshifts — No 2 to 1	No 3 to 2	Involuntary 3 to 2	Above normal speed	Below normal speed	Downshift Quality — Slip 2 to 1	Slip 3 to 2	Rough 2 to 1	Rough 3 to 2
SYMPTOM																												
ADJUSTMENT FAULTS																												
Fluid level low	2	1	1	1	1		1	1	1	1	1	1	1	1	1	1	1		1	1	1	1	1	1		1		1
Downshift cable incorrectly assembled or adjusted		2	1	1	1		1	2	2	2				2	2					2	2		2		1			
Manual linkage incorrectly assembled or adjusted	1	3	2	2		1	3	3	3					3	3													3
Incorrect engine idling speed																2	2		1									
Incorrect front band adjustment				2	2	2								4	4													
Incorrect rear band adjustment	4									2				4	4	2	2			3	2	1						
HYDRAULIC CONTROL FAULTS																												
Oil tubes incorrectly installed, missing or leaking	5	4	3	3	7					8	8	8	5	8	9				2			2	5	5	6	6		
Sealing ring missing or broken	3	7	4	3	6			7		9	9	8	5	9	10	4		5	3			5	5	5	7	7	3	6
Valve block screws missing or loose		6	5	2	5			5		10	9	9	6	10	11	5		6	4			6	6	6	8	8	5	7
Primary regulator valve sticking	4	5	6								10	10		6	7	3									4	4	8	8
Secondary regulator valve sticking														7		3												
Throttle valve sticking	4							1			6	2	2	7	8	4	4					4	4	4		5	4	4
Modulator valve sticking											7	7	2			5	5			3	2		2	2				
Governor valve sticking, leaking or incorrectly assembled											3	7	3	7		6	6			3	2		2	2				
Orifice control valve sticking		13			3							3										3						
1 to 2 shift valve sticking					4					4		4																
2 to 3 shift valve sticking											3	3	3			7							3	3			6	7
2 to 3 shift valve plunger sticking		8			4							4	4			8							3	3			7	8
Converter 'out' check valve sticking or missing												6																
Check valve sticking or missing																												
MECHANICAL FAULTS																												
Front clutch slipping	6	9		4	9		2	4		5	5			5	5	9	5				4					9	6	
Front clutch seized or plates distorted		10				2	2								6						5						7	6
Rear clutch slipping	7							6		5				6	6	7				4					2	2		7
Rear clutch seized or plates distorted																8					5				1			8
Front band slipping due to faulty servo or worn band		11		5	8									7	8	7	3	5	3			3						
Rear band slipping due to faulty servo or worn band														8		8	4	2	4									
Uni-directional clutch slipping or incorrectly installed																												
Uni-directional clutch seized			7																									
Input shaft broken			8																									
Front pump drive tangs on converter hub broken	12	12	9																									
Front pump worn			9																									
Converter blading and/or uni-directional clutch failed			10																									

NOTES

CHAPTER 8

THE PROPELLER SHAFT, REAR AXLE
AND SUSPENSION

8:1 Description

A rear view of the live rear axle is shown in **FIG 8:1**. It is located laterally by a Watts linkage which is bracketed to the body at its extremities and pivoted on the rear face of the differential housing cover. Longitudinal location is by two trailing links which straddle the axle casing and the body inner sills. Transmission and braking torque reaction is accommodated by a crossmember which is linked by a short bracket to the forward end of the pinion extension shaft housing which is, in effect, a torque tube. The pinion extension shaft is splined to the pinion shaft and coupled to the gearbox output flange by a propeller shaft which incorporates two constant velocity type universal joints. The drive line is slightly offset from the car centreline. The Watts linkage pivot and the crossmember torque reaction linkage point are both on the car centreline.

Suspension springing is by a pair of coil springs each of which is mounted between a seat which is integral with the axle casing and an upper seat on the body. A bump stop is incorporated in the upper seat. The arrangement is shown in **FIG 8:2**. Damping and supplementary springing is provided by telescopic hydropneumatic self-levelling Boge damper units. These are self-energising and their springing characteristics, in conjunction with the coil springs, provide a substantially constant rear spring 'rate' whether the car is lightly or fully laden.

The final drive and differential assembly is of conventional design with two sun wheels and two planet wheels. Bearing preload of the pinion and of the carrier bearings is induced by selective shim washers. Backlash adjustment of the crown wheel and pinion and of the sun wheel and planet wheel meshing is also by selective shim washers. Drive to the hubs is by halfshafts which spline into the sun wheels. A cross-section through a hub is shown in **FIG 8:3**. The single taper roller bearing is protected by an inner and an outer oil seal. The brake backplate is mounted on the axle casing and retained by the hub assembly nuts and bolts. The brake drums are spigotted to and retained to the halfshafts. The hub bearings require no routine maintenance.

8:2 Maintenance

Tyres:

Maintain the tyre inflation pressures, including the spare, at those quoted in the **Technical Data** section of

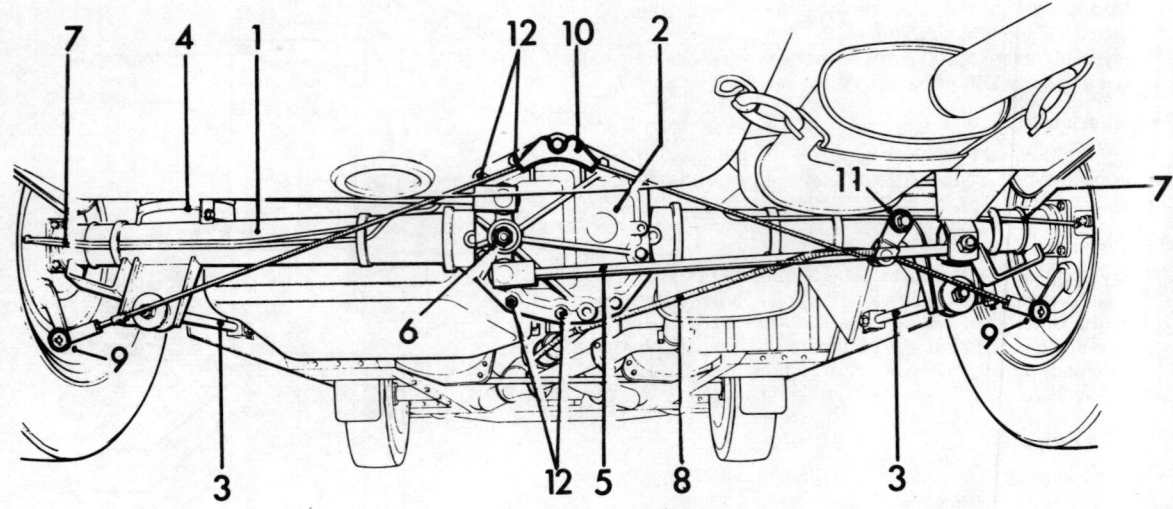

FIG 8:1 The axle assembly

Key to Fig 8:1 1 Axle casing 2 Cover 3 Trailing link 4 Spring seat 5 Watts linkage 6 Pivot stud 7 Brake hydraulic pipe 8 Handbrake cable 9 Handbrake lever clevis pins 10 Handbrake cable guide 11 Handbrake compensator 12 Cover retaining bolts

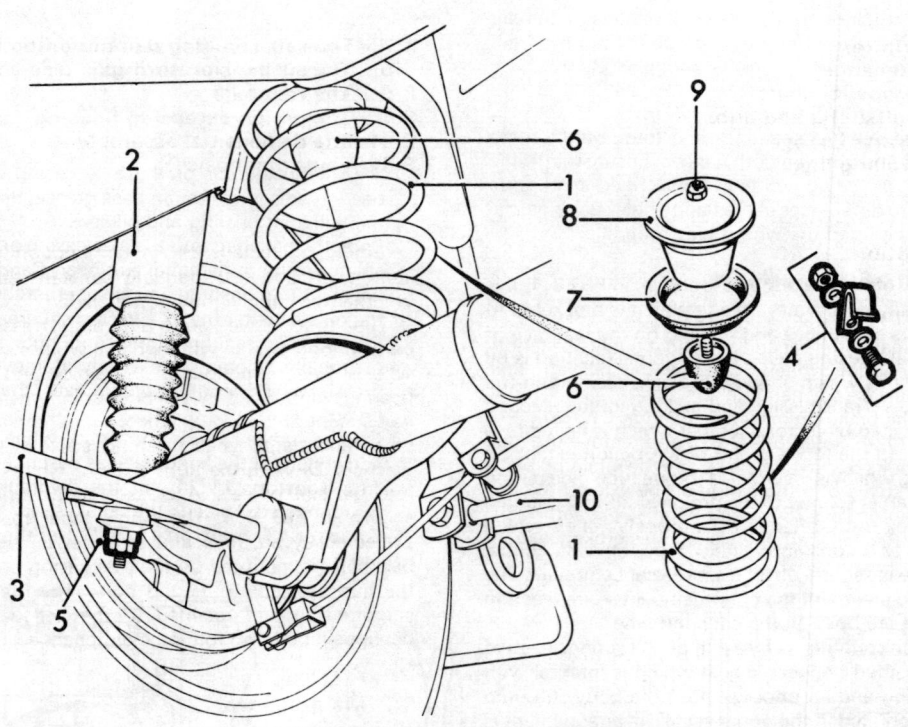

FIG 8:2 The righthand rear suspension

Key to Fig 8:2 1 Spring 2 Self-levelling damper unit 3 Trailing link rod 4 Spring clip assembly 5 Locknut, nut and dished washer 6 Bump stop 7 Insulating ring 8 Spring top mounting 9 Nut 10 Watts linkage

the **Appendix** for the size of tyres fitted and the anticipated car loading conditions.

Every 6000 miles (10,000km), have the wheel balance checked and corrected as necessary.

Propeller shaft:

Every 6000 miles (10,000km), check the tightness of the propeller shaft coupling bolts at the front and rear flanges.

Oil level:

Every 6000 miles (10,000km), check the level of the oil in the axle and top up as necessary. The filler plug is at the rear in the differential casing cover and the oil level is correct when it is just up to the bottom of the plug orifice. For preference, use the same brand of Hypoid 80 or 90 oil as that already in use. Torque tighten the filler plug.

8:3 The propeller shaft

The propeller shaft incorporates a constant velocity type of universal joint at each end. Gaiters prevent ingress of road dirt. No procedures are prescribed for the overhaul or repair of a propeller shaft by an owner but, for information purposes, a cross-section through the universal joints is shown in **FIG 8:4**. A worn, bent or damaged shaft must be removed and a new replacement fitted.

Removal:

Raise the rear of the car and support it firmly on stands. Chock the front wheels. Scribe marks on the gearbox flange, the propeller shaft front and rear flanges and the extension shaft flange to identify their relative alignment positions. Remove the four nuts and bolts from the front and rear flanges and dismount the propeller shaft.

Refitment:

Reverse the removal sequence and torque tighten the coupling nuts and bolts on both flanges. Ensure that, if the original shaft is being refitted, the scribed marks are aligned. Due to differences in the flange hole spacings, the shaft cannot be fitted the wrong way round.

8:4 The halfshafts and hubs

Halfshaft removal:

1 Raise the rear of the car and support it firmly on stands. Chock the front wheels. Remove the relevant rear wheels. Release the handbrake.
2 Remove the brake drum as described in **Chapter 11, Section 11:4**. Refer to **FIG 8:3** and remove the four nuts and bolts 5 and 4 which secure the retaining plate 7 and backplate 6 to the flange of the axle casing 8.
3 Using adaptor 18G 284-1 and impulse extractor 284, withdraw the halfshaft. If the shaft was broken, extract

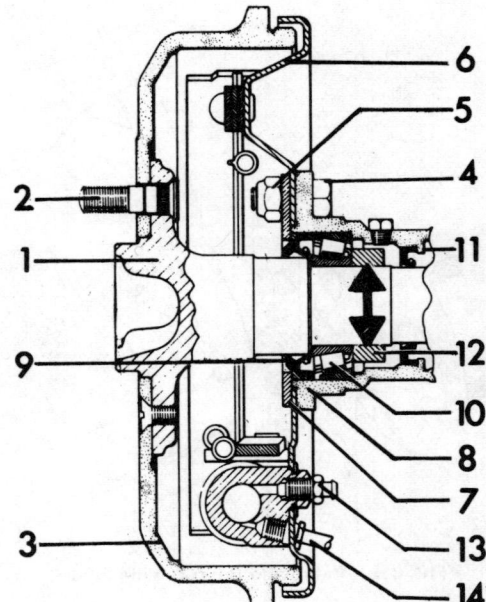

FIG 8:3 Cross-section through a rear hub and brake drum

Key to Fig 8:3 1 Halfshaft 2 Stud 3 Brake drum 4 Bolt 5 Nut 6 Backplate 7 Retaining plate 8 Axle casing 9 Outer oil seal 10 Bearing 11 Inner oil seal 12 Collar 13 Bleed nipple 14 Brake hydraulic pipe

the inner portion. If the backplate is to be separated, disconnect the brake hydraulic pipe and handbrake cable.

Halfshaft fitment:

1 Smear the interior of the axle casing and halfshaft bearing area with lithium base grease. Similarly grease the halfshaft bearing and oil seal.
2 Enter the halfshaft into the axle casing and engage the splines in the differential sun gear. Carefully slide the halfshaft into position and ensure that the bearing and the oil seal enter the axle casing squarely.
3 Fit the four securing bolts and nuts and, working diagonally, tighten them evenly. Remove any surplus grease which could contaminate the brake shoe linings.
4 Fit the brake drum and road wheel. Check the adjustment of the handbrake as described in **Chapter 11, Section 11:11**. If the hydraulic pipe was disconnected, bleed the brakes as described in **Chapter 11, Section 11:7**. Lower the car.

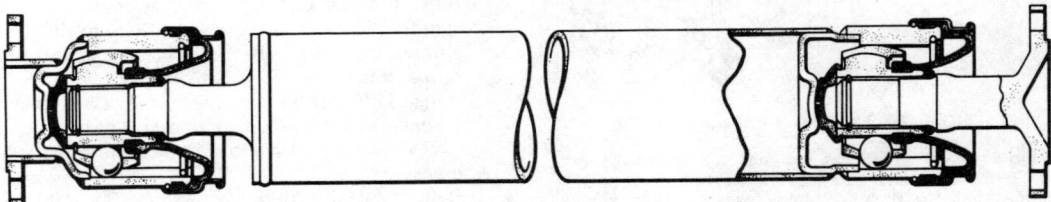

FIG 8:4 Cross-section through the propeller shaft joints

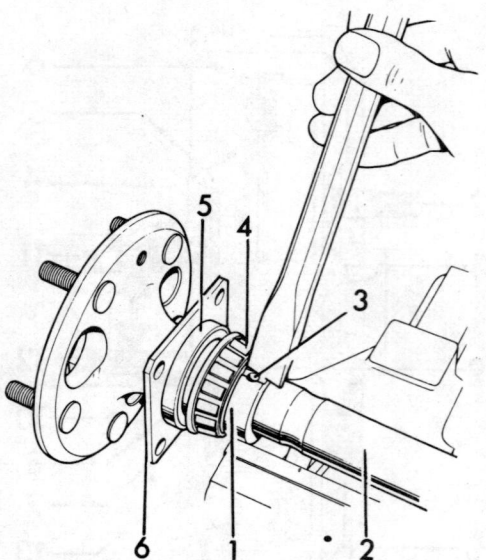

FIG 8:5　Removing the retaining collar

Key to Fig 8:5　1 Collar　2 Halfshaft　3 Drilled hole
4 Bearing　5 Oil seal　6 Retaining plate

Hub bearing and outer oil seal:

A new hub bearing and outer oil seal (10 and 9 in **FIG 8:3**) may be fitted to a serviceable halfshaft as follows.

Removal:

1 Remove the relevant halfshaft as described earlier. Refer to **FIG 8:5** and weaken the collar 1 by drilling into it as at 3. **Do not damage the halfshaft by allowing the drill to penetrate through the collar.**

2 Using a hammer and chisel as indicated in the illustration, burst the collar and remove it from the shaft. Under a press, remove the bearing, oil seal and retaining plate.

3 Using adaptor 18G 284AR and impulse extractor 284, hammer out the outer race of the bearing.

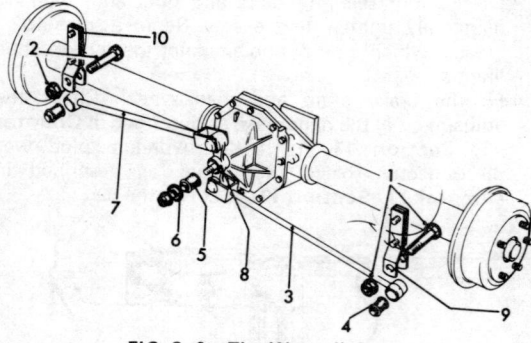

FIG 8:6　The Watts linkage

Key to Fig 8:6　1 and 2 Nut and bolt　3 Righthand rod
4 Bush　5 Pivot link bush　6 Nut and washer　7 Lefthand rod　8 Pivot link　9 Righthand body bracket　10 Lefthand body bracket

Fitment:

1 Fit the outer race of the hub bearing to the axle casing. Fit the retaining plate (welded member outwards) to the shaft. Lubricate the lip of the oil seal and slide the seal onto the shaft.

2 Fit the bearing (tapered face inwards). Refer to **FIG 8:3**. Wipe the arrowed section of the shaft inwards of the bearing clean of grease. Smear 'Loctite' on this diameter and also on the bore of a new retaining collar.

3 Fit the new collar and press it home until it butts against the bearing. The interference fit must be such that a load of **not less than three tons is required to press the collar along the final 3.2mm (0.125 in) of its travel.** If less than this load is required, remove the collar and fit another of greater interference.

4 Lubricate the bearing with grease (see earlier) and, following the procedure already described, refit the halfshaft.

Inner oil seal:

To fit a new oil seal 11 in **FIG 8:3**, remove the relevant halfshaft as described earlier and, using 'hook' tool 18G 1271, withdraw the inner oil seal.

Lubricate the lip of the new seal and install it squarely into the bore of the axle casing with the lip inwards. Refit the halfshaft as described earlier.

8:5 The Watts linkage

The function of the Watts linkage has been referred to in **Section 8:1**.

Removal:

Refer to **FIG 8:6**. Remove the bolt and nyloc nut 1 which secures the Watts link 3 to the righthand bracket 9. Similarly remove the bolt and nyloc nut 2 which secures the link 7 to the lefthand bracket 10. To facilitate removal of this bolt, slightly raise the car body. Remove the nut and plain washer 6. Withdraw the Watts linkage and collect the second plain washer from between the pivot link 8 and the differential cover.

Do not attempt to separate the linkage rods from the link pivot 8. If necessary, bushes 4 and 5 may be renewed by pressing them out and pressing in new bushes. If the linkage assembly 3, 7 and 8 is unserviceable, it must be renewed as an assembly.

8:6 The trailing links

The function of the trailing links has been referred to in **Section 8:1**.

Removal:

1 Raise the rear of the car and support the body on stands. Chock the front wheels. Refer to **FIG 8:7** and remove the nyloc nut 1, the washer 2 and the rear rubber bush 4.

2 Refer to **FIG 8:8** and remove the two 'powerlock' bolts 3 which secure the forked bracket 2 to the body inner sill. Withdraw the trailing link complete with the forked bracket.

3 Refer to **FIG 8:7**. Remove the sleeve 3 and the forward rubber bush 5 from the threaded end of the trailing link

rod. Refer to **FIG 8:8** and, if necessary, remove the nyloc nut 6, withdraw the bolt and separate the link rod from the bracket.

4 The bush in the forward end of the link rod may be renewed by pressing it out and pressing in a new bush. Renew the forward rubber bushes if they are worn, cracked or perished. Do not attempt to salvage a bent or damaged rod but obtain a new replacement part.

Refitment:

1 Fit the forward end of the rod to the bracket and torque tighten the assembly nut and bolt. Ensure that the bracket is parallel to the link rod. Fit the forward bush and sleeve to the threaded end of the rod.

2 Enter the rod into the axle casing bracket and align the fork bracket with the holes in the inner sill. Fit the two retaining bolts and torque tighten them.

3 Fit the remaining rubber bush, the washer and the nut. Torque tighten the nut. Raise the rear of the car, remove the stands and lower the car.

8:7 The self-levelling damper units

Boge Nivomat self-levelling telescopic dampers are incorporated into the suspension. A damper is fitted at each side and straddles the body and the axle casing. The upper damper mountings are secured to the body and access to them is from inside the car. The lower ends of the dampers are secured to brackets which project forward from the axle casing. Both the upper and the lower attachment points incorporate rubber mountings.

The object of fitting the self-levelling type dampers as against conventional units is that they maintain the same ground clearance irrespective of whether the car is lightly loaded or fully laden. By maintaining a constant 'datum', the characteristics of the 'ride' and so the handling of the car is substantially constant through the range of loading conditions.

The principle of operation of the Boge Nivomat self-levelling dampers is a combination of the conventional action of a hydraulic damper with that of the 'spring' action which is available from the compression and expansion of a volume of enclosed gas. In this application the gas in an annular chamber in the lower section of the unit forms the 'spring'. Movement of the damper piston allows hydraulic fluid to compress the gas 'spring' and, depending upon the position of the piston relative to the datum (the piston midway travel point), the pressure of the gas pumps the unit up (or lets the unit down) to the suspension level which corresponds with the datum.

Since the self-levelling units depend upon suspension movement to activate them, a stationary car will not 'self-level'. Once the car moves off, the distance which it must cover before the rear suspension has stabilised will vary with the condition of the road surface. It may be as little as two or three hundred yards on a rough road to several miles if the surface is even.

A Boge Nivomat unit cannot be overhauled or repaired by an owner. **No attempt should be made to open up a defective unit** (the gas content makes this dangerous) which should be removed and a replacement unit fitted.

Removal:

1 Raise the rear of the car and support the body firmly on stands. Chock the front wheels. Fold down the rear seat

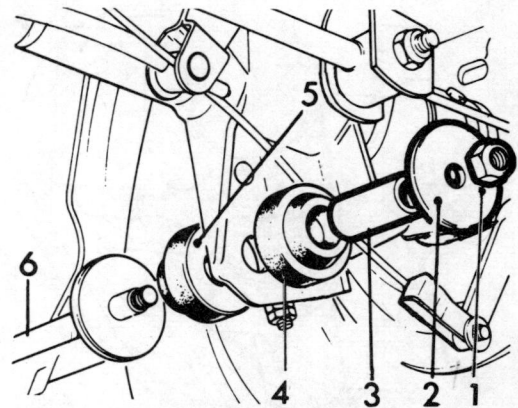

FIG 8:7 The rear end of the righthand trailing link

Key to Fig 8:7   1 Nut   2 Washer   3 Sleeve   4 Bush
5 Bush   6 Trailing link rod

and pull back the trim carpet from round the relevant wheel arch to gain access to the top mounting of the damper unit.

2 Position a jack under the axle and raise it to support the axle weight. From within the car, remove the locknut, nut and dished washer which secure the top of the unit to the body. Carefully lower the axle by letting down the jack.

3 Refer to **FIG 8:2**. Remove the locknut, nut and dished washer 5 which secure the damper unit to the bracket on the axle casing. Withdraw the unit from the car.

4 Remove the metal sleeves from the top and bottom mounting rubber bushes. Remove the top bush from the car body and the bottom rubber bush from the axle casing bracket.

Fitment:

To fit a self-levelling damper unit, reverse the sequence of the removal operations. Renew any rubber bush which may be worn, cracked or perished. Torque tighten the mounting nuts and the locknuts.

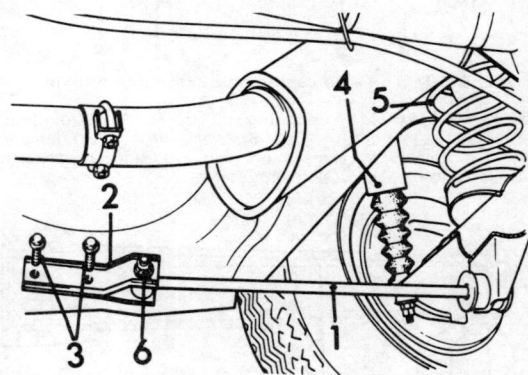

FIG 8:8 The forward end of the righthand trailing link

Key to Fig 8:8   1 Trailing link rod   2 Forked bracket
3 Powerlock screws   4 Self-levelling damper unit
5 Suspension spring   6 Nut

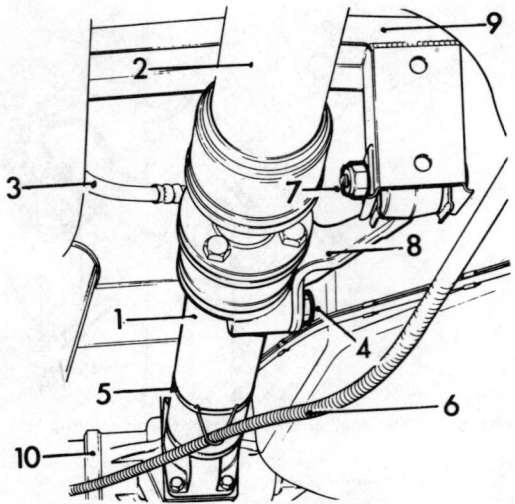

FIG 8:9 The pinion extension housing

Key to Fig 8:9 1 Pinion extension housing 2 Propeller shaft 3 Flexible hose 4 Bolts and spring washers 5 Jubilee clip 6 Handbrake cable 7 Bolt and nut 8 Bracket 9 Crossmember 10 Axle casing

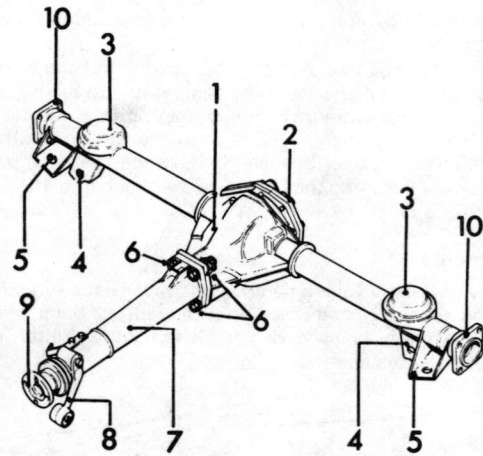

FIG 8:10 The axle casing and extension housing

Key to Fig 8:10 1 Axle casing 2 Cover 3 Spring seat 4 Bracket (trailing link) 5 Bracket (self-levelling damper unit) 6 Bolts 7 Extension housing 8 Bracket assembly 9 Drive flange 10 Casing flange

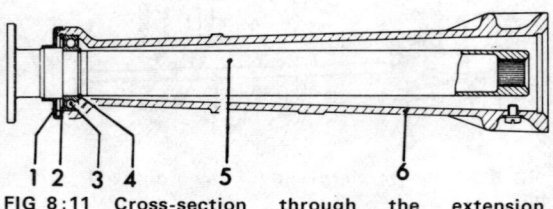

FIG 8:11 Cross-section through the extension housing

Key to Fig 8:11 1 Mud shield 2 Circlip 3 Bearing 4 Circlip 5 Extension shaft 6 Extension housing

8:8 The suspension springs

This section includes the description of the procedure for the removal and fitment of the bump stops.

Spring removal:

1 Raise the rear of the car and support the body firmly on stands. Chock the front wheels. Position a jack under the axle casing. Support the weight of the axle but do not raise the car off the stands.

2 Refer to **Section 8:6** and, by removing the two screws 3 in **FIG 8:8**, release the forked bracket at the forward end of the trailing link from the body inner sill.

3 Refer to **FIG 8:2** and remove the nyloc nut and washers and the clip which retains the spring to the axle casing. These parts are bracketed 4 in the illustration. Refer to **Section 8:7** and release the lower end of the damper unit from the axle casing bracket by removing the locknut, nut and dished washer 5 in **FIG 8:2**.

4 Carefully lower the jack. Withdraw the suspension spring and the insulating ring. Reject a cracked or distorted spring. Discard a worn, perished or cracked insulating ring.

Spring fitment:

To fit a spring, follow the reverse of the removal sequence. Ensure that the spring is correctly positioned with the squared end uppermost and the lower end located in the profile of the lower seat. Torque tighten the screws which retain the trailing link forked bracket to the body inner sill.

Bump stop removal and fitment:

Remove the relevant road spring as described earlier. Refer to **FIG 8:2**. Remove the suspension top mounting 8. Remove the retaining nut 9 and withdraw the bump stop 6. Discard a worn or perished bump stop.

Fitment of a bump stop is the reverse of the removal sequence.

8:9 The rear axle assembly

The procedures described in this Section cover the removal and refitment of the complete rear axle including the pinion extension housing. The procedures for the removal and refitment of only the pinion extension housing, its bracket and the torque reaction crossmember, leaving the rear axle assembly in position are described in **Section 8:10**.

Removal:

1 Raise the rear of the car and support the body securely on stands. Chock the front wheels. Remove both rear wheels and release the handbrake.

2 Position a jack under the axle casing. Refer to **Section 8:3** and uncouple the rear end of the propeller shaft from the pinion extension shaft flange.

3 Refer to **FIG 8:9**. Disconnect the flexible brake hose 3 from the bracket on the extension housing 1. Remove the two bolts and spring washers 4 and release the bracket 8 from the dowels in the extension housing. Loosen the jubilee clip 5 and remove the handbrake cable guide clip.

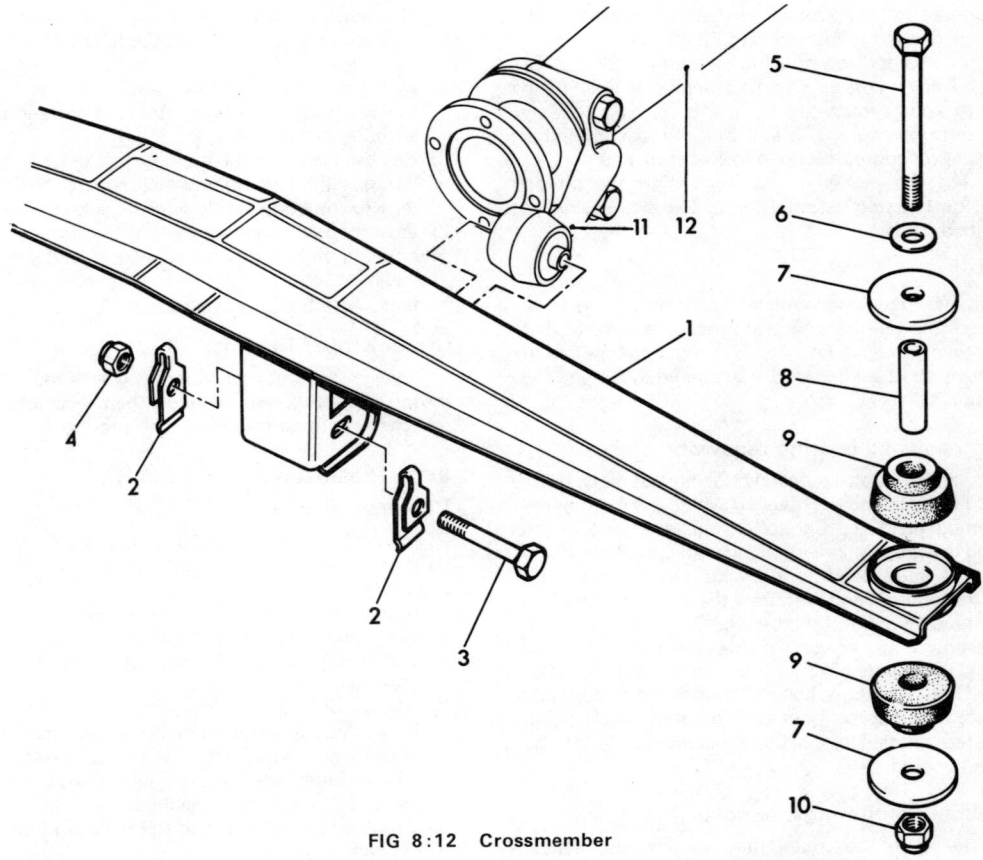

FIG 8:12 Crossmember

Key to Fig 8:12 1 Crossmember 2 Clip 3 Bolt 4 Nut 5 Bolt 6 Washer 7 Washer 8 Spacer tube 9 Mounting rubber 10 Nut 11 Bracket 12 Pinion extension housing

4 Refer to **FIG 8:1**. Remove the splitpins and clevis pins 9 which secure the handbrake cable forks to the backplate levers. Release the handbrake cable from the guide 10. Remove the nut and bolt 11 clamping the handbrake compensator and release the handbrake cable trunnion. Wire the cables clear of the axle casing.

5 Remove the Watts linkage as described in **Section 8:5**. Remove both trailing links 3 as described in **Section 8:6**. Refer to **Section 8:7** and release the both self-levelling damper units from their axle casing brackets. Refer to **Section 8:8** and remove the clips 4 in **FIG 8:2**.

6 Lower the axle casing assembly until the suspension springs, spring upper seats and bump stops can be dismounted. Withdraw the axle casing assembly. Remove the brake hydraulic pipes etc. as necessary.

Fitment:

If the axle assembly has been stripped down and rebuilt, ensure that it has been reassembled to the same completeness as when it was removed from the car. The refitment sequence will then be the reverse of that described earlier for removal. Refer to the relevant sectional texts and torque tighten nuts and bolts as indicated. On completion, refill or top up the axle casing oil

level as described in **Section 8:2** and bleed the brakes and adjust the handbrake as described in **Chapter 11, Sections 11:7** and **11:11**.

Dismantling and reassembly:

The procedures for the removal and refitment of the halfshafts are described in **Section 8:4**. The pinion extension housing removal and refitment procedures are covered in **Section 8:10** and the dismantling and reassembly procedures for the differential assembly (including the adjustment of the crown wheel and pinion meshing) are described in **Section 8:11**.

8:10 The pinion extension housing

The pinion extension housing is 7 in **FIG 8:10**. The pinion extension shaft is splined to the final drive pinion and is flange coupled to the propeller shaft. A cross-section through the shaft and housing is shown in **FIG 8:11**.

Removal:

If the complete rear axle assembly has been removed from the car as described in **Section 8:9**, the pinion extension shaft and housing may be separated from it after removing three bolts and spring washers and one nut, bolt and bracket. These are marked 6 in **FIG 8:10**.

If the pinion extension housing assembly only is to be dismounted leaving the axle casing assembly in position in the car, proceed as follows.

1 Carry out operations 1, 2 and 3 of the axle assembly removal procedure described in **Section 8:9**.
2 Carry out the procedure for separating the pinion extension housing assembly from the axle casing as described earlier.

Fitment:

To refit the extension housing assembly, reverse the sequence of the relevant removal procedure. Ensure that the joint faces are clean. Fit a new 'O' ring. Engagement of the extension shaft splines will be facilitated by turning the shaft flange.

Extension housing bearing renewal:

Dismount the pinion extension housing assembly. Refer to **FIG 8:11** and scribe the housing where it is overlapped by the mudshield 1. Carefully and evenly tap the mudshield towards the driving flange ensuring that, in the process, the mudshield is not buckled or distorted. Remove the circlip 2 and withdraw the shaft and bearing. Remove the circlip 4 and the bearing 3.

Reassembly is the reverse of this sequence. Carefully reposition the mudshield up to the original scribed location. There should, when the mudshield is correctly positioned, be a gap of 4mm (0.16in) between the rear edge of the mudshield and the machined lip of the extension housing.

Crossmember mountings, removal:

1 Raise the rear of the car and mount it firmly on stands. Chock the front wheels. Remove the rear seat cushion after removing the bolt and washer which secures the squab wing bracket to the body and disengaging the retainer from the bracket on the body.
2 Remove the tread plates from both rear doors and pull the door aperture sealing rubbers clear. Remove six tread plate retaining clips (three at each side) and pull back the carpet and felt to expose the crossmember mounting bolts.
3 Position a jack under the axle casing. Refer to **Section 8:3** and uncouple the propeller shaft from the extension housing shaft. Refer to **FIG 8:12** and remove the nut, large plain washer, bolt, spacer and lower rubber mounting (parts 10, 7, 5, 9) from both ends of the crossmember.
4 Lower the jack sufficiently to allow removal of the remaining mounting parts. **Ensure that the crossmember is not allowed to contact the brake flexible hose.**

Crossmember mountings, fitment:

Fitment of the crossmember mountings is the reverse of the removal sequence. Make sure that the upper and lower rubber mountings 9 are fitted the correct way round.

Crossmember removal:

1 Remove the mountings as described earlier. Position a jack under the front of the fuel tank (interpose a piece of wood), loosen the two clips of the filler neck hose and slide the hose clear of the filler pipe.
2 Refer to **FIG 8:9** and remove the two bolts which secure the bracket 8 to the housing 1. Release the bracket from the dowels. Remove nut and bolt 7 and withdraw the bracket.
3 Release the clips which secure the fuel pipe to the tank. Remove the two bolts which secure the front of the tank to the body and lower the jack and the tank.
4 Ease gently downwards on the pinion extension housing and let down the second jack sufficiently to facilitate removal of the crossmember over the fuel tank. Withdraw the crossmember.

Crossmember fitment:

Reverse the removal sequence. Check the condition of the mounting rubbers and renew them if necessary. Ensure that they are fitted the correct way round.

8:11 The differential assembly

Pinion oil seal renewal:

This seal is 8 in **FIG 8:13**. It can be renewed without removing the axle casing assembly from the car. Proceed as follows.

1 Remove the pinion extension housing as described in **Section 8:10**. Using tool 18G 2-1, remove the oil seal and seal housing 7. Using tool 6312, remove the old seal from the seal housing.
2 Using tool 18G 1273, fit a new seal to the housing with its lip facing away from the arrow marked on the housing face. Wrap a narrow strip of masking tape over the machined step on the pinion shaft (arrowed **T**) to prevent damage to the seal lip.
3 Lubricate the seal lip and the masking tape. With the marked face outwards and the arrow pointing downwards, fit the seal and housing squarely and evenly. Gently tap it into position. Refit the pinion extension housing.

Overhauling the differential assembly:

Overhaul of the final drive and differential assembly requires the use of a number of special tools and some experience of bearing preload and gearing backlash adjustment procedures. Unless an owner has such experience and access to the necessary tools, this overhaul work should be entrusted to a fully equipped agent.

Dismantling the differential assembly:

Remove the axle and pinion extension housing assembly from the car as described in **Section 8:9**. Refer to **FIG 8:1**. Remove bolts 12 and dismount the cover 2 and its gasket and the handbrake cable guide 10. Drain off the oil. Remove the halfshafts and brake backplates as described in **Section 8:4**. Separate the pinion extension housing assembly from the axle casing as described in **Section 8:10**.

Refer to **FIG 8:14**. Identify the differential bearing caps to their respective sides (they must not be interchanged), remove the four bolts and spring washers 1 and lift off the bearing caps. Carefully lever the crown wheel and differential unit out of the axle casing complete with carrier bearings and shim washers. If difficulty is experienced in removing the assembly, use spreader tools

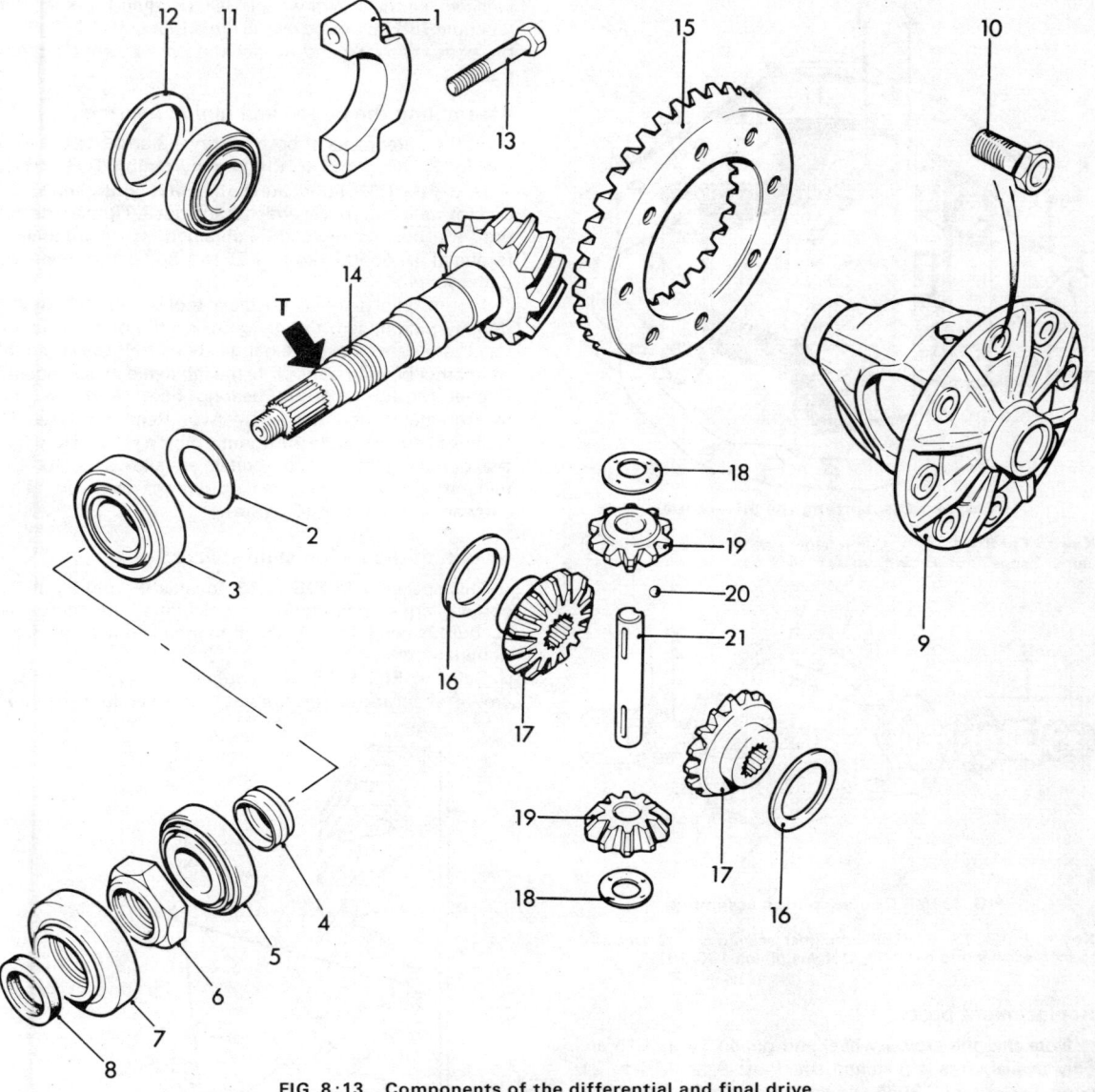

FIG 8:13   Components of the differential and final drive

Key to Fig 8:13   1 Bearing cap   2 Spacer (selective)   3 Bearing   4 Collapsible spacer   5 Bearing   6 Nut   7 Seal housing   8 Oil seal   9 Differential carrier   10 Bolt   11 Carrier bearing   12 Shim washer (selective)   13 Bolt   14 Pinion   15 Crownwheel   16 Thrust washer   17 Sun (side) wheel   18 Washer (selective)   19 Planet wheel   20 Locating ball   21 Pin   **T** See text

S101 and S101-1. Against the possibility that critical parts may not have to be renewed, identify the shim washers to their fitted positions.

If necessary and using adaptors S4221A under a press, withdraw the carrier bearings. Remove the eight bolts 4 and separate the crown wheel from the carrier. Refer to **FIG 8:13**. Withdraw the locating ball 20 and remove the pin 21. Rotate the sun wheels 17 to bring the planet wheels 19 and thrust washers 18 clear of the casing. Remove the planet wheels and washers. Remove the sun wheels 17 and washers 16.

To gain access to the pinion nut, remove the pinion oil seal and housing as described earlier. Using tools 18G 1272 and S98A, remove the pinion shaft nut 6. Using a hardwood block, carefully tap out the pinion complete with selective spacer 2, pinion head bearing 3 and collapsible spacer 4. Remove the pinion outer bearing 5 from the casing. Taking care not to damage the casing, drift out the pinion inner and outer bearing tracks. Remove and discard the collapsible spacer 4 from the pinion shaft 14. Using a press and adaptor 18G 47AJ, remove the pinion head bearing 3 and the selective spacer 2.

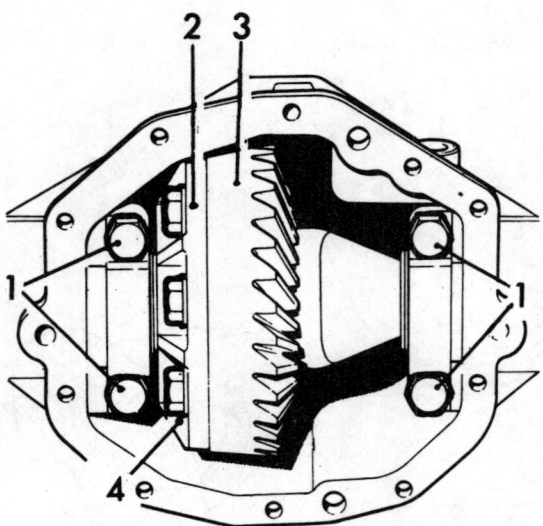

FIG 8:14   Dismantling the differential

Key to Fig 8:14   1 Cap retaining bolts   2 Differential carrier flange   3 Crown wheel   4 Bolts

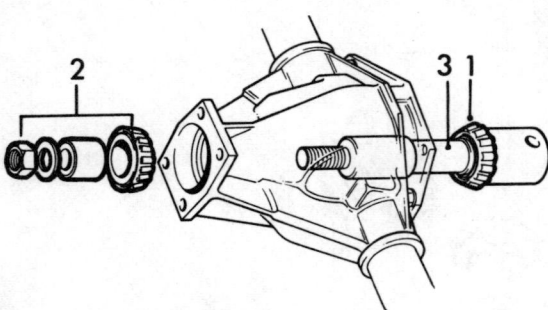

FIG 8:15   Dummy pinion assembly

Key to Fig 8:15   1 Pinion inner bearing   2 Bearing, spacer, washer and nut   3 Dummy pinion 18G 191-1

Replacement parts:

Note that the crown wheel and pinion 14 and 15 are only available as a matched set. Parts 9 and 16 to 21 comprise a kit RTC 2061 and are not available as separate items.

Assembling the differential carrier:

Fit bearings 11 to the carrier 9, lubricate the bearings lightly, fit the outer tracks and position the assembly in the axle casing. Slide the assembly fully to one side, rotate to centralise the bearings and, using a dial gauge set-up, check that the run out of the carrier crown wheel mounting flange does not exceed 0.08mm (0.003in). Using the dial gauge set up, measure the full lateral travel of the carrier in the axle casing. Record this measurement as **M**. Lift out the carrier assembly.

Carry out trial assemblies of the sun and planet wheels and select planet wheel thrust washers 18 of thickness which gives zero backlash of the planet wheels with the sun wheels. Assemble the gearing using the selected

washers. Fit the crown wheel. Use 'Locquic T' prime and 'Locquic 75' compound on the threads of bolts 10. Tighten the bolts gradually and evenly and finally torque tighten them.

Assembling the pinion and pinion bearings:

Fit the outer races of both bearings 3 and 5 to the axle casing. Fit bearing 3 to the dummy pinion 18G 191-1. Refer to **FIG 8:15**. Lubricate the bearings lightly and fit the dummy pinion 3, spacer, washer and nut 2. Tighten the nut until the bearing preload is obtained which requires a torque of 0.17 to 0.21kgm (1.25 to 1.50lb ft) to rotate the dummy shaft.

Mount a dial gauge (the official tool is 18G 191) on the dummy pinion, zero the gauge using the dummy pinion head as a base. Move the gauge stylus over the centre of one carrier bearing bore. Note the indicated measurement. Repeat for the opposite bearing bore. Add the two measurements and divide by two. Record this as **N**. Remove and dismantle the dummy pinion set up. Note that the dummy pinion incorporates an allowance for the minimum pinion head bearing spacer available. This allowance is 1.25mm (0.049in).

Selecting the pinion shim spacer:

This spacer, 2 in **FIG 8:13**, locates the pinion at the correct 'cone' point and, in calculating its thickness, account is taken of all relevant tolerance deviations from nominal.

Refer to **FIG 8:16**. **X** identifies the matching of the crown wheel and pinion as a set. **Y** is the variation in pinion

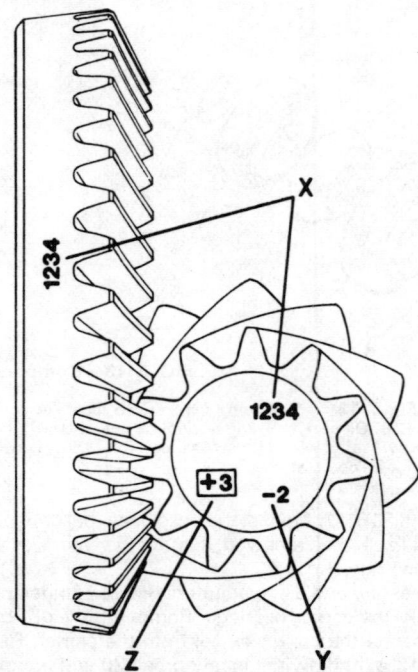

FIG 8:16   Crown wheel and pinion markings

Key to Fig 8:16   X Matching identification   **Y** Variation in pinion head thickness from nominal   **Z** Variation from nominal setting

head thickness from nominal. **Z** (the boxed figure) indicates the variation from nominal setting to obtain the best running position for the matched crown wheel and pin on set.

The required thickness **T** of the spacer is:

$$\mathbf{T} = \mathbf{N} + 1.25\text{mm} \ (0.049\text{in}) - \mathbf{Z}$$

Note that if **Z** has a negative value it will be added (double negative) to the other figures.

Spacers are available in six thicknesses from 1.25mm (0.049in) to 1.75mm (0.069in) in 0.10mm (0.004in) steps.

Assembling the pinion:

Fit a spacer of thickness nearest to that calculated (**T**). Assemble with a new collapsible spacer 4 (see **FIG 8:13**) and, using tools 18G 1272 and S98A, tighten nut 6 gradually until a bearing preload is obtained which requires a torque of 0.15 to 0.23kgm (1.1 to 1.7lb ft) to rotate the pinion. This tightening must be carried out with great care. If the nut is overtightened and the rotational torque exceeds 0.23kgm (1.7lb ft), the assembly must be dismantled, another new collapsible spacer 4 must be fitted and the tightening procedure restarted. **Under no circumstances may the rotational torque be reduced by backing off nut 6.**

Carrier bearing preload and gearing backlash adjustment:

A carrier bearing preload of 0.051 to 0.102mm (0.002 to 0.004in) is required. The total thickness of the two shim washers 12 in **FIG 8:13** must therefore be **M** (see earlier) plus this preload dimension and the total must be divided between the two positions to give a crown wheel to pinion backlash within the range of 0.102 to 0.150mm (0.004 to 0.006in). Eight thicknesses of carrier bearing shim washers are available. Their thicknesses range from 2.85mm (0.112in) to 3.45mm (0.136in) in 0.04mm (0.0016in) steps. Assess the division of the total thickness, select shim washers, fit them and carry out trial assemblies to confirm that the backlash is within the range specified. To fit the carrier with the preload thickness of shims, it will be necessary to expand the axle casing with tools S101 and S101-1. Torque tighten the bearing cap retaining bolts and fit the cover and gasket to the casing. Fit the halfshafts and the extension housing assembly as described in **Sections 8:4** and **8:10**.

8:12 Fault diagnosis

(a) Noisy final drive

1 Insufficient lubricant
2 Worn bearings
3 Worn gearing

(b) Excessive backlash

1 Check 2 and 3 in (a)
2 Worn extension shaft splines
3 Worn sun wheel splines
4 Worn propeller shaft joint(s)

(c) Oil leakage

1 Defective hub seal(s)
2 Defective pinion seal
3 Loose filler plug
4 Cover joint defective

(d) Vibration

1 Check 4 in (b)
2 Propeller shaft out of balance
3 Hub/wheel assembly out of balance

(e) Rattles

1 Worn Watts linkage bush(es)
2 Worn trailing link bush(es)
3 Worn damper attachment
4 Broken coil spring
5 Damper(s) loose

(f) 'Settling'

1 Weak or broken coil spring
2 Loose or broken damper mounting
3 Defective self-levelling of damper unit

(g) 'Bottoming' of suspension

1 Check (f)
2 Bump stops worn or missing

(h) Excessive tyre wear

1 Check 3 in (d); 1 and 2 in (e)
2 Wheel out of balance
3 Incorrect tyre pressure

CHAPTER 9

FRONT SUSPENSION AND HUBS

9:1 Description

Independent suspension is provided by a MacPherson type strut for each front wheel. The layout of the system is shown in **FIG 9:1**. Each strut incorporates a telescopic hydraulic damper and, at its upper end, a coil suspension spring which is offset to the strut centreline. This offset provides a biased spring load which counterbalances the bending moment on the strut arising from it being angled and not vertical. In this way the static friction between the piston and cylinder of the damper which is inherent in angled MacPherson type struts is counteracted. Bump stops are incorporated at the tops of the struts. A forward facing steering arm is bolted to each strut/stub axle flange which also carries a disc brake caliper assembly. The steering linkage is ball jointed to the steering arms.

Each strut swivels between an upper swivel assembly secured to the body and a ball joint which is integral with the bottom suspension link. The bottom suspension links swing on hinge pins in the front crossmember and these are shown in **Chapter 10, FIG 10:6**. Since there is no kingpin, the compound angle of the axis of the MacPherson type strut assembly is, in effect, the kingpin inclination and the camber and castor angles.

An anti-roll bar is mounted transversely to the front crossmember. Each rearward facing end of the bar is coupled to a bottom swinging link and, in addition to its anti-roll function, acts as a trailing arm to longitudinally control a bottom swinging link.

Each wheel hub runs on two taper roller bearings which are mounted directly onto a stub axle. A brake disc is spigotted and secured to each hub.

9:2 Maintenance

Tyres:

Maintain the tyre inflation pressures, including the spare, at those quoted in the **Technical Data** section of the **Appendix** for the size of tyres fitted and the anticipated loading conditions.

Every 6000 miles (10,000km), have the wheel balance checked and corrected as necessary.

Damper rubber boots:

At mileage intervals of, say, 6000 miles (10,000km), inspect these rubber boots for tears and deterioration.

9:3 The anti-roll bar

A cracked or broken anti-roll bar must be removed and a new replacement fitted. Do not attempt to salvage a bent or otherwise damaged bar.

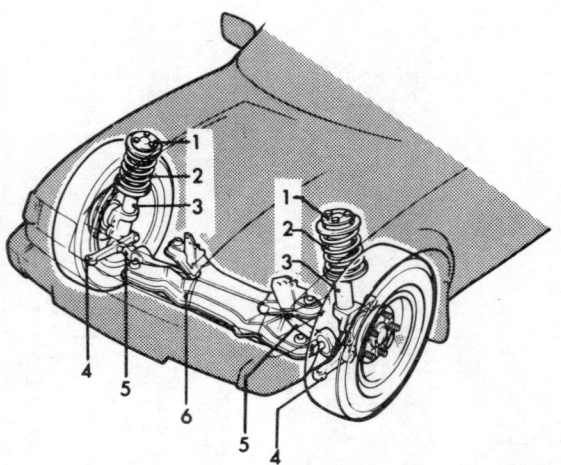

FIG 9:1 Layout of the front suspension

Key to Fig 9:1 1 Upper swivel   2 Spring   3 Strut
4 Steering arm   5 Bottom link   6 Front crossmember

Removal:

1 Refer to **FIG 9:2** and remove the nuts 2 which retain the bracket 1 on each of the two mountings. Remove the brackets. Refer to **FIG 9:3**. Withdraw the splitpin 1. Remove the nut, washers, flanged polyurethane outer bush and foam polyurethane inner bush (parts 2 to 6) from both ends of the anti-roll bar.

2 Refer to **Chapter 10, FIG 10:6** and remove the nut and hinge bolt 5 from either of the bottom links to front crossmember hinge points. Disconnect the bottom link from the hinge point and disengage the anti-roll bar from the bottom link.

3 Withdraw the anti-roll bar and remove the other (inner) sets of three parts from the bar. If a new bar is being installed, remove the washers and clamps 5 in **FIG 9:2** for transfer to the new bar.

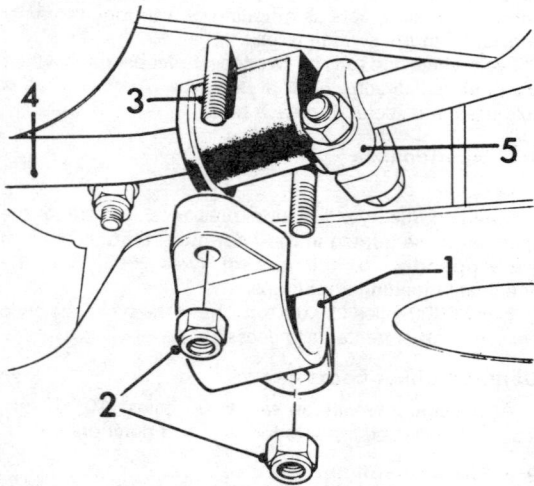

FIG 9:2 Anti-roll bar mounting

Key to Fig 9:2   1 Bracket   2 Nut   3 Rubber bush
4 Anti-roll bar   5 Clamp

Fitment:

Fit the anti-roll bar by reversing the removal sequence. Torque tighten the relevant nuts and bolts. Use new split-pins 1 in **FIG 9:3**.

Anti-roll bar mounting bushes:

To renew the mounting bushes 3 in **FIG 9:2**, remove the bar as described earlier, cut through the old rubbers and remove them from the bar. Clean the bar thoroughly and smear it with rubber grease between both ends and the location clamps. Slide the new mounting rubbers along the bar and into position against the washer and clamp. Refit the bar.

9:4 The suspension springs

Weak, cracked or broken springs must be removed and new components fitted. Ensure that the correct replacement springs are obtained. Springs fitted to cars in which air conditioning equipment has been installed differ from those fitted to standard equipment models. The spring removal and fitment procedures are as follows

Removal:

1 Dismount the complete suspension strut as described in **Section 9:6**. Clean all road dirt from the assembly.

2 Using a set of suitable spring compressing clamps (the official tools are a pair of P 5045 clamps), compress the coils of the spring evenly and note the extent of the compression required to relieve the spring load from the swivel assembly.

3 Refer to **FIG 9:4**. Remove the plastic grommet 14 from the top of the swivel assembly. Using tool 18G 1063, remove nut 13 and washer 12 from the damper piston rod 4. Lift off the upper swivel assembly 11, the spring upper seat 10 and the shim(s) 9.

4 Dismount the clamped road spring 7 from the strut 1 and gradually loosen off the clamping load until the clamp(s) can be removed. Dismount the spring, the rubber boot retaining plate 8, the boot 5 and the two bump stop rubbers 6.

Inspection:

Refer to **Sections 9:6** and **9:7** and check that the damper strut, upper swivel, boot, bump stops etc are serviceable.

Fitment:

The fitment procedure for a new spring, assembly and installation of the strut unit follows the reverse of the removal and dismantling sequences but note the following points.

Compress the new spring to approximately the same extent as that noted when the old spring was being removed. Extend the damper rod 4 in **FIG 9:4** fully before proceeding. Use tool 18G 1063 when fitting nut 13 and, as the clamp(s) are gradually released, check that the spring is seating correctly and that the shim(s), insulating ring, boot etc are locating correctly. Torque tighten nut 13 and fit the grommet 14.

Refer to **Sections 9:6** and **9:7** and to **Chapter 11, Section 11:8** and, on completion of the installation, bleed the brakes as described in **Chapter 11, Section 11:7**.

9:5 The hubs

A cross-section through a hub is shown in **FIG 9:5** and the hub components are shown in **FIG 9:6**.

Hub end float:

If end float adjustment is required, carry out operations 1 and 3 (omitting operation 2) of the hub removal procedure described later. Refer to **FIG 9:5** and torque tighten nut 3 to a torque of 0.7kgm (5lb ft) and then back off by one-sixth of a turn (one hexagon flat). **Do not overtighten or damage may be caused to the bearings and bearing tracks.** Fit retainer 2, lock with a new splitpin 1 and fit cap 14. Fit the road wheel and lower the car.

Hub removal:

1 Apply the handbrake firmly. Raise the front of the car and support the body on stands. Remove the relevant road wheel.
2 Refer to **FIG 9:7** and to **Chapter 11, Section 11:8** and disconnect the brake caliper pipe 5 from the brake hose. Untab the two bolts which secure the brake caliper to the stub axle assembly (rearward 8 and 9), remove the two bolts and withdraw the caliper clear of the brake disc.
3 Refer to **FIG 9:5**. Prise off the grease cap 14 and clean the grease from the now exposed end of the stub axle. Remove and discard splitpin 1. Withdraw the retaining cap 2.
4 Remove nut 3 and washer 4. Withdraw the hub assembly 8 complete with the brake disc 12, bearings 5 and 10 and oil seal 11. If necessary, remove bolts 16 and dismount the disc guard 15. If this is done, clean off the black sealant.

Brake disc:

The procedures for the removal and fitment of the brake disc are included in **Chapter 11, Section 11:3**.

Oil seal renewal:

Remove the hub as described earlier. Extract and discard the oil seal. Fit the new seal evenly and squarely and ensure that the lip is facing the bearing. Lubricate the seal lip with all purpose grease. Check that the projecting deflector on the disc guard is not damaged and that it does not foul the hub or seal. Refit the hub as described later.

Inner hub bearing renewal:

This bearing is 10 in **FIGS 9:5** and **9:6**.

Remove the hub as described earlier. Extract and discard the oil seal 11. Remove the bearing 10 and, using a suitable puller, withdraw the bearing track 9. Ensure that the new bearing is fitted the correct way round. Fit a new oil seal as described earlier. Fit the hub as described later.

Outer bearing renewal:

This is bearing 5 in **FIGS 9:5** and **9:6**.

Remove the hub as described earlier. Remove the bearing 5 and, using a suitable puller, withdraw the bearing track 6. Ensure that the new bearing is fitted the correct way round. Fit the hub as described later.

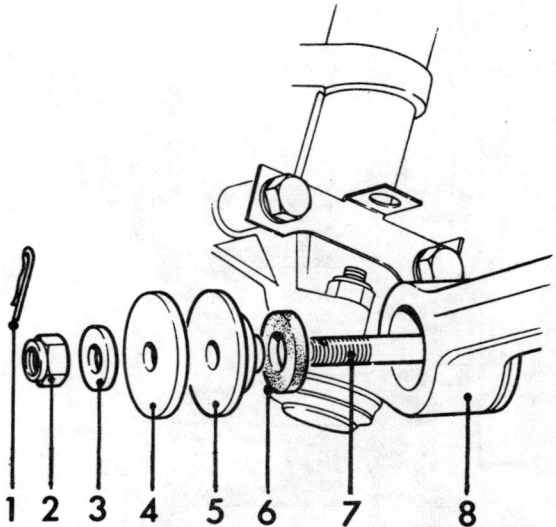

FIG 9:3 Removing the anti-roll bar from a bottom link

Key to Fig 9:3 1 Splitpin 2 Nut 3 Washer 4 Washer 5 Flanged bush 6 Inner bush 7 Anti-roll bar 8 Bottom link

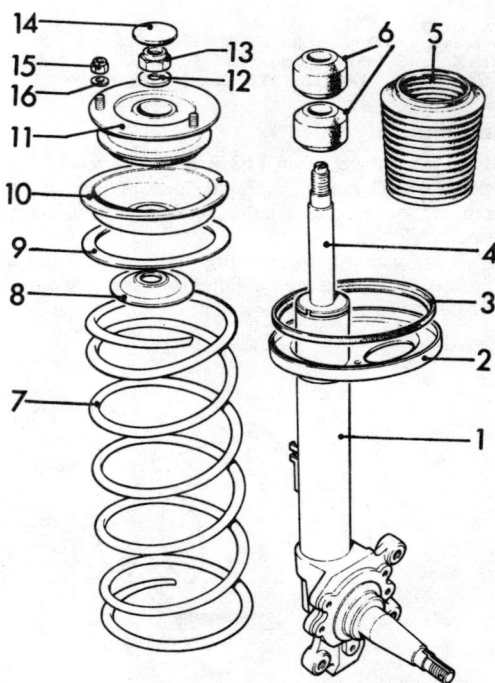

FIG 9:4 Suspension strut components

Key to Fig 9:4 1 Stub axle and damper unit 2 Spring bottom seat 3 Seat rubber 4 Damper piston rod 5 Rubber boot 6 Bump stop 7 Spring 8 Boot retaining plate 9 Shim 10 Spring upper seat 11 Upper swivel 12 Washer 13 Nut 14 Grommet 15 Nut 16 Washer

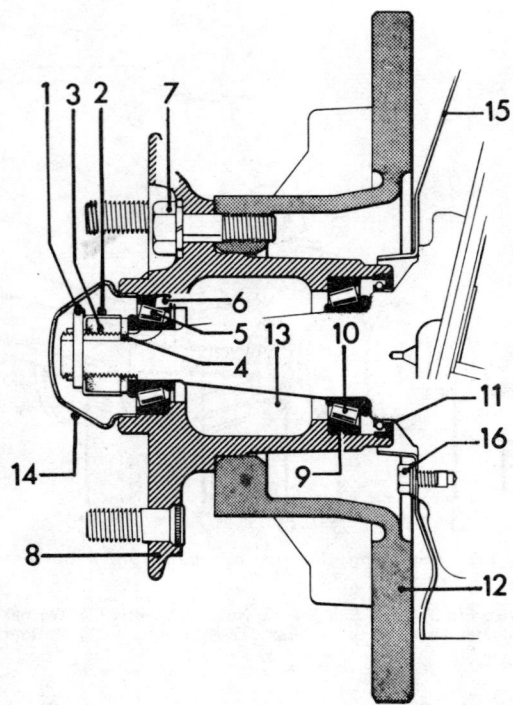

FIG 9:5   Cross-section through a wheel hub

Key to Fig 9:5   1 Splitpin   2 Retaining cap   3 Nut
4 Washer   5 Outer bearing   6 Track   7 Bolt   8 Hub
9 Track   10 Inner bearing   11 Oil seal   12 Brake disc
13 Stub shaft   14 Cap   15 Guard   16 Bolt

Hub refitment:

If the disc guard 15 in **FIG 9:5** was removed, apply black 'sealastik' sealer round the base of the stub axle before refitting the guard and its retaining spring washers and bolts.

With the bearings in position, partially pack the hub with fresh all purpose grease. Enter the assembly onto the stub axle and fit the washer 4 and nut 3. Check that the nut

turns freely on the stub axle threads. If it does not, correct the fault before proceeding to the torque tightening. Torque tighten the nut to 0.7kgm (5lb ft) and then back off by one-sixth of a turn (one hexagon flat). **Do not overtighten or damage may be caused to the bearings and bearing tracks.** Fit the retainer 2 and lock with a new splitpin 1. Fit the cap 14. Refer to **Chapter 11, Sections 11:3, 11:8** and **11:7** and fit the caliper, reconnect the brake pipe to the hose and bleed the brakes. Fit the road wheel and lower the car.

9:6   The stub axle and damper assemblies

No procedures are prescribed for the overhaul or repair of an unserviceable or damaged strut which must be removed and a new replacement fitted.

Removal:

1 Open the bonnet. Apply the handbrake firmly. Raise the front of the car and support the body securely on stands. Remove the relevant road wheel. Refer to **FIG 9:7**.
2 Refer to **Chapter 11, Section 11:8** and disconnect the brake caliper pipe 5 from the brake hose. Loosen the locknut which secures the hose to the bracket on the strut and disengage the hose from the bracket
3 Remove the nyloc nut and plain washer 6 from the track rod ball joint 2 and, using tool 18G 1063 (or an equivalent ball joint extractor), release the track rod ball joint from the steering arm 11.
4 Remove the nyloc nut and plain washer 7 and, using a suitable lever, separate the bottom link 10 from the strut.
5 Refer to **FIG 9:4**. Remove the three nyloc nuts and plain washers 15 and 16 which secure the upper swivel to the wing valance. The strut assembly may now be dismounted.

Dismantling:

Remove the suspension spring as described in **Section 9:4**. Refer to **FIG 9:4**. The retainer 8, rubber boot 5 and bump stops 6 may now be removed. Remove the brake caliper, hub assembly and disc guard as described in **Section 9:5**.

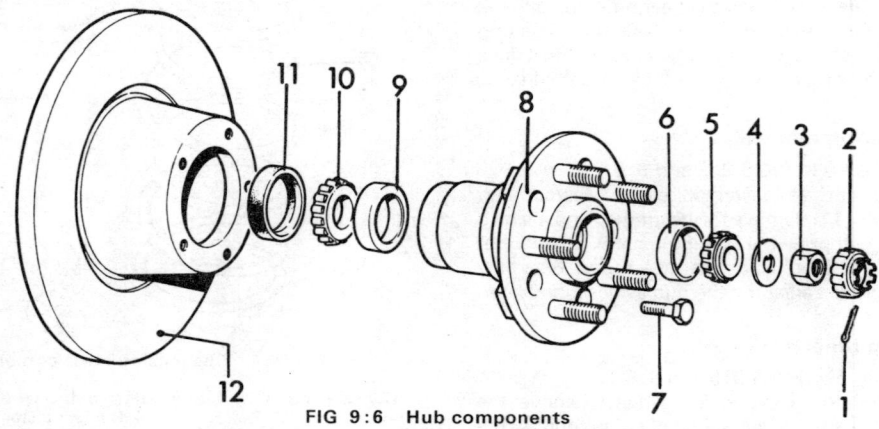

FIG 9:6   Hub components

Key to Fig 9:6   1 Splitpin   2 Retaining cap   3 Nut   4 Washer   5 Outer bearing   6 Track   7 Bolt   8 Hub   9 Track   10 Inner bearing   11 Oil seal   12 Brake disc

Check the serviceability of the components and obtain new replacements as necessary.

Reassembly:

Reverse the removal sequence and refer to **Sections 9:4** and **9:5** as relevant.

Fitment:

Offer up the assembled strut unit to the wing valance, engage the studs of the upper swivel, fit the washers and tighten the nuts. Refer to **FIG 9:7**. Locate the bottom link ball joint stud into the stub axle assembly, fit the washer and torque tighten the nut 7. Similarly connect the track rod and torque tighten nut 6. Refer to **Chapter 11, Section 11:8** and connect the brake pipe to the hose and bracket. Bleed the brakes, fit the road wheel and lower the car. Depending upon the replacement parts which may have been fitted, refer to **Chapter 10, Section 10:9** and check the wheel alignment.

9:7 The upper swivel

Each strut assembly pivots between an upper swivel which incorporates a ball bearing and a ball joint which is integral with each bottom suspension link.

Upper swivel removal:

Dismount the stub axle and damper assembly as described in **Section 9:6**. Refer to **Section 9:4** and carry out the spring compression operation. With the spring load relieved from the upper swivel, the washer and nut 12 and 13 in **FIG 9:4** may be removed from the damper rod using tool 18G 1063. The upper swivel assembly can now be lifted off.

Upper swivel fitment:

Reverse the removal sequence. Refer to **Sections 9:4** and **9:6** as relevant.

Bottom link ball joint:

Refer to **Section 9:8**.

9:8 The bottom links

Removal:

1 Apply the handbrake firmly. Raise the front of the car and support the body on stands. Remove the relevant road wheel.
2 Refer to **FIG 9:3**. Withdraw and discard the splitpin 1. Remove the nut 2, washers 3 and 4, the flanged bush 5 and the inner bush 6 from the end of the anti-roll bar.
3 Refer to **FIG 9:7**. Remove the nut and washer 7 which retains the ball joint of the bottom link to the stub axle. Using a suitable lever, separate the ball joint stud from the stub axle.
4 Refer to **Chapter 10, FIG 10:6**. Remove the nut and bolt 5 on which the bottom link pivots in the front crossmember. Dismount the bottom link.

The bottom link pivot bush may be renewed by pressing it out and pressing in a new bush. No procedure is prescribed for the renewal of the ball joint and, if this is unserviceable, a new bottom link **of the correct hand must be fitted**.

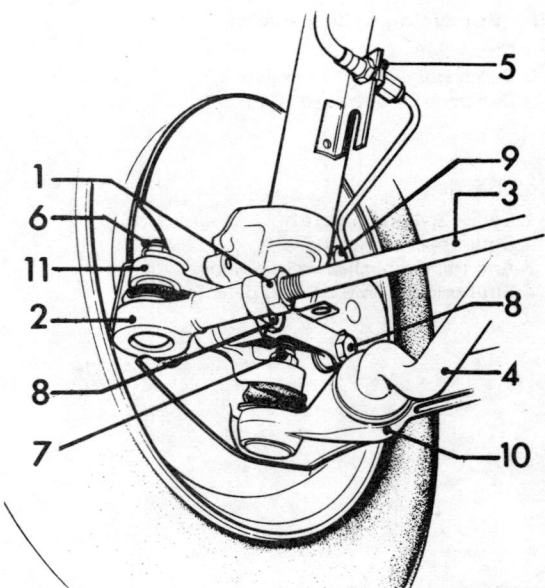

FIG 9:7 Steering linkage and suspension components

Key to Fig 9:7   1 Locknut   2 Ball joint   3 Track rod   4 Anti-roll bar   5 Pipe/hose joint   6 Nut   7 Nut   8 Bolt   9 Bolt   10 Bottom link   11 Steering arm

Fitment:

Reverse the removal sequence. Torque tighten the relevant nuts.

9:9 Camber and castor

No procedures are prescribed for the adjustment of camber or castor angles. These, and the strut inclination angle, are determined by the position of the upper swivel in its location in the wing valance. They will be affected by any distortion of the bottom suspension links, struts, stub axles or front crossmember.

In the event of accident damage, measurement of the camber and castor angles will provide a check on possible distortion of these components or of a wing valance. Professional experience and equipment will be required to measure the angles and to advise on replacements and repairs. Refer to the **Technical Data** section of the **Appendix** for specification angles. Note that data is given for a laden and an unladen car. In this context a vehicle is laden when the fuel tank is full and a driver and two passengers are on board.

Wheel alignment adjustment is covered in **Chapter 10, Section 10:9**.

9:10 Fault diagnosis

(a) Wheel wobble

1 Worn hub bearings
2 Broken or weak front springs
3 Uneven tyre wear
4 Worn bottom link pivot bush
5 Loose or broken anti-roll bar
6 Excessive hub end float
7 Loose wheel nuts

(b) Bottoming of suspension

1 Check 2 in (a)
2 Bump stops worn or missing
3 Damper(s) inoperative

(c) Rattles

1 Check 2, 4 and 5 in (a)
2 Strut upper swivel loose
3 Anti-roll bar bushes worn or loose
4 Strut upper swivel bearing defective

(d) Excessive rolling

1 Check 2 in (a); 3 in (b) and 3 in (c)
2 Anti-roll bar broken

(e) Car sways on corners

1 Check 4 and 5 in (a); 3 in (b); 3 in (c) and 2 in (d)
2 Distorted suspension geometry

(f) Excessive tyre wear

1 Check 4 and 5 in (a); 3 in (b); 3 in (c) and 2 in (e)
2 Incorrect tyre pressures
3 Incorrect wheel alignment

CHAPTER 10

THE STEERING GEAR

10:1 Description

The layout of the power assisted rack and pinion steering system is shown in **FIG 10:1**. The steering rack 1 is mounted on the front crossmember and is connected with the steering arms by track rods 2 which are ball jointed to them. Wheel alignment is adjusted by altering the effective lengths of the track rods. Steering wheel motion is transmitted to the rack pinion via the steering column 3 and the steering shaft 4. A universal type joint couples the steering column with the steering shaft and a flexible type joint couples the steering shaft with the rack pinion. The steering column is adjustable for both reach and rake.

Power for the assisted steering is provided by the pump 5 which is belt driven from a pulley on the forward end of the crankshaft. Belt tension is adjustable. A reservoir 6 maintains the supply of hydraulic fluid to the system. The vane type pump operates at up to 67 to 70kg/sq cm (950 to 1000lb/sq in) and any work carried out on the hydraulic system requires meticulous cleanliness and a very high standard of competence.

A combination steering lock/ignition/starter switch is provided and a multi-purpose switch block is mounted on the steering column.

10:2 Maintenance

Fluid level:

At least every 3000 miles (5000km), check the hydraulic fluid level in the reservoir (see **FIG 10:2**) and top up as necessary. The level is correct when the fluid is 25mm (1in) below the base of the filler neck. Refer to **Section 10:3** and use an ATF type F fluid (this is the same as that approved for the automatic transmission) of reputable brand and, preferably, of the same brand as that already in the power steering hydraulic system.

Pump drive belt:

Every 6000 miles (10,000km), check the tension and the condition of the pump drive belt. The procedures for the tensioning and renewal of the belt are given in **Section 10:4**.

Wheel alignment:

Every 6000 miles (10,000km), check and, if necessary, adjust the wheel alignment. The procedure is described in **Section 10:9**.

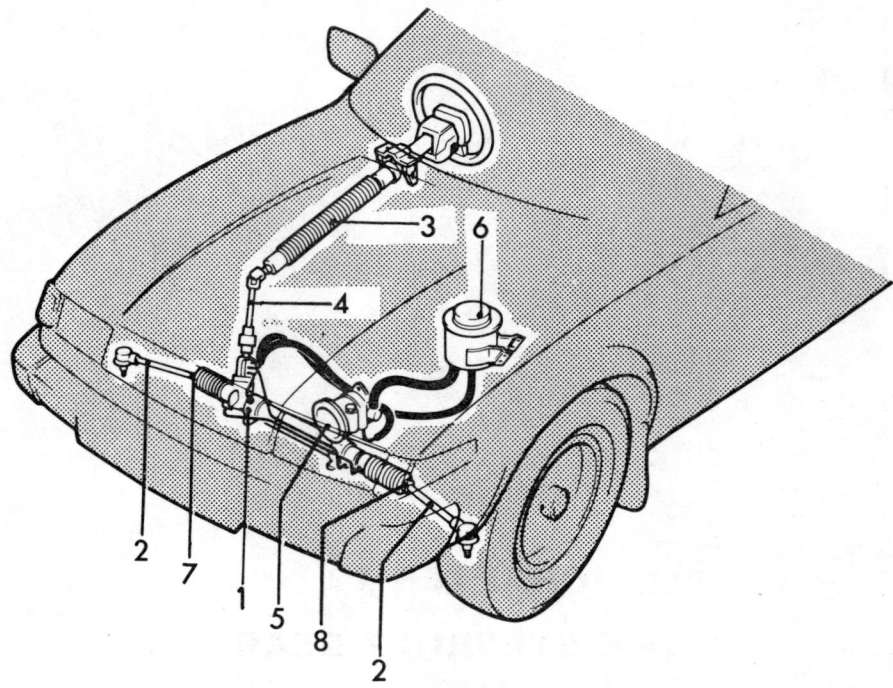

FIG 10:1 Layout of the steering gear

Key to Fig 10:1 1 Rack and pinion unit   2 Track rod   3 Steering column   4 Steering shaft   5 Pump   6 Reservoir
7 and 8 Boot outer clip

General:

Maintain regular checks for fluid leaks from the steering rack, pump and pipe joints and rectify any fault without delay. Maintain regular checks on the condition of the boots which enclose the rack to track rod connections and on the condition of the flexible hoses.

10:3 The hydraulic system

Observe meticulous cleanliness when working on the hydraulic system. **Do not re-use drained fluid** as, even if it is perfectly clean, it will be aerated.

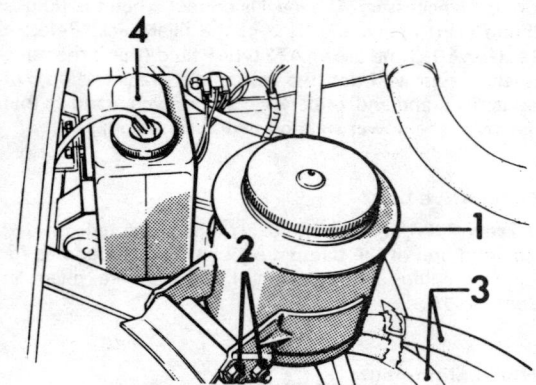

FIG 10:2 The fluid reservoir

Key to Fig 10:2 1 Reservoir   2 Retaining bolts   3 Feed and return pipes   4 Windscreen washer reservoir

Bleeding:

No routine bleeding of the system is required. If, however, the pump or rack and pinion unit have been newly installed, if the reservoir has been emptied or the pipelines disturbed, proceed as follows.

Fill the reservoir to the correct level as described in **Section 10:2**. Refer to **Section 10:4** and release the pump drive belt tension. With the belt slackened, turn the pump pulley by hand to prime the system. Re-tension the drive belt, run the engine at idling speed and, to minimise tyre scrub, **slowly** turn the steering wheel to one full lock then to the other full lock and then to the straight ahead position. Finally top up the fluid reservoir.

Pressure tests:

Heavy steering may result from mechanical faults such as incorrect wheel alignment, incorrect tyre pressures, seized strut pivots, distorted steering geometry, worn hub, suspension and steering components or from lack of power assistance. If the suspension and steering are mechanically serviceable and lack of power assistance is suspected, the efficiency of the pump should be checked.

Fit a three-way adaptor and pressure gauge JD 10 and adaptor pipe JD 10-2. The gauge has a range of zero to 140kg/sq cm (2000lb/sq in). Open the tap in JD 10-2 and bleed the system as described earlier.

Run the engine at 1000rev/min. With the steering wheel held hard on full lock, the pressure should be 67 to 70kg/sq cm (950 to 1000lb/sq in) or, at idling speed 32kg/sq cm (450lb/sq in). **Do not hold full lock for more than 30 seconds** in any one minute or fluid

overheating may occur. Release the steering wheel. With
the engine idling the pressure should now be a maximum
of 4kg/sq cm (55lb/sq in).

If the pressure recorded is outside the ranges specified,
have the pump relief valve renewed or substitute a pump of
known serviceability. If, on retest, the pressure is still
outside the specified ranges, the fault is in the rack and
pinion unit or in the control valve housing.

10:4 The pump

Tensioning the pump drive:

The belt is correctly tensioned when thumb pressure
applied to a point midway between the crankshaft pulley
and the pump pulley gives a belt deflection of 6 to 8mm
(0.25 to 0.30in). Adjustment is made by loosening the two
pivots 1 and the quadrant nut and bolt 2 in **FIG 10:3**,
swinging the pump away from the engine and retightening
the nuts and bolts. Recheck the belt tension and re-adjust
if necessary.

Belt renewal:

Refer to **Chapter 12, Section 12:5** and remove the
alternator/fan drive belt. Refer to **Chapter 1, FIG 1:35**.
Remove bolt 7 and move the transducer 1 aside. Refer to
Chapter 3, FIG 3:3. Remove the retaining bolts and
dismount the timing pointer. Refer to **Chapter 4, Section
4:4** and remove the fan drive/water pump pulley. Refer to
FIG 10:3. Loosen nuts and bolts, swing the pump
towards the engine, disengage the belt from the pulley and
remove the belt.

Fitment of a new belt is the reverse of this sequence.

Pump removal:

Remove the cap from the reservoir. Disconnect the inlet
hose from the pump, drain off and discard the drained
fluid. Disconnect the fluid delivery hose from the pump.
Refit the reservoir cap and blank off the hose and pump
orifices. Refer to **FIG 10:3**. Remove nuts and bolts 1 and
2, disengage the belt from the pulley and withdraw the
pump.

Pump fitment:

Reverse the removal sequence. Fill the reservoir to the
correct level (see **Section 10:2**). Refer to **Section 10:3**.
Prime the pump and bleed the system.

10:5 The steering shaft

Removal:

1 Apply the handbrake firmly. Raise the front of the car
   and support the body on stands. Refer to **FIG 10:4**.
   Turn the steering wheel to give access to the nut and
   remove nut and bolt 2.
2 From inside the car, draw back the steering column
   shaft by about 13mm (0.5in). Remove nut and bolt 4.
   Remove nut and bolt 5. Slide the steering shaft and
   coupling downwards and disengage it from the
   column shaft.
3 Release the shaft from the lower coupling and
   withdraw the shaft. The lower coupling may now be
   removed from the pinion shaft by withdrawing it
   upwards after marking its alignment with the pinion
   shaft.

FIG 10:3   The pump

Key to Fig 10:3   1 Pivot nuts and bolts   2 Clamping
bolt

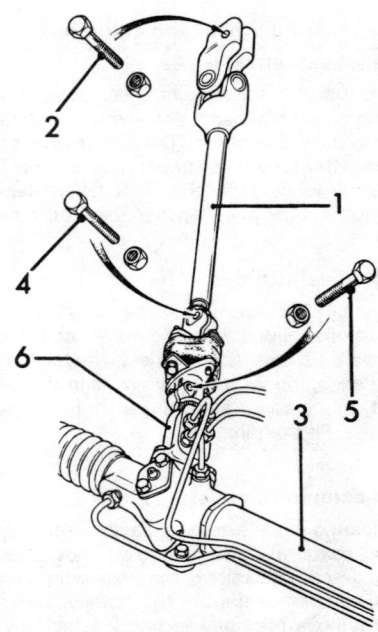

FIG 10:4   Removing the steering shaft

Key to Fig 10:4   1 Steering shaft   2 Upper joint bolt
3 Rack and pinion unit   4 Lower joint upper bolt
5 Lower joint lower bolt   6 Valve housing

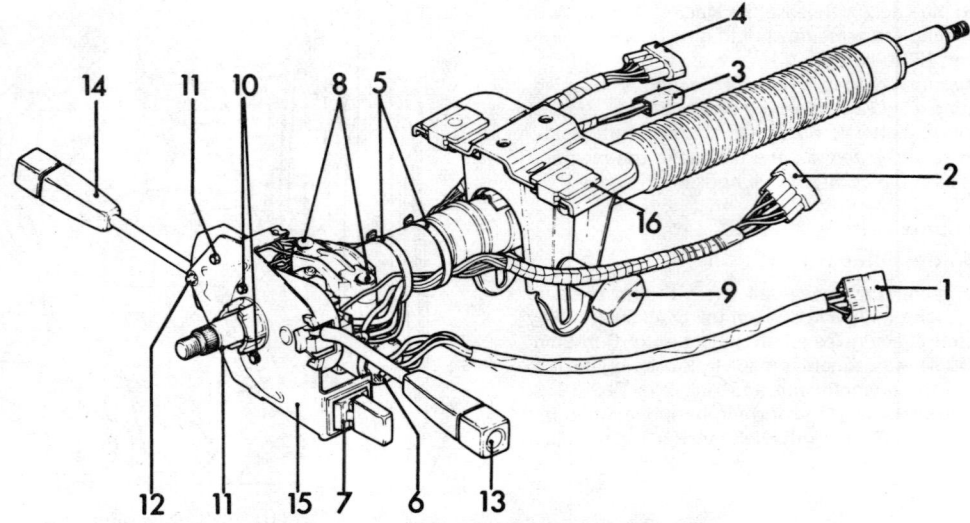

FIG 10:5   The steering column switches

Key to Fig 10:5   1 Ignition/starter switch connector   2 Horn, dip, direction indicator switch connector   3 Lights switch connector   4 Windscreen wiper and washer switch connector   5 Harness clips   6 Ignition/starter switch   7 Lights switch   8 Sheared off bolts   9 Column clamp   10 Switch retaining bolts   11 Switch retaining bolts   12 Switch retaining clip   13 Horn, dip, direction indicator switch   14 Windscreen wiper and washer switch   15 Switch assembly plate   16 Steering column bracket

Fitment:

Set the road wheels and the steering shaft in the straight ahead positions and reverse the shaft removal sequence.

10:6 The steering wheel and column

Steering wheel removal:

With the wheel in the straight ahead position, prise off the steering wheel trim pad. Loosen the nut which retains the wheel to the column shaft. **Do not attempt to drive or tap the wheel from the shaft** but use tool 18G 1014 to release the wheel from the shaft taper. Remove the retaining nut and the plain washer and lift off the wheel.

Steering wheel fitment:

Ensure that the arrow on the direction indicator cancelling collar aligns with the centre of the direction indicator stalk. Fit the steering wheel with the two lugs on the wheel engaging with the two slots in the cancelling collar. Fit the washer and torque tighten the wheel retaining nut. Fit the trim pad.

Steering column removal:

If the steering wheel is to be separated from the column shaft, it will be found convenient to do so by following the procedure described earlier before removing the column.

Disconnect the leads from the battery. Refer to **FIG 10:4** and remove the nut and bolt 2 which clamps the steering shaft upper joint to the column shaft. Refer to **Chapter 13, Section 13:10** and remove the glovebox from the driver's side. Refer to **FIG 10:5**. Identify and disconnect the four multi-pin connectors 1, 2, 3 and 4.

Remove the two nyloc nuts, washers and bolts which secure the steering column mounting bracket 16 to the body. Withdraw the steering column assembly rearwards into the car. If the steering wheel was removed earlier, the assembly will be as shown in **FIG 10:5**.

Steering column fitment:

Enter the column assembly into the lower bush and, with the road wheels in the straight ahead position, engage the column shaft into the splines of the steering shaft upper joint. Fit and tighten the nut and bolt 2 in **FIG 10:4**. Align the column bracket with the body and fit the two retaining bolts. Torque tighten these bolts. Reconnect the multi-pin connectors, refit the glovebox and reconnect the battery leads.

10:7 The steering rack

If pressure tests (see **Section 10:3**) indicate that lack of power assistance is due to a defective rack and pinion unit, remove the unit. The following procedures assume a righthand drive car. In the case of a lefthand drive vehicle, read lefthand for righthand where relevant.

Rack removal:

1 Remove the air cleaner as described in **Chapter 2, Section 2:3**. Remove the steering shaft and lower coupling as described in **Section 10:5**. Disconnect the track rods from the steering arms as described in **Section 10:8**.

2 Remove the bolt which secures the clip for the flexible hose from the rack. Refer to **FIG 10:6**. Disconnect the feed and return flexible hoses 11 from the valve housing 7. Drain off and discard the hydraulic fluid. Blank off the hose and valve housing orifices.

3 Position a jack under the engine sump (interpose a piece of wood) and support the engine. Refer to **Chapter 1, Section 1:18** and release both engine front mountings by removing nuts and bolts 2 and 1 in **Fig 1:32**. Remove the two bolts which secure the engine righthand tie rod to the front crossmember and remove the tie rod.

4 Raise the engine to clear the rack unit. Turn the righthand road wheel to full righthand lock. Remove the four nuts and bolts 9 in **FIG 10:6** and release the rack unit from the crossmember. Carefully manoeuvre the rack unit out of the righthand wheel arch.

Rack overhaul:

No procedures are prescribed for the overhaul of a rack unit by an owner but those who have the necessary expertise should note that the following kits are available: AAU 3357, shim kit (top of pinion); AAU 3358, shim kit (adjuster button); AAU 3359, pinion housing (valve) kit; AAU 3353, rack oil seal kit; AAU 3354, pinion oil seal kit; AAU 3356, pinion race kit; AAU 3360, inner ball joint kit. Refer to **Section 10:8** for details of the rubber boot (bellows) kit.

Rack fitment:

If the position of the rack was disturbed, remove the plug in the rack damper assembly and, using a suitable probe, locate the dimple in the rack shaft. Refit and tighten the plug. Refitment will now be the removal sequence in reverse. Torque tighten nuts and bolts where applicable and refer to sectional and chapter texts where relevant. On completion, refill the reservoir to the correct level as described in **Section 10:2** and bleed and test the system as described in **Section 10:3**.

10:8 The steering linkage

A track rod connects each end of the steering rack with a steering arm which is bolted to each suspension strut assembly. The connection is through an axial ball joint at the rack (enclosed in a bellows type rubber boot) and an outer righthand ball joint at the steering arm. The outer ball joints are screwed onto a threaded section of the track rods and this arrangement allows alteration to the effective lengths of the rods and provides the means of adjusting the wheel alignment as described in **Section 10:9**.

To disconnect a track rod from its steering arm, refer to **Chapter 9, FIG 9:7** and remove nut 6 and its dust shield. Using a ball joint extractor (the official tool is 18G 1063) separate the ball joint stud from its steering arm. If the ball joints are to be renewed, loosen locknuts 1 and unscrew the ball joints 2 from the track rods 3. Screw the new ball joints into position so that the distance between the track rod ball joint centres (inner to outer) is a nominal 336mm (13.23in) on both sides. Recouple the rods to the steering arms and adjust the wheel alignment as described in **Section 10:9**.

To renew the rubber boots, remove the outer ball joints, unclip and remove the old boots, fit the new boots but tighten only the large (inner) clips, fit the outer ball joints, recouple and adjust the wheel alignment. The small clips are then tightened. The kit covering replacement boots and clips is AAU 3355.

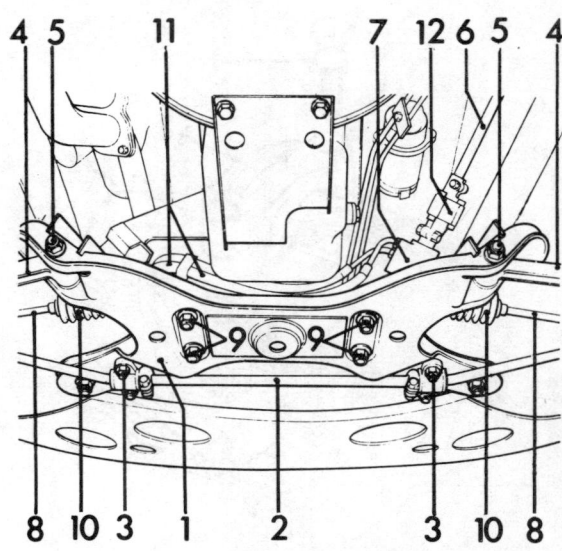

FIG 10:6   The front crossmember

Key to Fig 10:6   1 Front crossmember   2 Anti-roll bar   3 Anti-roll bar bracket   4 Suspension bottom link   5 Bottom link pivot bolt   6 Steering shaft   7 Valve housing   8 Track rod   9 Steering unit retaining nuts and bolts   10 Track rod boot   11 Pump feed and return pipes   12 Lower joint

10:9 Wheel alignment

First class equipment (preferably optical) should be used when checking and adjusting the toe-in which should be zero to 3.17mm (0.125in) with the car laden or unladen.

Adjustment:

With the car on level ground and the wheels in the straight ahead position, refer to **Chapter 9, FIG 9:7** and loosen the locknuts 1 on **both** track rods. Refer to **FIG 10:1** and loosen the boot outer retaining clips 7 and 8. Shorten or extend both track rods by equal amounts to give the specified toe-in. Tighten the locknuts and the boot clips.

10:10 The steering lock/ignition/starter switch

Ignition/starter switch:

The electrical section of the combined switch may be removed without disturbing the lock section.

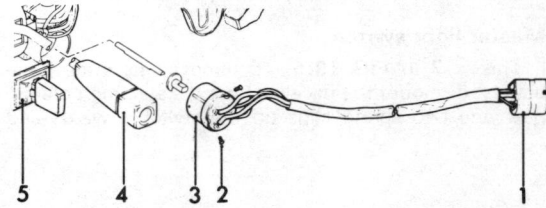

FIG 10:7   Removing the ignition/starter switch

Key to Fig 10:7   1 Connector   2 Retaining screws   3 Switch   4 Horn, dip, direction indicator switch   5 Lights switch

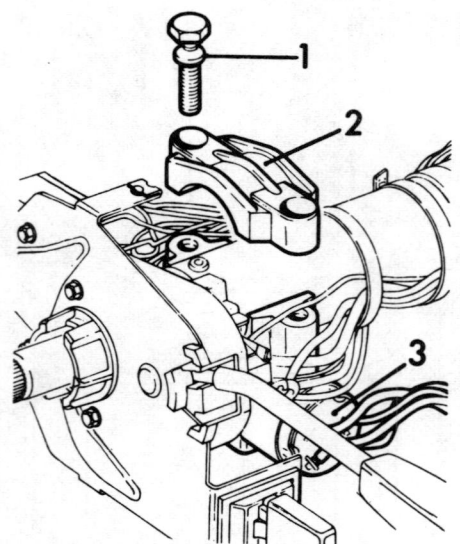

FIG 10:8 Renewing the lock/ignition/starter switch unit

Key to Fig 10:8   1 New (unsheared) bolt   2 Cap
3 Ignition/starter switch

Disconnect the battery leads. Remove two screws and dismount the nacelles from the steering column. Remove the harness straps. Manoeuvre the harness rearwards and disconnect the multi-pin connector 1 in **FIG 10:7** (this is 1 in **FIG 10:5**). Remove two small screws 2 and withdraw the switch 3.

Fitment is the reverse of this sequence.

Steering lock removal and fitment:

Disconnect the battery leads. Dismount the nacelles from the steering column. Refer to **FIG 10:5**. Disconnect the multi-pin connector 1. Remove the two anti-tamper (sheared off heads) bolts either by unscrewing them with a small chisel or by drilling and extracting with an 'Easiout'. Fit the new lock/switch, refer to **FIG 10:8** and, using headed bolts 1, fit the cap. Evenly tighten the bolts until their heads shear off. Connect up and fit the nacelles.

10:11 The column multi-purpose switches

The three separate switches may be renewed separately. The multi-pin connectors are identified in **FIG 10:5**.

Master light switch:

This is 7 in **FIG 10:5**. To remove, disconnect the battery, dismount the nacelles from the steering column, push the two spring clips on the switch inwards and

withdraw the switch. Identify and disconnect the leads from the switch. The associated multi-pin connector is 3.

Fitment is the reverse of this sequence.

Multi-purpose switches:

To remove the complete unit, proceed as follows. Disconnect the battery leads. Remove the steering wheel as described in **Section 10:6**. Dismount the nacelles from the column. Unclip the harnesses from the column (clips 5 in **FIG 10:5**). Uncouple the three multi-pin connectors 2, 3 and 4 in **FIG 10:5**. Remove the switch assembly clamp screw and withdraw the switch assembly from the column. Bolts 11 and spire clip 12 retain the lefthand switch. Bolts 10 retain the righthand switch.

Reassembly is the reverse of the removal sequence.

10:12 Fault diagnosis

(a) Wheel wobble

1 Check (a) in **Chapter 9, Section 9:10**
2 Loose ball joint connections
3 Excessive wear in steering linkage

(b) Wander

1 Check (a)
2 Distorted steering geometry
3 Defective dampers

(c) Heavy steering when driving

1 Check 2 in (b)
2 Very low tyre pressures
3 Pump defective (see **Section 10:3**)
4 Alignment incorrect
5 Steering column bearings tight
6 Low fluid level in reservoir
7 System requires bleeding
8 Pump drive belt slipping or broken
9 Rack binding

(d) Heavy steering when parked

1 Check 2, 3, 5, 6, 7, 8 and 9 in (c)
2 Restricted hose
3 Low fluid pressure due to heavy leakage

(e) Fluid leaks

1 Loose pipe or hose connections
2 Defective seal(s)
3 Reservoir fluid level too high

(f) Rattles, noisy operation

1 Check (c) in **Chapter 9, Section 9:10**
2 Pump drive belt slipping
3 Worn pump
4 Worn rack and pinion unit
5 Rack and pinion unit loose on crossmember

CHAPTER 11

THE BRAKING SYSTEM

11:1 Description

The general layout of the braking system in a righthand drive car is shown diagrammatically in **FIG 11:1**. The layout in a lefthand drive vehicle is similar except for the servo and master cylinder assembly and the associated pipeline runs.

The hydraulic system:

The brake pedal 1 operates the master hydraulic cylinder 3 via the servo assistance unit 2. Power for the servo assistance unit is derived from the difference in pressure between atmosphere and the partial vacuum in the engine induction manifold. The manifold to servo pipeline is not included in **FIG 11:1**. The master cylinder has tandem pistons and a two-section hydraulic fluid reservoir and separate feed lines 4 and 5 for the front and rear brakes. Pressure fluid from the two sections of the master cylinder are fed to separate sections of the regulating/reducing valve 6. The primary function of this valve is to limit the pressure of the fluid to the rear brake wheel cylinders. This, by biasing braking effort in favour of the front wheels, precludes locking of the rear wheels under normal circumstances. The valve is failure sensitive and, should there be a pipeline failure in the front brakes circuit, increased pressure is available to the rear brakes. If there should be a failure in the rear brakes circuit, the valve passes full pressure to the front brakes in the normal way.

Front brakes:

These are disc brakes. A rigidly mounted caliper which straddles each disc is bolted to the hub section of each suspension strut. The calipers are twin piston type units and carry two friction pads. Compensation for wear of the pad friction linings is automatic and operates through hydraulic action.

Rear brakes:

These are drum brakes and each carries two brake shoes. The hydraulic wheel cylinders are fitted with two pistons each acting on a shoe. This gives a leading/trailing shoe arrangement. Compensation for wear of the shoe friction linings is automatic through a self-adjusting mechanism incorporated in the brake shoe handbrake linkage which maintains a fixed running clearance between the shoe linings and the brake drum. Self-adjustment occurs on application of the foot brake.

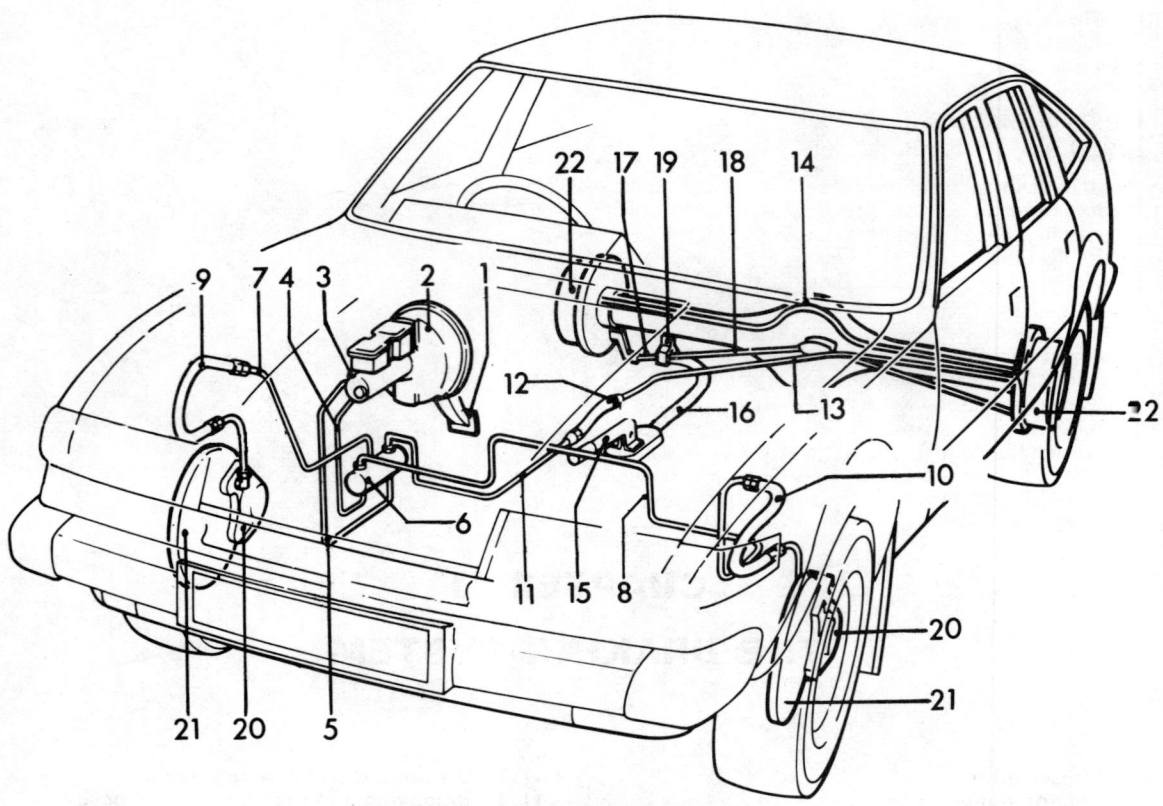

FIG 11:1   Layout of the braking system

Key to Fig 11:1   1 Brake pedal   2 Servo unit   3 Master cylinder   4 Front brakes feed to PR   5 Rear brakes feed to PR
6 Pressure regulator (PR)   7 and 8 Rigid pipe (front feed)   9 and 10 Flexible hose (front feed)   11 and 13 Rigid pipe (rear
feed)   12 Flexible hose (rear feed)   14 Rigid pipe (rear righthand feed)   15 Handbrake lever   16 Bowden type cable
17 Direct cable to righthand drum   18 Reaction cable to lefthand drum   19 Compensator   20 Caliper   21 Brake disc
22 Brake drum

Handbrake:

The handbrake acts on the rear wheels only. It operates through an adjustable Bowden type cable. The inner cable acts directly on the righthand rear wheel. The outer cable is anchored to a swinging compensator from which a reaction cable acts on the lefthand wheel.

11:2 Maintenance

General:

Every 3000 miles (5000km), check over the pipelines (including the servo to manifold hose) for condition, secure connections, leaky joints etc. Correct or renew as may be necessary.

Fluid level:

At least every 3000 miles (5000km), check and, if necessary, top up the level of the fluid in the reservoir. Use, for preference, the same brand of fluid as that already in the system. Approved fluids (they are the same as those approved for the clutch hydraulic system) are given in **Chapter 5, Section 5:2**. If these are not available, use a fluid of reputable brand which meets specification SAE J1703d.

Brake pads and shoes:

Every 6000 miles (10,000km), check the thickness of the front pad friction linings and the rear shoe linings. Pads should be renewed when the linings have worn down to 1.5mm (0.06in) and brake shoes should be renewed when the linings have worn down to 2.5mm (0.10in). The procedures are described in **Sections 11:3** and **11:4**.

Handbrake:

Every 6000 miles (10,000km), lubricate the compensator and lever pivot points and, if necessary, adjust the operating cable as described in **Section 11:11**.

Fluid renewal:

Every 18,000 miles (30,000km) or every 18 months (whichever is the sooner), refer to **Section 11:5** and drain off and discard the fluid from the hydraulic system. Refill with new fluid.

Hydraulic system overhaul:

Every 36,000 miles (60,000km) or every three years (whichever is the sooner), overhaul the front calipers, the rear wheel cylinders and the master cylinder. The procedures are described in **Sections 11:3, 11:4** and **11:5** respectively.

11:3 The front brakes

Pad renewal:

Both pads in both calipers should be renewed at the same time. Kit GBP 242 contains an axle set of splitpins, retaining springs and pads (2, 3 and 4 in **FIG 11:2**).

1 Raise the front of the car and remove a road wheel.
2 Straighten the splitpins 2. Depress the pad retaining spring 3 and withdraw the splitpins. Remove the retaining spring. Note their positions and lift out the old pads and shims from the recess in the caliper. Provided that the shims are undamaged and are not corroded, they may be re-used.
3 Remove the cap from the fluid reservoir and, as fluid is displaced during the following operation, keep a careful watch on the fluid level. Ease the caliper pistons into their bores until the increased thickness of the new pads can be accommodated.

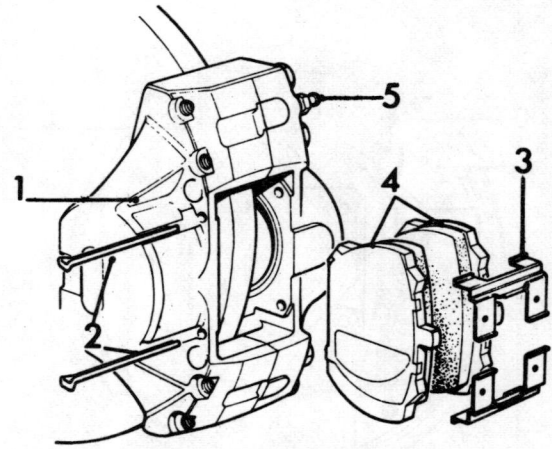

FIG 11:2   Caliper pad renewal

Key to Fig 11:2   1 Caliper body   2 Splitpins   3 Retaining spring   4 Pads   5 Bleed nipple

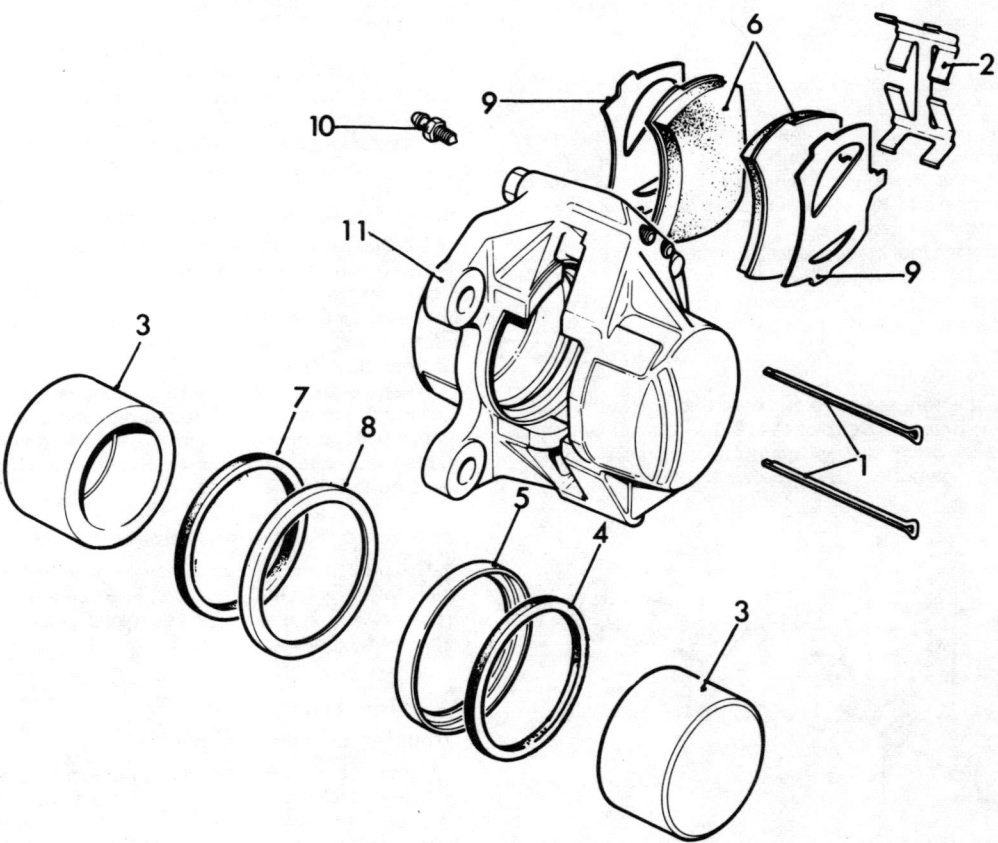

FIG 11:3   Components of a caliper

Key to Fig 11:3   1 Splitpins   2 Retaining spring   3 Piston   4 Seal   5 Wiper   6 Pads   7 Seal   8 Wiper   9 Shim   10 Bleed nipple   11 Caliper body

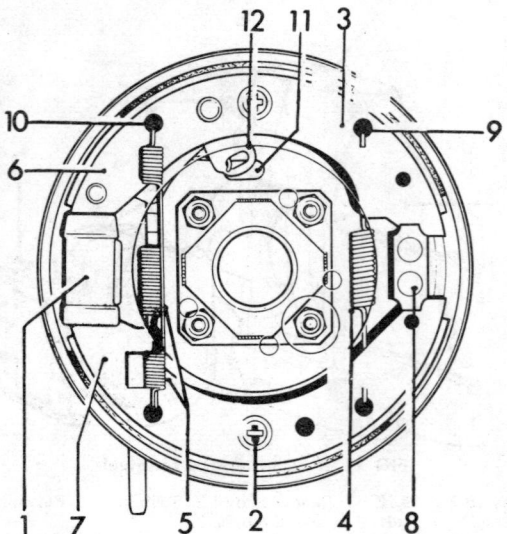

FIG 11:4 A rear brake with the drum removed

Key to Fig 11:4   1 Wheel cylinder   2 and 3 Steady pins
4 and 5 Springs   6 and 7 Brake shoes   8 Pivot block
9 Spring hooked outwards   10 Spring hooked inwards
11 Hole in backplate   12 Adjuster lever

4 Remove fluid as necessary as the level rises and ensure
that the fluid does not come in contact with the
paintwork. Use a soft brush to remove the dust and
clean the caliper pad locations.

5 Insert the new pads and shims (larger cutout
uppermost), fit the retaining spring and the splitpins.
Open the splitpin legs to lock the assembly. Firmly
depress the foot brake pedal a number of times to locate
the pads. Refit the road wheel.

6 Repeat operations 2 to 5 on the opposite wheel. Lower
the car and adjust the fluid to the correct level.

Caliper removal:

1 Raise the front of the car and remove the relevant road
wheel. Refer to **Section 11:8** and disconnect the
brake line union at the suspension strut bracket. Blank
off the pipe orifices to preclude entry of dirt.

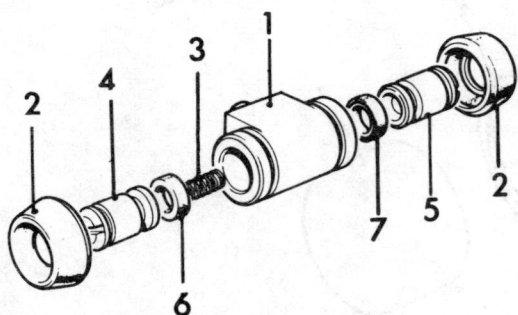

FIG 11:5   Components of a wheel cylinder

Key to Fig 11:5   1 Cylinder body   2 Boot   3 Spring
4 and 5 Piston   6 and 7 Piston seal

2 Refer to **Chapter 9, FIG 9:7**. Untab and remove the
two bolts (rearward 8 and 9) which retain the caliper to
the strut assembly and dismount the caliper.

Caliper fitment:

Align the caliper over the disc and fit but do not tighten
the upper retaining bolt. Fit the lower bolt. Torque tighten
both bolts and retab to lock. Reconnect the brake pipe.
Bleed the caliper as described in **Section 11:7**.

Caliper overhaul:

Dismount the calipers and remove the friction pads and
shims as described earlier. The components of a caliper are
shown in **FIG 11:3**.

Identify the pistons to their respective positions and,
using low pressure air, carefully blow them from their
bores. **Pistons must not be interchanged in the
bores.** If a piston has seized, the complete caliper
assembly must be renewed. Using a blunt screwdriver and
taking great care not to damage the caliper bores, carefully
prise out and discard the seals and wipers. Do not separate
the two halves of a caliper.

Using new brake fluid or methylated spirit, thoroughly
clean the pistons and caliper bores. If they show any signs
of corrosion, scuffing or wear, new parts must be obtained.
Obtain new seals and wipers. These are contained in kit
AAU 2067.

Using only the fingers, fit the new seals into the grooves
in the caliper bores and check that they are correctly
seated. Fit the new wipers. Lubricate the bores with clean
brake fluid and insert the pistons squarely. Fit the caliper
and, preferably, new pads as described earlier. Bleed the
system as described in **Section 11:5**.

Brake disc removal and fitment:

The brake discs are spigotted and bolted to the hubs as
shown in **Chapter 9, FIG 9:5**.

To separate a disc from a hub, dismount the hub as
described in **Chapter 9, Section 9:5**, remove the five
retaining bolts and spring washers 7 and separate the disc
12 from the hub 8.

When reassembling, ensure that the spigot faces are
clean and free of burrs. Working diagonally, tighten the
retaining bolts gradually and evenly and finally torque
tighten them. Refit the hub as described in **Chapter 9,
Section 9:5**.

Disc guard removal and fitment:

The procedures for the removal and refitment of this
guard which is 15 in **Chapter 9, FIG 9:5** are included in
Section 9:5. A distorted or damaged guard should be
replaced by a new component.

11:4 The rear brakes

Drum removal and fitment:

Chock the front wheels. Raise the rear of the car and
remove the relevant road wheel. Release the handbrake.
Refer to **Chapter 8, FIG 8:3** and remove the countersunk
screw which retains the drum 3 to the halfshaft 1. Pull off
the drum.

If, due to wear or ridging, difficulty is experienced in
withdrawing the drum, remove the rubber plug from the

rear of the backplate, refer to **FIG 11:4**, insert a small screwdriver through hole 11 and engage it in the slotted hole in the adjusting lever 12. Press downwards to release the mechanism.

Fitment is the removal sequence in reverse. If the brake shoes were disturbed or were renewed, they may require to be centralised on the backplate to allow the drum to pass over them. With the road wheels again on the ground, apply the footbrake a number of times to adjust the shoes.

Brake shoes, renewal:

Both shoes on both rear brakes should be renewed at the same time. Kit GBS 635 will be required.

1 Remove both brake drums as described earlier.
2 Refer to **FIG 11:4** and, before proceeding, carefully relate and note the positions of the shoes and springs with the illustration. Note, in particular, the handing of the lefthand and righthand assemblies.
3 Remove the shoe steady pins 2 and 3 by removing their cups and springs and withdrawing the pins from the rear of the backplate.
4 Ease the toe of the leading shoe 7 and the heel of the trailing shoe 6 from the slots in the heads of the wheel cylinder pistons. Refer to **Section 11:11** and disconnect the handbrake cables from the levers by removing the clevis pins.
5 Unhook and remove the pull-off springs and the cross tension springs 4 and 5. Remove the brake shoes and the operating lever.
6 Fit the new shoes by reversing operations 5 to 3. Check the operation of the adjusters as described in operation 7 before refitting the brake drums.
7 Gently operate the footbrake pedal. Following expansion of the brake shoes, the ratchet will be seen to operate. Brake shoe expansion can be cancelled by raising the ratchet plate to separate the ratchet teeth and allowing the pull-off springs to retract the shoes.
8 Refit the brake drums as described earlier. Apply the footbrake heavily a number of times to centralise and adjust the new shoes. Refer to **Section 11:11** and check the adjustment of the handbrake.
9 Road test the car. If the operation of the rear brakes including the handbrake is poor, make four or five brake applications. Apply moderately high pedal efforts to decelerate the car from 20 miles/hr to rest. This will ensure correct adjustment of the shoes.

Backplate:

Refer to **Chapter 8, Section 8:4**, halfshaft removal operation 3.

Wheel cylinder removal and fitment:

Remove the brake shoes as described earlier. Disconnect the feed pipe and, in the case of a lefthand brake, the transfer pipe or, in the case of a righthand brake, the bleed nipple. Remove the retaining spring clip and withdraw the wheel cylinder.

Fitment is the reverse of this sequence. Adjust the brake shoe clearance as described earlier and bleed the brakes as described in **Section 11:7**. Road test the car as described earlier.

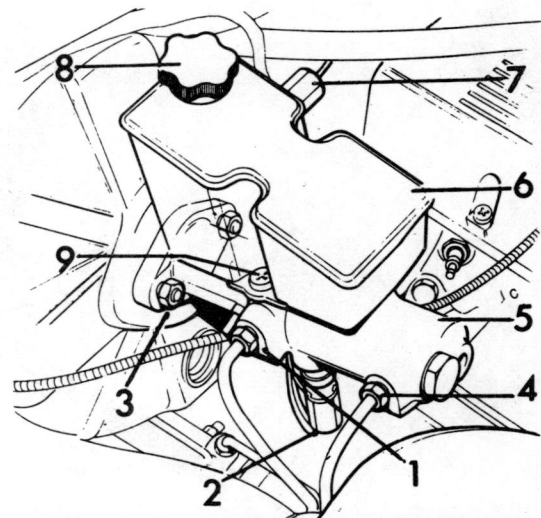

FIG 11:6   The fluid reservoir and master cylinder

Key to Fig 11:6   1 Feed to front brakes   2 Brake failure switch   3 Servo unit   4 Feed to rear brakes   5 Master cylinder   6 Reservoir   7 Fluid level warning switch   8 Cap   9 Screw

Wheel cylinder overhaul:

For each wheel cylinder a kit AAU 2066 will be required.

Remove the wheel cylinder as described earlier. Refer to **FIG 11:5**. Remove and discard both boots 2 and withdraw the pistons 4 and 5 and the spring 3. Remove and discard the piston seals 6 and 7. Clean the cylinder bores and pistons with fresh brake fluid or with methylated spirit. If they show signs of corrosion, scuffing or wear, renew the assembly.

Assemble with the internal parts wetted with fresh brake fluid. Refitment and brake assembly follows the relevant sequences described earlier.

11:5 The hydraulic system

Observe scrupulous cleanliness when working on the hydraulic system. **Do not re-use drained fluid as, even if it is perfectly clean, it will be aerated.**

Draining and refilling the system:

1 Refer to **FIG 11:6**. Remove the brake failure switch 2 from the master cylinder. Chock the wheels and release the handbrake.
2 Attach a tube to the bleed nipple on the lefthand caliper (righthand drive cars) or to the righthand caliper (lefthand drive cars) and open the bleed nipple.
3 With the tube leading to a container, pump the brake pedal until no further fluid emerges from the tube. Discard the drained fluid.
4 Transfer the tube and container to the opposite caliper, open the bleed nipple and pump the brake pedal until no further fluid emerges. Discard the drained fluid.
5 Transfer the tube and container to the bleed nipple of the righthand rear brake and again pump the brake pedal until no further fluid emerges. Discard the drained fluid. Close all the bleed nipples.

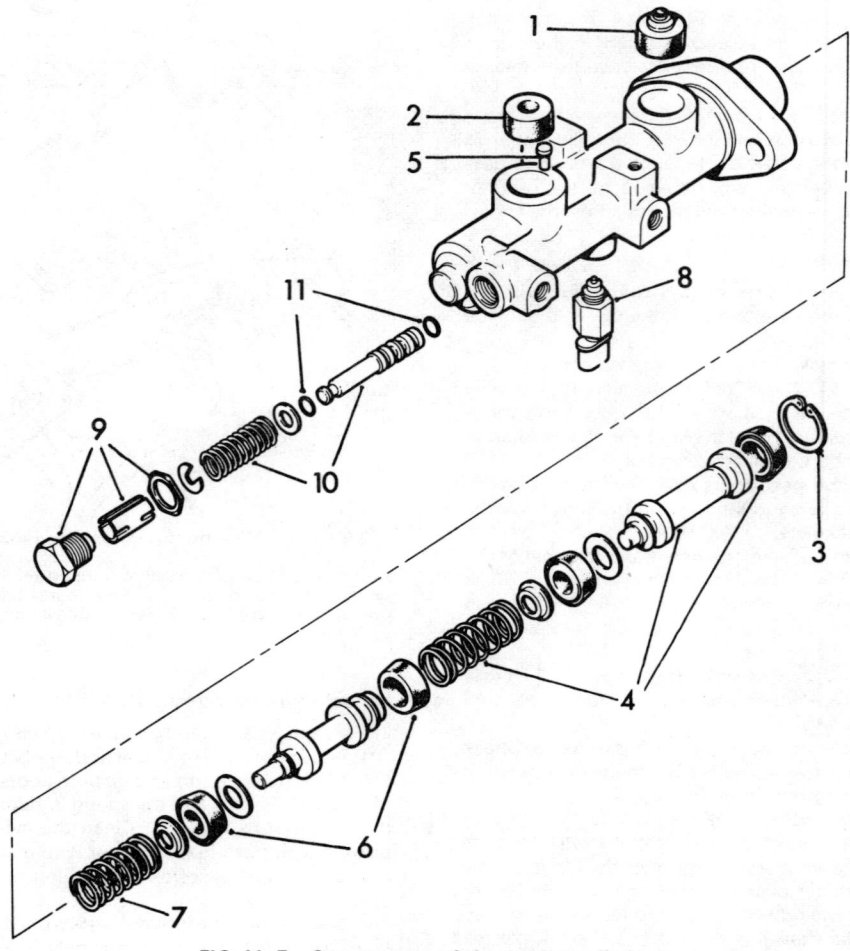

FIG 11 : 7   Components of the master cylinder

Key to Fig 11 : 7   1 Seal (primary)   2 Seal (secondary)   3 Circlip   4 Primary piston and return spring assembly   5 Stop pin   6 Secondary piston assembly   7 Spring   8 Brake failure warning switch   9 End plug, distance piece and copper washer   10 Piston and spring   11 Seals

6 Fill the reservoir with fresh fluid. Bleed the system as described in **Section 11:7**. Refit the brake failure warning switch and reconnect the wiring.

Master cylinder removal and fitment:

Refer to **FIG 11:6**. Identify and uncouple the feed pipes 1 and 4. Blank off the pipe ends and the master cylinder orifices. Identify and disconnect the wiring from switches 2 and 7. Remove the two nuts and washers which retain the master cylinder assembly to the servo unit flange 3 and dismount the assembly.

To refit the master cylinder assembly, reverse the removal sequence and, on completion, bleed the system as described in **Section 11:7**.

Master cylinder overhaul:

Kit AAU 3069 will be required.
1 Remove the master cylinder assembly as described earlier. Drain off and discard the fluid from the reservoir.

Refer to **FIG 11:6**, remove the two screws 9 which retain the reservoir to the cylinder body and dismount the reservoir.
2 Refer to **FIG 11:7**. Note their positions and remove the two seals 1 and 2 from the recesses in the master cylinder body. Remove the retaining circlip 3 and withdraw the primary piston assembly and return spring 4.
3 Insert a soft metal rod into the cylinder, depress the secondary piston and spring assembly, remove the stop pin 5 and withdraw the secondary piston assembly 6 and the return spring 7.
4 Remove switch 8. Remove the end plug, copper washer and distance piece 9. Withdraw the piston and spring assembly 10 and seals 11.
5 Discard all seals after carefully identifying the new replacement parts contained in the repair kit. Clean all components in fresh brake fluid or in methylated spirit. If the bores or pistons are corroded, scuffed or worn,

obtain a new assembly. Check that all ports, orifices and the cap vent are clear and clean.

Assemble with all internal parts wetted with fresh brake fluid. Ensure that all seals are correctly located and properly seated. Torque tighten the end plug against a new copper washer. Do not overtighten the two reservoir retaining screws.

Refit the master cylinder assembly as described earlier. Refil the reservoir. Bleed the system as described in **Section 11:7**.

11:6 The pressure regulator

The function of the pressure regulator (or pressure reducing valve) has been indicated in **Section 11:1**. A cross-section through the valve is shown in **FIG 11:8**. The master cylinder primary feed is connected to port **A** and two primary outlet ports **C** and **D** connect with the front brake calipers. The master cylinder seconday feed is connected to port **B** and the single secondary port **E** connects with the single feed to the rear brakes.

Pressure acting on annular area **a1** minus **a2** forces the plunger towards the end plug. Pressure acting on annular area **a1** plus **a4** minus **a3** tends to move the plunger to the right (away from the plug end) so closing the metering valve **F**. Pressure at the outlet port **E** (the pressure to the rear brakes) therefore falls relative to the input pressure and, since there is no reduction in pressure between inlet port **A** and outlet ports **C** and **D**, the braking effort is biased in favour of the front brakes. The pressure at **E** is reduced after cut-off in proportion to the areas **a2** and the difference between the annular areas **a1** minus **a2** and **a4** minus **a3**. The cut-off is equal to the preload from spring **S** divided by the combined pressure loads from **a2** plus **a4** minus **a3**.

Should the front brake circuit fail there will be no pressure acting on **a4** minus **a3** and, since the load on **a2** and the spring preload are unchanged, the cut-off pressure will increase (approximately threefold). Should the rear circuit fail, the valve becomes inoperative and pressure continues to be fed from port **A** to ports **C** and **D**.

No procedures are prescribed for the repair or overhaul of the pressure reducing/regulator valve by an owner and a defective unit should be removed and a replacement fitted.

Removal and fitment:

The location of the unit is shown at 6 in **FIG 11:1**.

Loosen the two pipes 1 and 4 in **FIG 11:6** at the master cylinder. Refer to **FIG 11:9**. Identify and uncouple the five pipes 1, 2, 4, 5 and 6. Blank off the open pipe ends and the valve orifices to preclude entry of dirt. Remove nut and washer 3 and dismount the unit.

To fit a unit, follow the removal sequence in reverse. Bleed the system as described in **Section 11:7**.

11:7 Bleeding the hydraulic system

This procedure, for which two operators are required, is only necessary if air has entered the system. This may result from the fluid level in the reservoir having fallen too low; because the system has been drained of old fluid or because part of the system has been dismantled. **Do not allow the fluid level in the reservoir to fall below half capacity during the procedure and, when topping up, use fresh fluid. Do not re-use fluid**

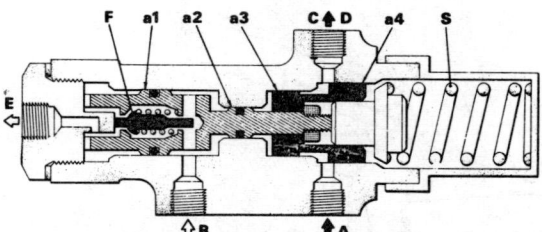

FIG 11:8 A cross-section through the pressure regulator

Key to Fig 11:8   **A** Primary feed   **B** Secondary feed **C** and **D** To front brake calipers   **E** To rear brakes **F** Metering valve   **S** Spring   **a1, a2, a3** and **a4** Annular areas (see text)

which has been bled from the system as it will be aerated. Do not bleed the system with the servo in operation (that is with the engine running).

Note that each front caliper is bled separately but that both rear brake wheel cylinders are bled from the righthand side since the nipple position on the lefthand wheel cylinder takes the transfer pipe which connects the two wheel cylinders.

1 Refer to **FIG 11:6**. Remove the brake failure warning switch 2 from the master cylinder. Chock the wheels and release the handbrake.
2 Attach a bleed tube to the bleed nipple on the front caliper furthest from the master cylinder (lefthand on righthand drive cars, righthand on lefthand drive cars). Submerge the free end of the tube in a transparent container partially filled with brake fluid.
3 Open the bleed nipple by one quarter to one half turn. Fully depress the brake pedal and follow with three rapid successive pedal strokes. Release the pedal.
4 Repeat this sequence until fluid which is free of air bubbles emerges from the bleed tube. Depress the

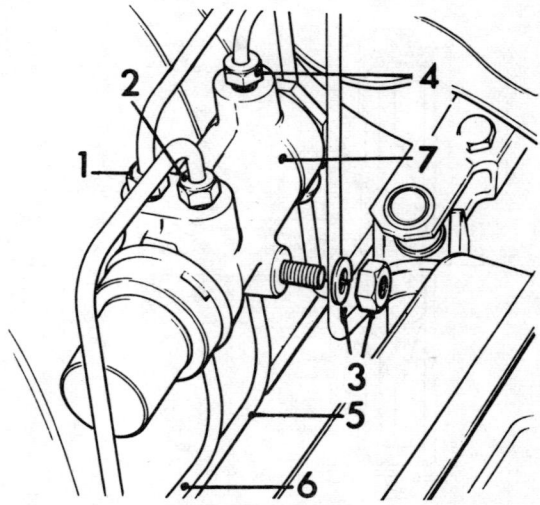

FIG 11:9 Removing the pressure regulator

Key to Fig 11:9   1 and 2 To front calipers   3 Retaining nut and washer   4 To rear brakes   5 Primary feed 6 Secondary feed   7 Pressure regulator

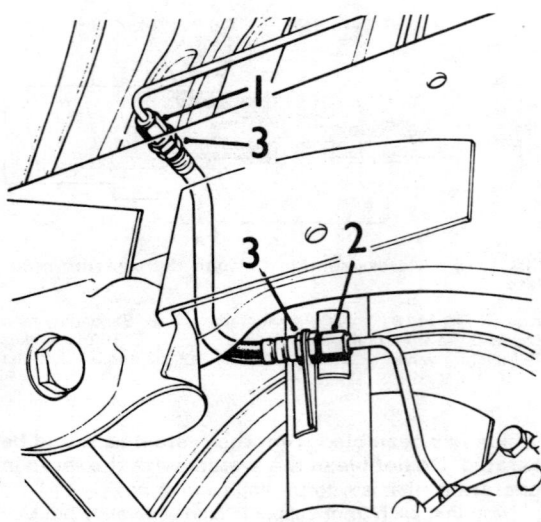

FIG 11:10   Removing a flexible hose

Key to Fig 11:10   1, 2 and 3 See text

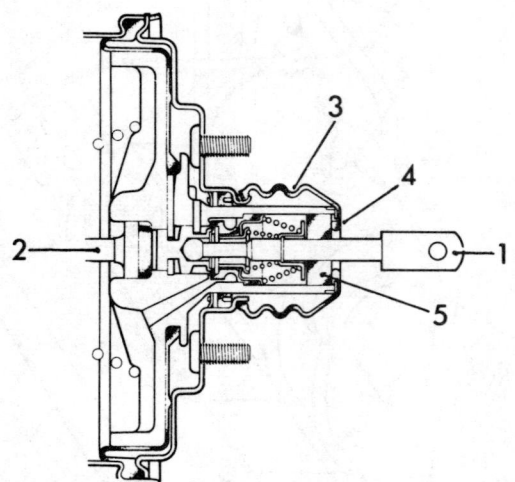

FIG 11:11   Cross-section through the rear of a servo unit

Key to Fig 11:11   1 Servo rod clevis   2 Pushrod   3 Boot
4 Steel ring   5 Filter

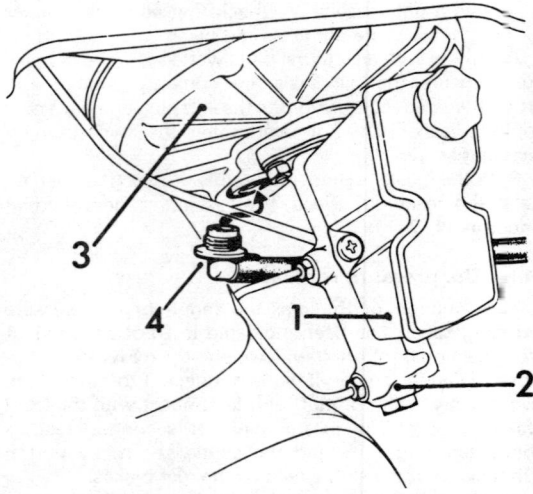

FIG 11:12   The servo non-return valve

Key to Fig 11:12   1 Fluid reservoir   2 Master cylinder
3 Servo unit   4 Non-return valve

pedal, close the bleed nipple, release the pedal and disconnect the bleed tube. Top up the reservoir.

5 Transfer the bleed tube and container to the opposite front caliper and carry out operations 3 and 4.

6 Transfer the bleed tube and container to the righthand rear wheel cylinder and carry out operations 3 and 4.

7 Finally refit and connect up the brake failure switch and top up the reservoir fluid to the correct level as described in **Section 11:2**.

11:8 Removing and fitting a flexible hose

It is important that flexible hoses are not twisted when they are being removed or fitted. Always hold the hose hexagon with a second spanner before unscrewing or tightening an adjacent locknut or connecting union if there is a possibility that, otherwise, the hose would twist.

As an example of the correct procedure, the following is the sequence of operations which should be followed when removing a front brake hose (9 or 10 in **FIG 11:1**).

Refer to **FIG 11:10** and follow the sequence of the key numerals:

1 Disconnect the brake pipe and union from the inboard end of the flexible hose.

2 Disconnect the brake pipe and union from the outboard end of the flexible hose.

3 Using two spanners, remove the locknuts and washers securing the hose to the support brackets and remove the hose.

When fitting the hose, reverse this sequence and confirm that the hose is neither kinked nor twisted when installed.

11:9 The servo unit

The servo unit is interposed between the brake pedal and the hydraulic master cylinder. It augments the foot effort applied by the driver to the brake pedal. The air entry is from the interior of the car via a filter 5 which is shown in **FIG 11:11**. The vacuum supply is via a flexible hose and a non-return valve 4 in the forward face of the unit and is shown in **FIG 11:12**. This maintains a partial vacuum on the forward side of a diaphragm when the engine is running. When the brake pedal is depressed, air enters the rear of the unit and acts on the rear of the diaphragm. The pressure difference provides the servo assistance. In the event of there being no vacuum assistance available, unassisted driver's foot effort acts on the master cylinder when the pedal is depressed.

If power assistance does not appear to be fully effective, confirm that the vacuum hose is not leaking and that the non-return valve is serviceable. If these are in order, renew the air filter as described later. If no improvement results,

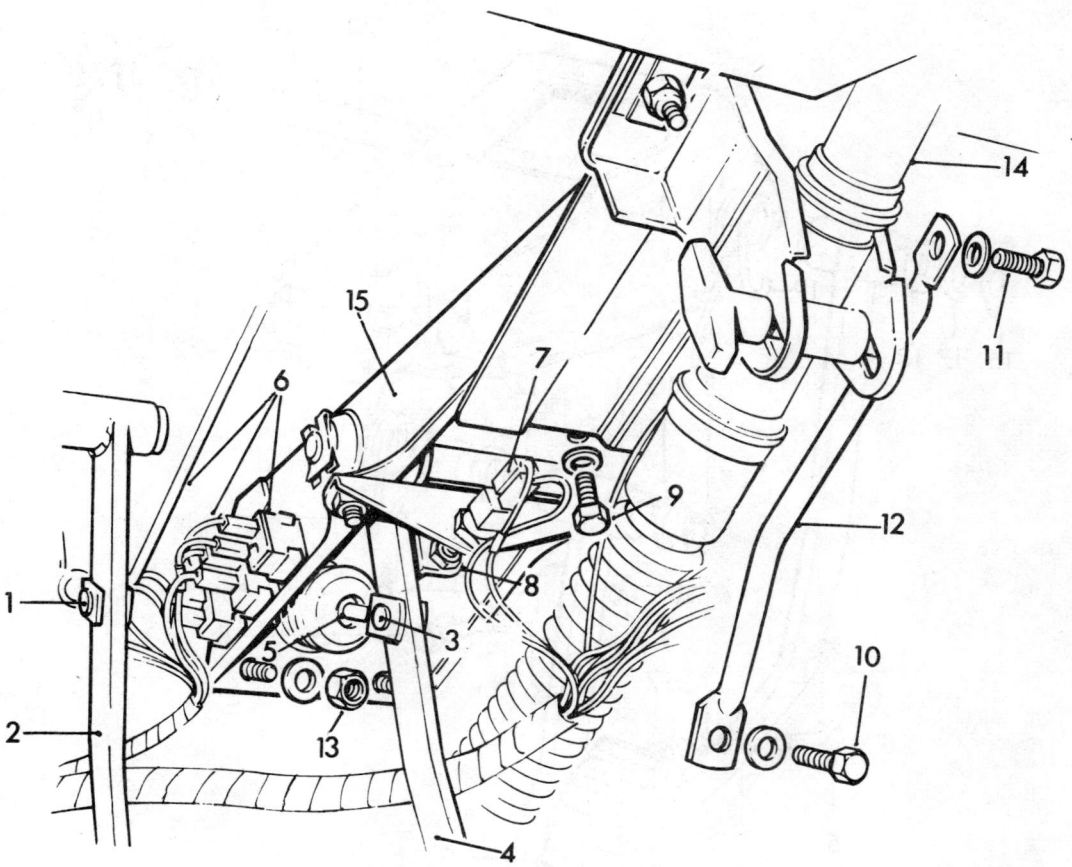

FIG 11 : 13   Lefthand drive pedal box installation

Key to Fig 11 : 13   1 Clutch clevis pin   2 Clutch pedal   3 Brake clevis pin   4 Brake pedal   5 Servo air filter   6 Flasher and relay units   7 Stop light switch   8 Stop light switch adjuster   9, 10 and 11 Bolt   12 Steady bracket   13 Retaining nut   14 Column   15 Pedal box

the servo unit must be suspect. No procedures are prescribed for the repair or overhaul of the servo unit by an owner and a defective unit should be removed as described later and a replacement fitted.

Renewing the servo air filter :

Remove the driver's glovebox as described in **Chapter 13, Section 13 : 10**. Refer to **FIG 11 : 11**. Remove the split-pin, washer and clevis pin which connects the servo rod 1 to the brake pedal. Pull back the boot 3 and remove the steel ring 4 from the housing. Withdraw the filter 5.

To fit the new filter and reassemble, follow the reverse of the filter removal sequence.

Removing and refitting the non-return valve :

The non-return valve is 4 in **FIG 11 : 12**.

With the engine stationary, depress and release the brake pedal a number of times to destroy the vacuum in the servo unit. Release the hose from the non-return valve. Withdraw the valve from the servo unit.

Renew the sealing rubber as necessary and press the valve into place. Connect the hose and tighten the clip.

Servo unit removal and fitment :

1 Remove the driver's glovebox as described in **Chapter 13, Section 13 : 10**. Disconnect the servo rod 1 in **FIG 11 : 11** from the brake pedal as described earlier.

2 Uncouple the vacuum hose from the non-return valve as described earlier. Dismount the master cylinder from the servo unit as described in **Section 11 : 5**.

3 Refer to **FIG 11 : 13** and remove the four nuts and washers 13 which retain the servo unit. Withdraw the servo unit.

Fitment is the reverse of this sequence. On completion of the installation, bleed the hydraulic system as described in **Section 11 : 7**.

11 : 10   The pedal box

The pedal box installation in a lefthand drive car is shown in **FIG 11 : 13**. The components of a righthand drive pedal box are shown in **FIG 11 : 14**.

Brake stop lights are controlled by switch 7 in **FIG 11 : 13** and the adjustable stop bolt 8 which opens the switch contacts when the pedal is in the released position.

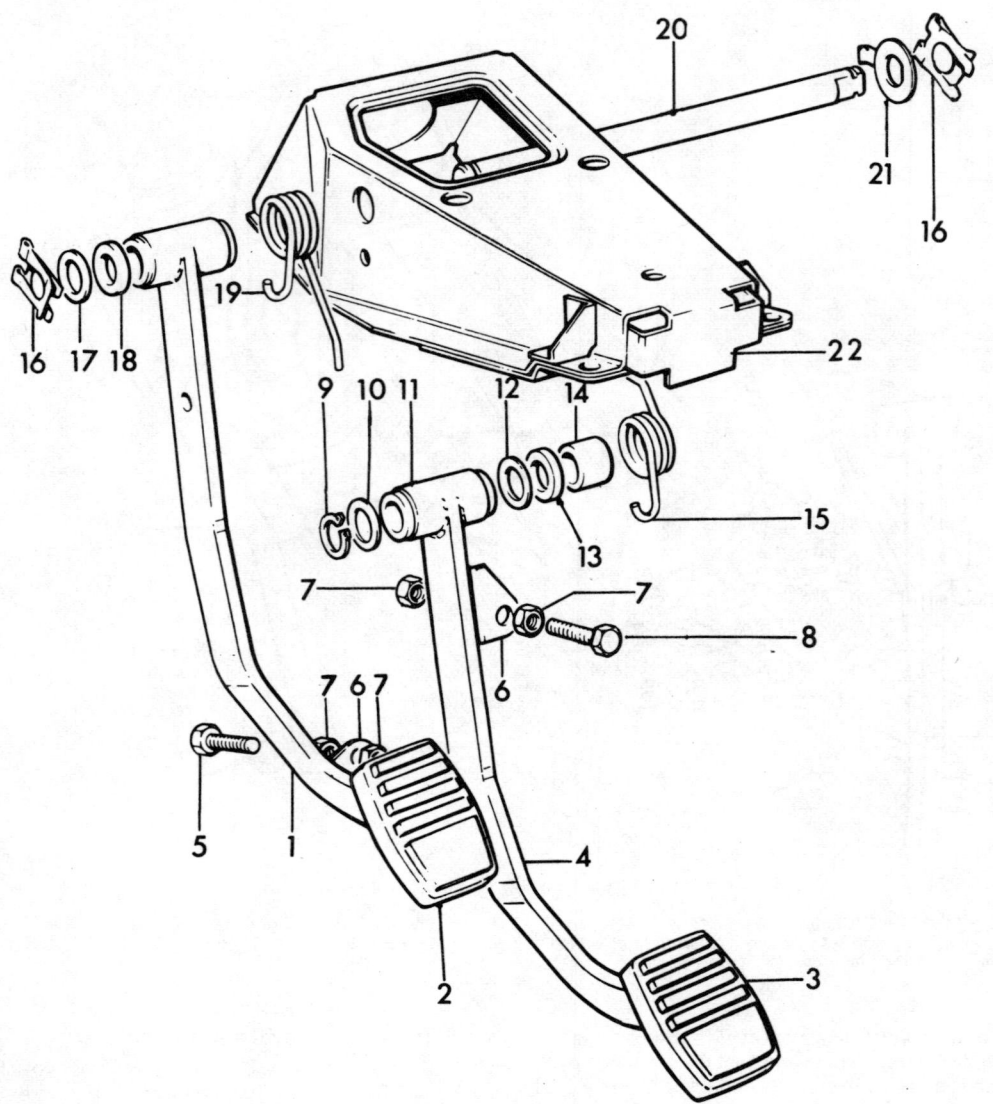

FIG 11:14   Components of a righthand drive pedal box

Key to Fig 11:14   1 Clutch pedal   2 and 3 Pedal rubber   4 Brake pedal   5 Pedal stop adjuster   6 Bracket   7 Locknut
8 Stop light switch adjuster   9 Circlip   10 Washer   11 Bushed pedal boss   12 Washer   13 Felt washer   14 Spacer
15 Return spring   16 Clip   17 Washer   18 Felt washer   19 Return spring   20 Spindle   21 Lockwasher   22 Pedal
box

This adjuster is carried in a bracket on the brake pedal and retained by two locknuts. A similarly adjustable clutch pedal stop is carried in a bracket on the clutch pedal. Note that the pedals are provided with torsion type return springs.

Stop light switch adjustment:

Refer to **FIG 11:15**. Adjustment is correct when, in the pedal released position, there is a gap of 1.50 to 1.75mm (0.06 to 0.07in) between the face of the adjuster bolt 2 and the face of the special nut 3. To adjust, loosen both locknuts 1, reposition the adjuster bolt 2 and retighten the locknuts. **Note that the switch 4 must bottom against the shoulder in the special nut 3.**

11:11   The handbrake

Refer to **FIG 11:16**. The handbrake operates on the rear brakes only. The inner cable 5 actuates the righthand brake; the lefthand brake is actuated by the reaction cable 6 which is anchored to the outer cable at the swinging compensator lever 12.

Handbrake adjustment:

1 Loosen the cables completely at points 4 and 11. Release the lever 1. Depress the brake pedal hard three times.

2 Using the fork adjuster 11, take up all the slack in the reaction cable 6 but maintain the compensator lever at 15° to the left vertical as shown in **FIG 11:17**. Tighten the adjuster locknut.

3 Take up the slack in the inner cable 5 by pulling the adjuster 6 in the direction of the arrow (rearwards) and move the locknut 2 against the bracket 7 to hold this position.

4 With 11.35kg (25lb) effort applied to the handbrake lever, the rear brakes should be hard on at the third ratchet notch but fully off at the first notch. If necessary, repeat operation 3 to achieve this condition and then tighten locknut 1 against the bracket 7 and locknut 2.

Cable removal and fitment:

Loosen the cable completely. Refer to **FIG 11:16**. Withdraw the three clevis pins 3 and 8 (two), remove the compensator pivot bolt and also bolt 10. Release the cable trunnion loosen clips 7 and withdraw the cable assembly.

Fitment is the reverse of this sequence and must be followed by carrying out the adjustment procedure described earlier.

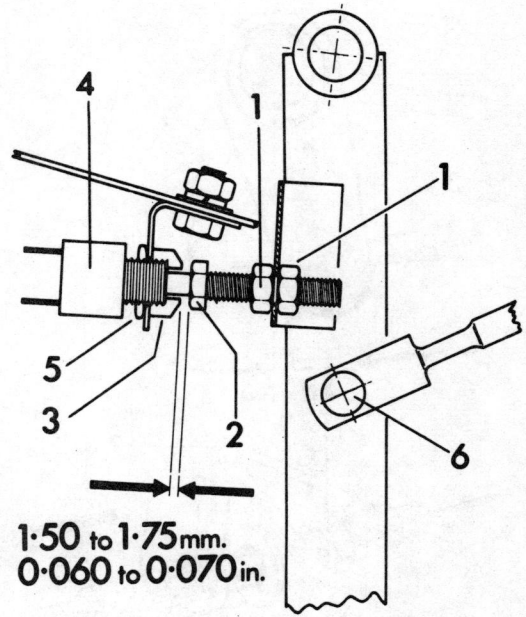

1·50 to 1·75mm.
0·060 to 0·070 in.

FIG 11:15   Stop light switch adjustment

Key to Fig 11:15   1 Locknut   2 Adjuster bolt   3 Special nut   4 Switch   5 Locknut   6 Clevis pin

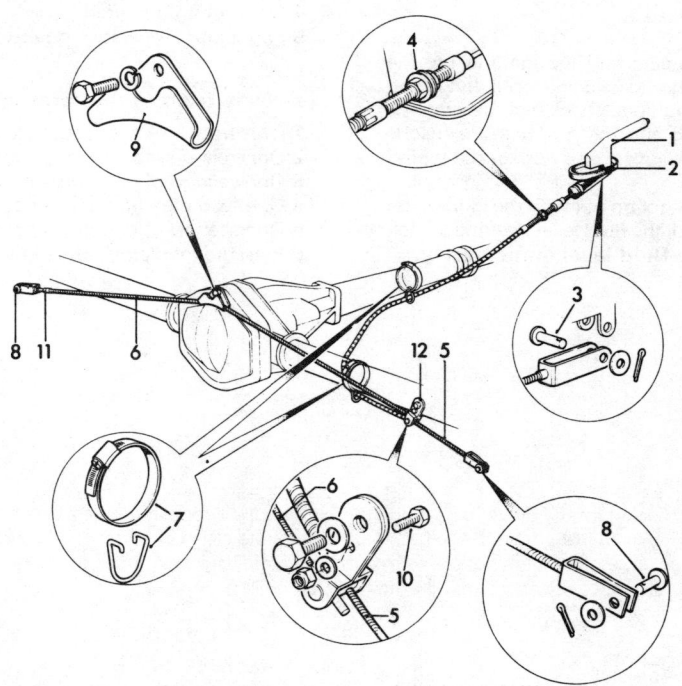

FIG 11:16   Layout of the handbrake cables

Key to Fig 11:16   1 Handbrake lever   2 Warning light switch   3 Clevis pin   4 Adjuster   5 Inner cable   6 Reaction cable   7 Clip   8 Clevis pin   9 Cable guide   10 Bolt   11 Adjuster   12 Compensator lever

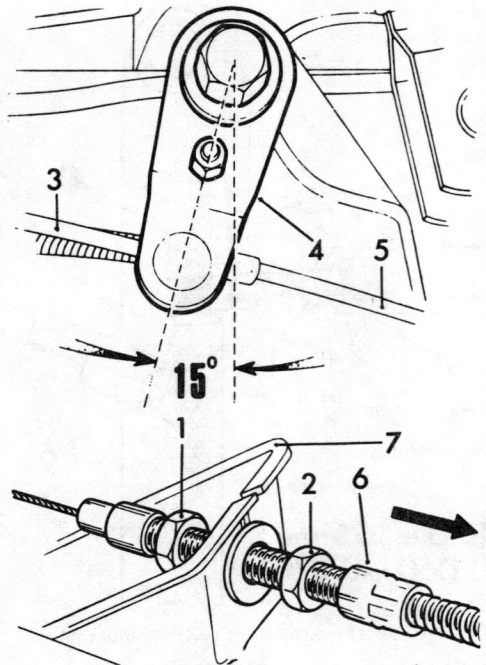

FIG 11:17 Handbrake cable adjustment

Key to Fig 11:17   1 and 2 Locknut   3 Reaction cable
4 Compensator lever   5 Inner cable   6 Adjuster
7 Bracket

Warning light:

With the handbrake applied and the ignition on, the handbrake warning light should be illuminated. If it is not, check the bulb. If this is unblown, check that the switch 2 in **FIG 11:16** is operating and that the relevant fuse is intact. If these are in order, locate and correct the wiring discontinuity.

If the warning light does not go out with the ignition on and the handbrake released, the fluid level warning switch has operated. **Top up the fluid level immediately.**

11:12 Fault diagnosis

(a) 'Spongy' pedal

1 Leak in hydraulic system
2 Worn master cylinder
3 Defective master cylinder seals
4 Defective caliper seals
5 Defective wheel cylinder seals
6 Air in hydraulic system

(b) Excessive pedal travel

1 Check 1 and 6 in (a)
2 Rear self-adjusting mechanism faulty
3 Very low fluid reservoir level

(c) Brakes grab or pull to one side

1 Distorted disc or drum
2 Wet or oily friction pads or shoe linings
3 Loose caliper unit
4 Loose disc
5 Worn suspension or steering connections
6 Uneven tyre pressures
7 Seized piston on caliper or wheel cylinder
8 Blocked flexible or rigid pipe
9 Seized handbrake cable or pivot

(d) No servo assistance

1 Air filter blocked
2 Vacuum pipe blocked, broken or adrift
3 Non-return valve defective
4 Servo unit punctured
5 Servo unit inoperative due to internal fault

(e) Only front or rear brakes operative

1 Only front brakes operating, pipe to rear brakes broken
2 Only rear brakes operating, pipe to front brakes broken
3 One section of reservoir empty
4 One feed pipe from master cylinder broken
5 One section of master cylinder defective
6 Pressure regulator/reducing valve defective

CHAPTER 12

THE ELECTRICAL EQUIPMENT

12:1 Description

A wiring diagram for the 12-volt system in which **the battery negative terminal is earthed** is included in the **Technical Data** section of the **Appendix**.

The battery is positioned in the engine compartment. Twelve fuses are located in the instrument panel as shown in **FIG 12:1**. There are, in addition, three in-line fuses. The flasher units and relays are mainly located behind the gloveboxes but the starter motor relay is housed in the engine bay and the two relays for the door locking system are in the side of the luggage compartment.

The starter motor incorporates a solenoid and positive engagement of the pinion gear. The solenoid is energised through a relay.

The generator is belt driven from the crankshaft by the same belt that drives the water pump and cooling fan. It is a 3-phase AC machine with an integral transistorised rectifier. An electronic regulator controls the charging circuit and a 'no charge' warning light is provided.

Although information for the servicing of electrical equipment is given in this chapter, parts of it are only intended to assist those who have appropriate experience of working on this type of equipment and it must be accepted that it is not sensible for those with limited experience to attempt repairs to units which may be seriously defective, electrically or mechanically. Such defective equipment should be replaced by new or exchange replacement units. Testing and adjustment of certain equipment requires specialist facilities.

12:2 The battery

The negative terminal is earthed. **Do not, under any circumstances, reverse the terminal connections.** The connections must be tight on the battery posts and a light coating of petroleum jelly (Vaseline) should be applied to the terminal clamps and posts to retard corrosion and oxidation.

Keep the fluid in the cells topped up to 5mm (0.2in) above the plates and separators by adding distilled water. **Never add undiluted acid. If it is necessary to prepare a new solution of electrolyte due to spillage or loss, add the acid to the distilled water. It is highly dangerous to add water to acid.**

If the charge state of the battery is suspect, test the electrolyte with a hydrometer. The indications from the

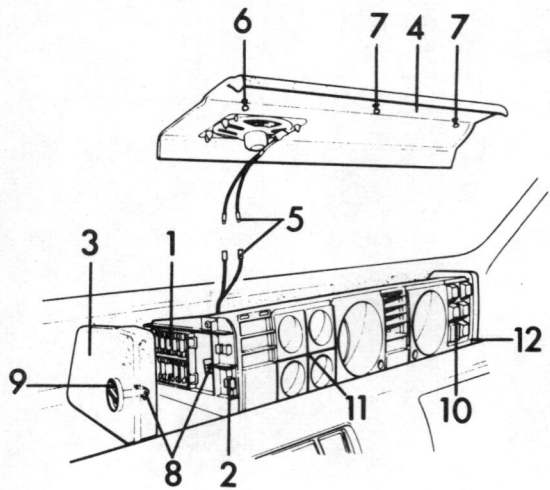

FIG 12:1 Instrument panel and fuses

Key to Fig 12:1   1 Fuses   2 Spare fuse holders   3 End
cover   4 Top cover   5 Speaker leads   6 and 7 Location
pegs   8 Prong and catch   9 Control   10 Switches
11 Gauges   12 Rheostat end cover

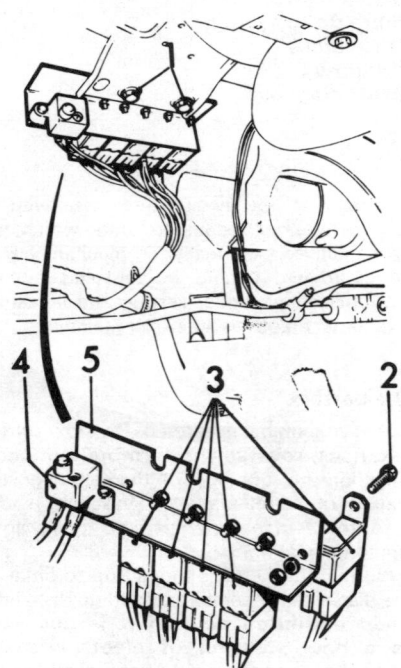

FIG 12:2 Location of relays

Key to Fig 12:2   1 Bolts   2 Bolt   3 Relays   4 Thermal
cut-out switch (window lifts)   5 Carrier

specific gravity readings given by the hydrometer are
approximately as follows:

   Cells fully charged—Specific gravity 1.270 to 1.290
   Cells half charged —Specific gravity 1.190 to 1.210
   Cells discharged   —Specific gravity 1.110 to 1.130

   These readings will apply when the battery temperature
is about 16°C (60°F). For the same cell condition, specific
gravity will increase when the electrolyte temperature is
higher than 16°C and vice versa. Add 0.002 for every 3°C
(5°F) above 16°C and subtract 0.002 for every 3°C below
16°C.

   If the state of the battery is low take the car for a long
daylight run or put the battery on charge at 4 to 5amp. If
this does not correct the battery charge state, have the
individual cells voltage tested to ascertain whether the
battery should be replaced by a new one. If the battery is to
be put on charge without dismounting it from the car,
disconnect both leads from the battery.

   If the battery is to stand for a long period, give it a
freshening-up charge every month. If it is left discharged, it
will deteriorate and be ruined.

12:3 The fuses and relays

Fuses:

   Access to the fuses requires the removal of the
instrument panel end cover 3 in **FIG 12:1** by turning the
recessed control 9 until the prong and catch 8 unlock.

   There are 12 fuses in this location and, in addition, there
are three in-line fuses. **Never fit a replacement fuse of
greater capacity than that specified for the circuit**
being protected since, by doing so, proper protection may
be jeopardised. If a fuse blows repeatedly, trace the reason
for it doing so without delay.

   The following tabulation identifies the fuses to the
wiring diagram **FIG 14:1** in the **Appendix** and quotes
their correct capacities.

Fuse no.	FIG 14:1	Capacity amps	Main circuit*
1-2	—	—	Available for extra accessories
3-4	19j	25	Heater motor
5-6	19g	25	Horns, interior lights
7-8	19h	25	Flasher units
9-10	19k	25	Instruments, stop/reversing lights
11-12	19m	35	Windscreen wiper/washer
13-14	19a	25	RH main beam
15-16	19b	25	LH main beam
17-18	19c	15	RH dipped beam
19-20	19d	15	LH dipped beam
21-22	19e	15	Side and panel lights
23-24	19f	25	Front fog lights
x	90	50	Backlight heater
y	3	50	Central door locking system
z	14	2	Radio

* Refer to **FIG 14:1** for full circuit(s). x, in-line
near fusebox; y, in-line in RH footwell; z, in-line
behind radio.

Relays:

   Relays are located in three positions. The main location
is behind the passenger's glovebox and access requires
this to be removed as described in **Chapter 13, Section
13:10**. To renew one of these relays, disconnect the
battery leads, remove the glovebox and refer to **FIG 12:2**.

Loosen the two bolts 1 and lower the carrier 5. Identify the relevant relay 3 from the wiring colours and the tabulation given later, remove the retaining bolt 2 and dismount the relevant relay. Identify and disconnect the four wires. To fit the new relay, reverse this sequence.

Relay	FIG 14:1	Wiring colours+
Heated backlight	89	N/Y, N/R, W/S, B
Heater motor	48	N, N/U, W, B
Lighting supply	49	N, R/U, R/G, B
Window lifts, front		N/G, G, N/P, B
Window lifts, rear		N/G, LG, N/P, B

+ B, black; G, green; LG, light green; N, brown; P, purple; R, red; S, slate; U, blue; W, white; Y yellow.

Starter motor relay:

This relay is located in the engine compartment. Refer to **Section 12:4**.

Door lock relays:

These relays are built into the control assembly which is located in the righthand side of the luggage compartment. Refer to **Section 12:13**.

12:4 The starter motor

Tests for a starter which does not operate:

Check the condition of the battery and its connections. If these are in order, switch on the lights and operate the starter switch. Current is reaching the starter if the lights go dim. If they do not, check with a voltmeter or test lamp if there is voltage at the relay and the solenoid when the switch is operated. If there is, and depending upon the indications from the checks, suspect a defective relay or solenoid. If there is not, suspect the ignition switch or a wiring discontinuity. If these are in order, remove the starter motor for investigation and to check the brush gear.

Starter motor relay:

This relay is located in the engine bay adjacent to the radiator expansion tank and is 1 shown in **FIG 12:3**. It is 47 in **FIG 14:1**, the wiring diagram. To dismount the relay, remove the retaining Pozidriv screw and pull off the harness plug. Fitment is the reverse of this sequence.

Renewing a solenoid:

Carry out operations 1 and 2 of the starter motor removal procedure described later. Prise out the grommet. Remove two bolts and spring washers and withdraw the solenoid from the plunger. Unhook the plunger from the engaging lever. Remove the spring and the spring cup from the plunger.

Fit the spring cup and spring to the plunger. Insert a finger through the grommet hole and push the engaging lever forwards. Insert the plunger, compress the spring and hook the plunger to the lever. Carefully insert the solenoid over the plunger ensuring that the plunger does not come unhooked from the engaging lever. Fit the two retaining bolts and spring washers. Reverse operations 2 and 1 of the motor removal sequence.

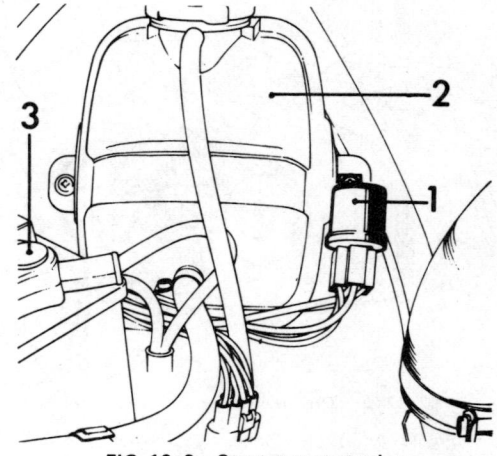

FIG 12:3   Starter motor relay

Key to Fig 12:3   1 Starter motor relay   2 Expansion tank   3 Battery

Starter motor removal and fitment:

1 With the car on a hoist or over a pit, disconnect the battery leads. Refer to **FIG 12:4**. Remove the retaining nut and washer and disconnect the lead 1 from the solenoid 4.
2 Remove the small Pozidriv screw and spring washer and disconnect the white/yellow wire 2. Remove the larger Pozidriv screw and spring washer and disconnect the white/brown wire 3.
3 Using a socket in an extension bar and ratchet, remove the starter motor lower mounting bolt and spring washer. Remove the upper mounting bolt and washer and manoeuvre the motor downwards from the car.

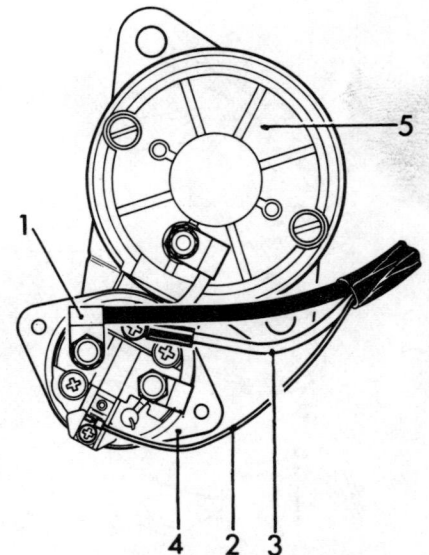

FIG 12:4   Starter motor solenoid

Key to Fig 12:4   1 Battery lead   2 White/yellow lead   3 White/brown lead   4 Solenoid   5 Starter motor

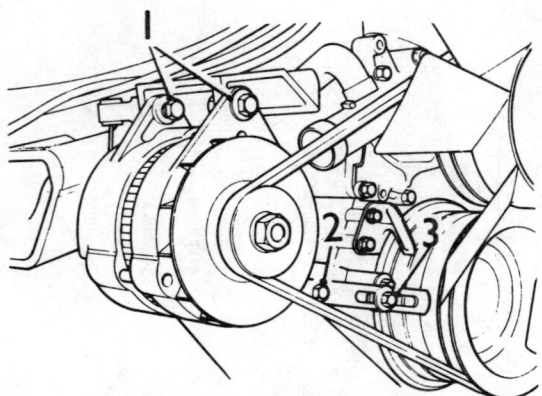

FIG 12:5 The alternator and drive belt

Key to Fig 12:5 1 Pivot bolts   2 Link bolt   3 Adjuster bolt

Fitment is the reverse of the removal sequence. Ensure that the mounting bolts do not become cross-threaded in the aluminium cylinder block and that they are correctly torque tightened.

Starter motor overhaul:

No procedures are prescribed for the repair or overhaul of a starter motor by an owner who, unless he has experience of this type of work, should pass the unit to a specialist or fit a replacement motor.

Those who have the requisite experience should note the information given in the **Technical Data** section of the **Appendix** and that the following kits are available: kit GSB 112, brushes; kit 608352, bushes; kit 608363, roller clutch.

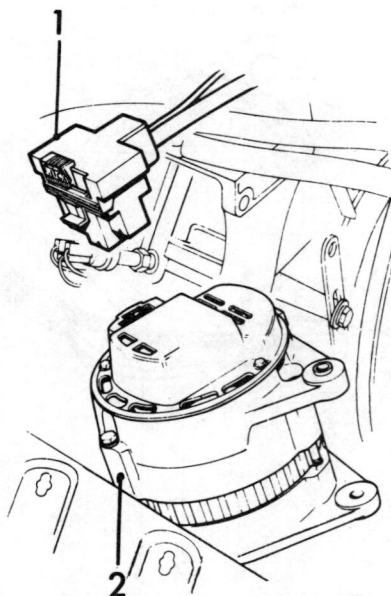

FIG 12:6 Removing the alternator

Key to Fig 12:6 1 Harness plug   2 Alternator

12:5 The alternator

The alternator is a 3-phase AC machine with an integral diode rectifier and a built-in regulator. It carries its own cooling fan and is belt driven from the crankshaft by the same belt that drives the water pump and cooling fan.

Observe the following precautions:

1 Never disconnect the regulator or battery while the alternator is being driven.
2 Never disconnect or dismount the alternator without first disconnecting the battery.
3 Never test the alternator either in the car or on a test bench unless the battery is in circuit. Ensure that the battery is in good condition and fully charged and that the negative is earthed. **Never reverse the polarity.**

Tests on an alternator which is not charging:

Check that the connections to the battery and to the alternator are intact and firm. Check that the drive belt is correctly tensioned as described later. Check that the brushes are of serviceable length and that they are not sticking in their holders. If these are in order, remove the alternator for further investigation.

Tensioning the drive belt:

The belt is correctly tensioned when thumb pressure applied at a point midway between the alternator pulley and the water pump pulley gives a belt deflection of 5 to 8mm (0.20 to 0.30in). Adjustment is made by loosening the two pivots 1, the link point 2 and the adjuster nut and bolt 3 in **FIG 12:5**, swinging the alternator away from the engine and retightening the nuts and bolts 1, 2 and 3. Recheck the tension and re-adjust if necessary.

Renewing the drive belt:

Refer to **FIG 12:5**. Loosen nuts and bolts 1, 2 and 3, swing the alternator towards the engine and disengage the belt from the alternator pulley. Remove the belt.

Engage the new belt in the three pulley grooves and carry out the belt tensioning procedure described earlier.

Brushes:

The length of new brushes is 12.7mm (0.50in). They should be renewed if less than 5.0mm (0.20in) protrudes from the brushbox when free. Kit GGB 504 contains a set of new brushes.

Alternator removal and fitment:

Disconnect the leads from the battery. Disengage the drive belt from the alternator pulley as described earlier. Refer to **FIG 12:5**. Remove nuts, bolts and washers 1, 2 and 3 after noting which way round they are fitted and dismount the alternator. Slide the harness plug lock downwards to the unlock position and disconnect the plug 1 (see **FIG 12:6**). Disconnect the capacitor from the suppressor terminal.

Fitment is the reverse of this sequence and must be followed by adjusting the drive belt tension as described earlier.

Alternator overhaul:

No procedures are prescribed for the repair or overhaul of an alternator by an owner who, unless he has experience

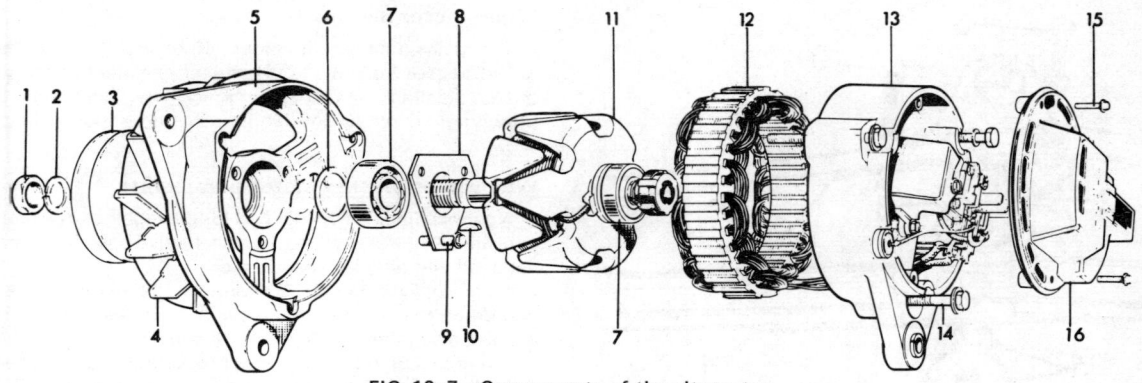

FIG 12:7   Components of the alternator

Key to Fig 12:7   1 Nut   2 Washer   3 Pulley   4 Fan   5 Pulley end casing   6 Washer   7 Bearing   8 Plate
9 Bolt   10 Key   11 Rotor   12 Stator   13 Slip ring end casing   14 Bolt   15 Bolt   16 End cover

of this type of work and also some knowledge of electronics, should pass the unit to a specialist or fit a replacement alternator.

The component parts of an alternator are shown in **FIG 12:7**.

Those who have the requisite experience should note the information given in the **Technical Data** section of the **Appendix** and that, in addition to the brushes kit quoted earlier, the following kits are available: kit AAU 3172, drive end bearing; kit 606832, slip ring end bearing; AAU 2871, rectifier; AAU 2870, regulator; AAU 2872, surge protector; DRC 1068, suppressor.

12:6   Windscreen wiper and washer

Wiper blades:

Renew wiper blades immediately they become inefficient. Depress the spring lever at the end of the arm and withdraw the blade. Do not allow the arm to scratch the windscreen glass.

Wiper motor and linkage, removal and fitment:

1 Disconnect the battery leads. Remove the air cleaner as described in **Chapter 2, Section 2:3**. Refer to **FIG 12:8**. Remove the bonnet lock fixings 3 and move the lock 1 aside.

2 Remove the plastic caps, nuts and wiper arms 4. Remove the nut, shim washer and seal 5 from each wiper arm spindle 6. Disconnect the earth strap from the wiper motor mounting plate.

3 Remove the fixings 7 which secure the wiper motor mounting plate to the body, uncouple the electric plug from the motor and withdraw the motor and linkage.

Fitment is the reverse of this sequence except that the wiper arms should be fitted last after switching the motor on and off to bring the spindles to the PARK positions. The arms are then fitted in their PARK positions.

Wiper motor overhaul:

Remove the motor and linkage as described earlier. Refer to **FIG 12:9** and separate the motor and gearbox unit from the linkage.

Refer to **FIG 12:10** and dismantle the motor and gearbox by following the sequence of the component key

numerals. Note the cover/gearbox alignment marks. Do not allow the brushes 8 to become contaminated with lubricant. Lift and slide the limit switch 9 out sideways to release the spring clip. Inspect and renew parts as necessary.

On reassembly, lubricate the self-aligning bearing and the cover bearing with Shell Turbo oil. Saturate the felt washer with this oil also. **Keep the brushes clear of lubricant.** The armature shaft end float should be within the range of 0.05 and 0.20mm (0.002 and 0.008in). Align the cover and gearbox to the original position. Lubricate the final gear bushes with Ragosine Listate grease. Fit the dished washer with its concave side next to the final gear. Pack Ragosine grease round the worm and final gears. Ensure that the rubber seal 1 is in good condition.

Recouple the unit to the linkage and fit the assembly to the car.

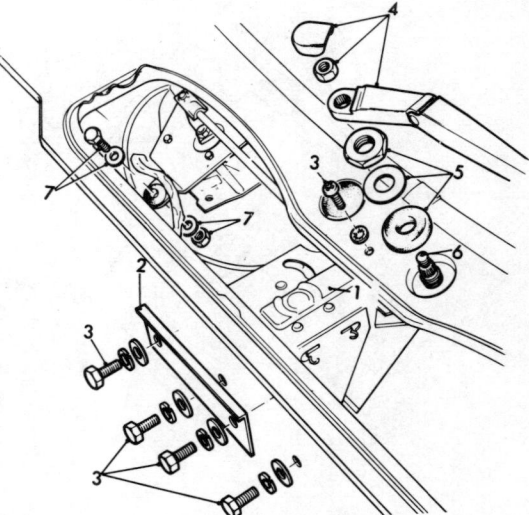

FIG 12:8   Removing the windscreen wiper mechanism

Key to Fig 12:8   1 Bonnet lock   2 Plate   3 Lock fixings
4 Plastic cap, nut and arm   5 Nut, washer and seal
6 Spindle   7 Nut, washers and bolt

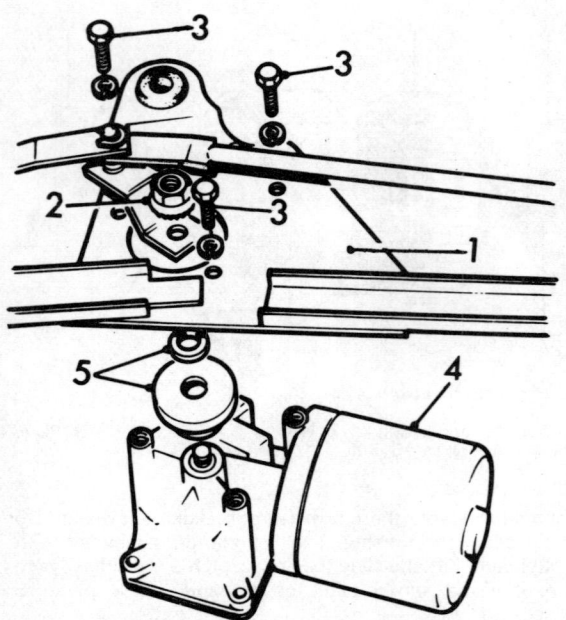

Wiper motor delay unit:

The delay unit is clip mounted behind the driver's glovebox (see **Section 12:9**) and may be identified from the connecting wire colours which are: white/green, brown/light green, yellow/light green and brown/green

Windscreen washer motor/pump unit:

No procedures are prescribed for the repair or overhaul of a washer motor or pump and a defective unit should be removed and a replacement fitted.

Refer to **FIG 12:11**. Disconnect the battery leads, withdraw the washer reservoir 3 from its mounting bracket, disconnect the leads 4, remove the retaining bolts and washers 5, withdraw the pump sufficiently to allow the inlet and delivery tubes 6 to be disconnected and dismount the pump 7.

To fit, follow the reverse of this sequence.

FIG 12:9 Separating the motor and gearbox from the linkage

Key to Fig 12:9 1 Mounting plate 2 Nut 3 Bolt 4 Motor 5 Shim washer and seal

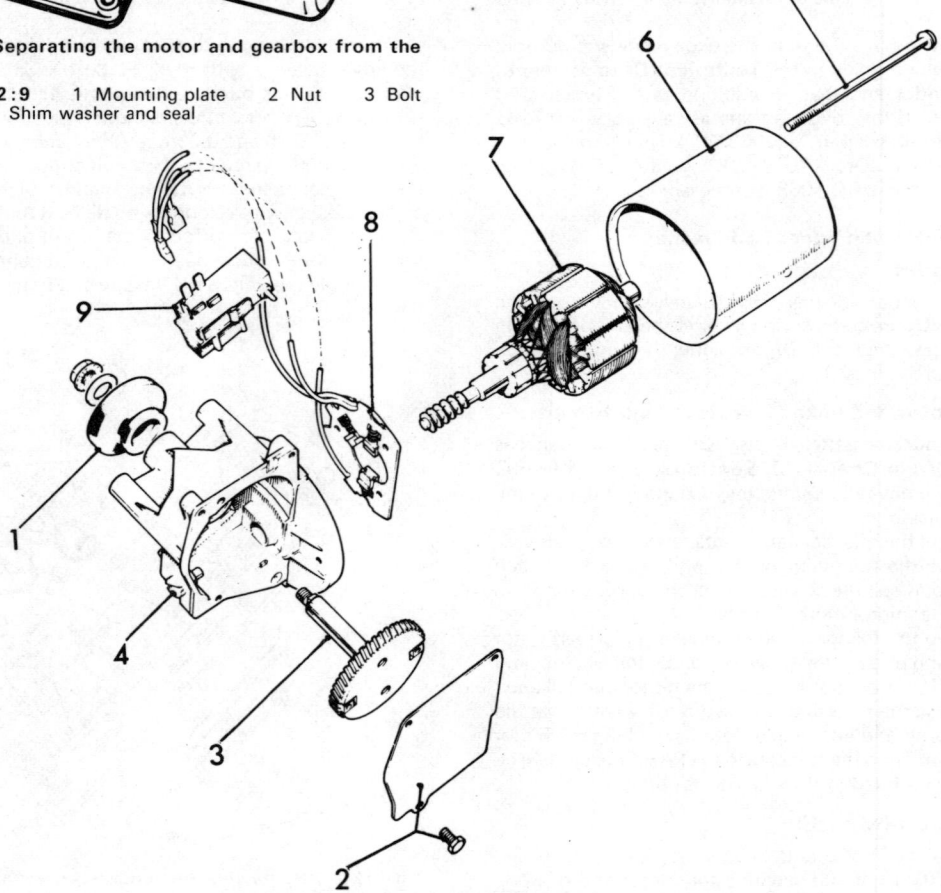

FIG 12:10 Motor and gearbox components

Key to Fig 12:10 1 Seal 2 Cover and retaining screws 3 Shaft 4 Thrust screw or thrust screw and locknut 5 Bolt 6 Cover 7 Armature and worm gear assembly 8 Brush assembly 9 Limit switch

12:7 Front and rear lights

Headlamp beam setting:

Beam aiming adjustments are best carried out by an agent who is equipped with free standing equipment such as the Lucas 'Beamsetter' or 'Beam Tester'. Note that equipment which is attached against lens aiming pads such as the Lucas 'Lev-L-Lite' cannot be used.

The three hand-knob adjusters 1 are shown in **FIG 12:12**.

Main/dip beam bulb renewal:

Refer to **FIG 12:12**. Remove the rubber cover 2, disengage and swing back the wire clip 3 and withdraw the bulb 4. When fitting the new bulb, do not handle the glass envelope.

Main beam bulb renewal:

Refer to **FIG 12:12**. Release the cover 5 by disengaging the forward lip and pulling it along the two wires 6. Disconnect the connections from the earth and from the bulb. Disengage the wire clip and swing it upwards. Withdraw the bulb. When fitting the new bulb, do not handle the glass envelope.

Front parking and flasher bulbs:

Access to the bulbs is achieved by withdrawing the lens which is retained by three screws. The bulbs have bayonet fittings.

Front fog lamp bulb renewal:

Carefully prise the rim from the housing. Support the weight of the lamp. Disconnect two connectors, disengage and swing back the wire clip and withdraw the bulb. When fitting the new bulb, do not handle the glass envelope.

Rear lamp assembly:

Open the tailgate, remove two special nuts and withdraw the cover. Refer to **FIG 12:13**. Four of the bulb holders have two connectors each. The tail lamp bulb holder (the centre of the five) has one connector and one terminal. This holder may be pulled out after disconnecting the two wires. Each of the other four holders is removed by rotating anticlockwise after pulling off the two connectors. The bulbs have bayonet fittings.

Number plate illumination bulb renewal:

Withdraw the forward edge first when removing the festoon type bulb.

Luggage compartment bulb renewal:

Prise the lens from the aperture. **Depress the plunger of the switch** (to preclude blowing the fuse if the bulb shorts the terminals) and withdraw the bulb. Again depress the switch plunger when fitting the new bulb.

12:8 Lighting circuits

Refer to the wiring diagram **FIG 14:1** in the **Technical Data** section of the **Appendix** for details of the lighting circuits. The relevant fuses and relays and their locations are identified in **Section 12:3**.

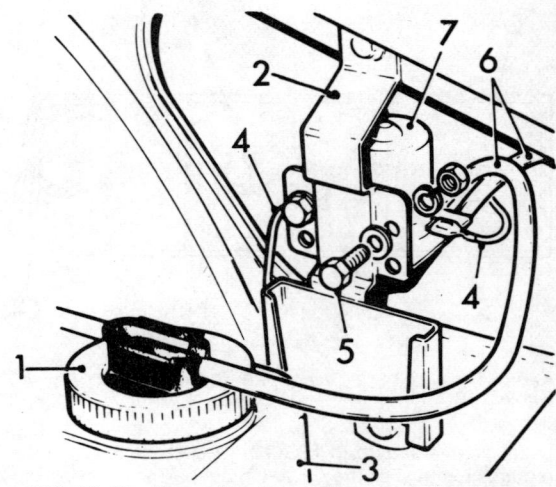

FIG 12:11   Removing the washer motor/pump unit

Key to Fig 12:11   1 Reservoir cap   2 Bracket
3 Reservoir   4 Leads   5 Bolt   6 Inlet and delivery tubes
7 Pump/motor unit

If bulbs burn out frequently, suspect that the alternator regulator is defective. If the brilliance of the lights varies with engine speed, check that the battery connections are clean and making good contact. Confirm that the alternator drive belt is correctly tensioned as described in **Section 12:5**.

12:9 Flasher units

The direction indicator flasher unit and the hazard warning flasher unit are located on the outboard side of the

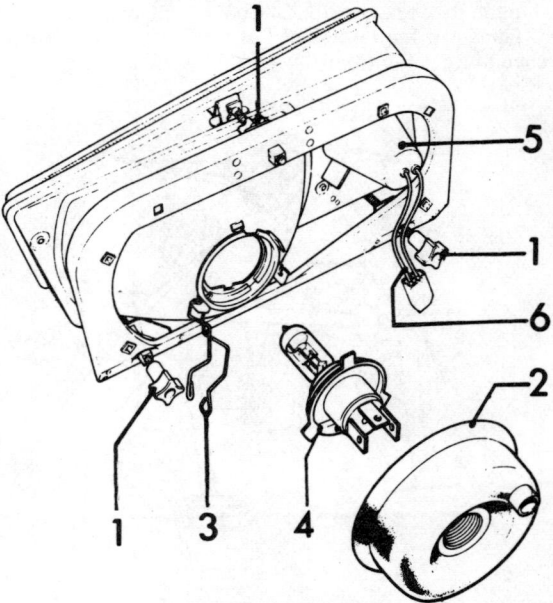

FIG 12:12   Headlamp unit

Key to Fig 12:12   1 Beam aiming adjusters   2 Cover
3 Spring clip   4 Main/dip bulb   5 Main beam bulb cover
6 Leads

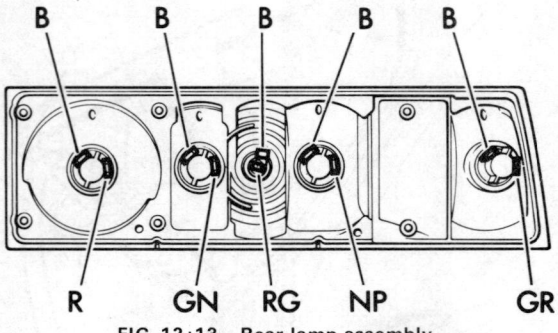

FIG 12:13   Rear lamp assembly

Key to Fig 12:13   **B** Black   **GR** Green/red   **NP** Brown/
purple   **RG** Red/green   **GN** Green/brown   **R** Red

pedal box as shown in **FIG 12:14**. Access to the units requires removal of the driver's glovebox as described in **Chapter 13, Section 13:10**.

Identify the relevant unit from the colour of the two connecting wires. Those connected to the indicator unit are both light green/brown. Those connected to the hazard unit are blue/brown and light green/purple.

Removal and fitment of the indicator switch is covered in **Chapter 10, Section 10:11**. Removal and fitment of the hazard switch is covered in **Section 12:11**. The relevant fuse is 7-8 (19h).

12:10 Horns

Removal and fitment:

Disconnect the leads from the battery. Locate the relevant horn forward of the radiator, remove the single nut and lock washer and withdraw the horn downwards through the upper air slot. Disconnect the two wires.

Fitment is the reverse of this sequence. The relevant circuit fuse is 5-6 (19g).

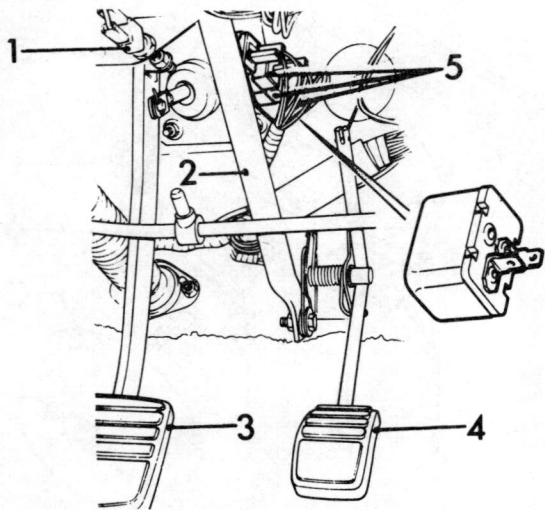

FIG 12:14   Flasher and delay units

Key to Fig 12:14   **1** Stop light switch   **2** Steady bracket
3 Brake pedal   **4** Accelerator pedal   **5** Flasher and delay
units

12:11 Instruments

With the exception of the speedometer which is mechanically driven from the transmission by a cable, the instruments are electrically operated.

Access to instruments, switches etc:

Access to the fuses requires removal of the panel end cover 3 (see **FIG 12:1**) as described in **Section 12:3**. With the end cover removed, the top cover 4 may be detached from its locating pegs 6 and 7 and lifted off. This gives access to the warning lights, switches 10 and instruments 11. Further dismantling is required to allow removal of the panel lighting rheostat end cover 12.

Panel lighting rheostat:

To remove the end cover 12, disconnect the battery, remove the fusebox cover as described in **Section 12:3**, lift off the top cover and disconnect the radio speaker wiring. Refer to **FIG 12:15**. Remove the three bolts 6. Release two plastic clips on the fusebox, swing the fusebox into the instrument panel and remove the single bolt 4. Carefully raise the rheostat end of the panel, remove two screws 10 and withdraw the rheostat end cover 11.

Tachometer removal and fitment:

Refer to **FIG 12:16**. The tachometer is actuated from the ignition system. Disconnect the battery and remove the panel side and top covers. Withdraw the plug connection 3 from the back of the tachometer, depress the top lugs 4 and lift the front cover 9 clear. Remove two screws 5, draw the tachometer forwards and withdraw the bulb holders 7.

To fit, reverse the removal sequence.

Speedometer removal and fitment:

Disconnect the battery and remove the side and top covers. Depress the locking prong and uncouple the drive cable 3 in **FIG 12:15**. Proceed as described earlier for the tachometer.

To fit, reverse the removal sequence.

Gauges, removal and fitment:

Refer to **FIG 12:17**. Disconnect the battery and remove the panel side and top covers. Depress the lugs 3 and remove the cover 1. Remove two screws 4 and draw the gauge housing 5 forwards. Depress the prong 6 and disconnect the multi-plug connector. Withdraw the bulb holder 7 from the triangular plate. Disconnect the white/green lead 8. Lift the gauge housing clear, remove two screws 9 and lift off the lens holder 2. Refer to **FIG 12:18**, remove the relevant gauge retaining nuts and withdraw the selected gauge from the housing 6.

Gauge fitment is the reverse of this sequence.

Transmitters:

There are three transmitters which actuate three of the block of gauges 11 in **FIG 12:1** (2 in **FIG 12:15**).

The location of the **oil pressure transmitter** is shown in **Chapter 1, FIGS 1:17** and **1:18**. The location of the **coolant temperature transmitter** is shown in **FIG 12:19**. The **fuel tank contents gauge transmitter** is integral with the fuel pump assembly and is shown in **Chapter 2, FIG 2:9**. It can only be removed with the fuel pump as described in **Chapter 2, Section 2:6**.

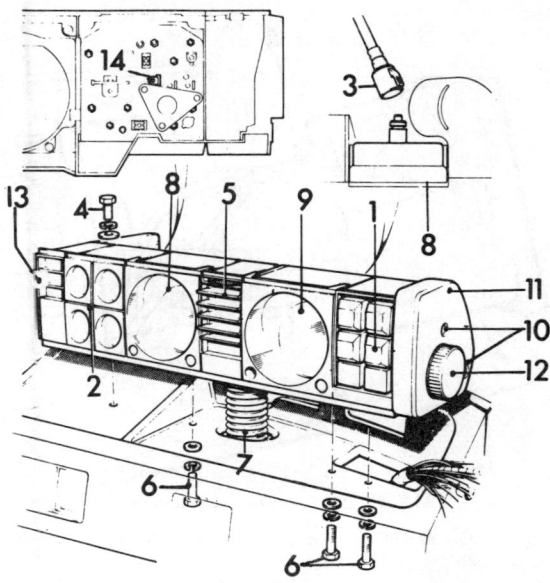

FIG 12:15 Removing the instrument panel

Key to Fig 12:15 1 Switches 2 Gauges 3 Speedometer drive cable 4 Bolt 5 Centre block 6 Bolt 7 Duct 8 Speedometer 9 Tachometer 10 Screws 11 Rheostat end cover 12 Rheostat control 13 Warning light lens unit 14 Terminal for white/green lead

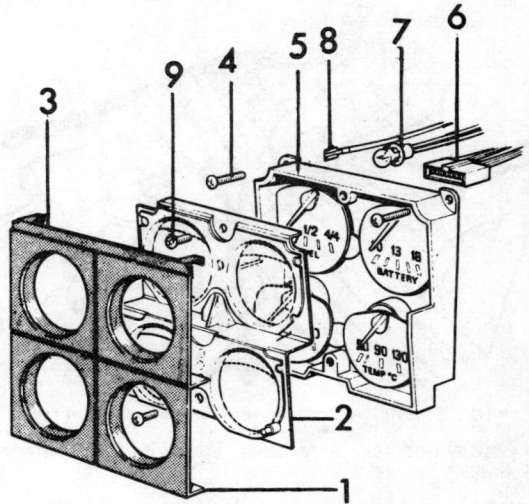

FIG 12:17 Dismounting the gauges

Key to Fig 12:17 1 Front cover 2 Lens holder 3 Lugs 4 Screws 5 Gauge housing 6 Locking prong 7 Bulb holder 8 White/green lead 9 Screws

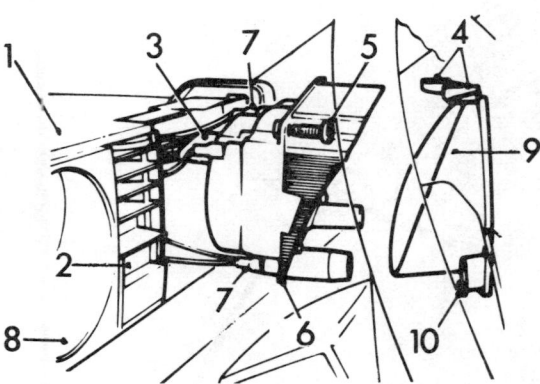

FIG 12:16 Removing the tachometer

Key to Fig 12:16 1 Instrument panel 2 Centre block 3 Plug connector 4 Retaining lugs 5 Screws 6 Tachometer 7 Bulb holders 8 Speedometer 9 Front cover 10 Lugs

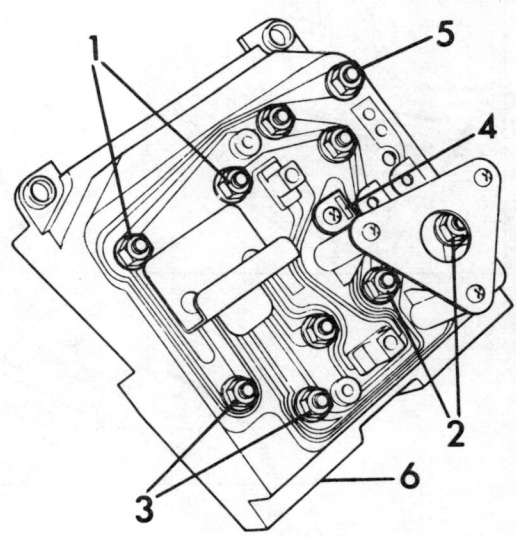

FIG 12:18 Removing the gauge(s)

Key to Fig 12:18 1 Battery condition indicator 2 Oil pressure gauge 3 Coolant temperature gauge 4 Terminal for white/green lead 5 Fuel gauge 6 Gauge housing

Warning light bulbs:

Disconnect the battery and remove the panel side and top covers. For access to the warning lights 13 in **FIG 12:15**, lift one spring clip and remove the warning light lens unit. For access to the warning lights 5 in **FIG 12:15**, remove the tachometer and speedometer face panels as described earlier and withdraw the centre block to the limit of the harness length.

Switches, removal and fitment:

To remove any of the block of switches 10 in **FIG 12:1** (1 in **FIG 12:15**), disconnect the battery, remove the panel side and end covers and push out the selected switch rearwards to release the two retaining clips. Disconnect the relevant harness plug and withdraw the switch.

Fitment is this sequence in reverse.

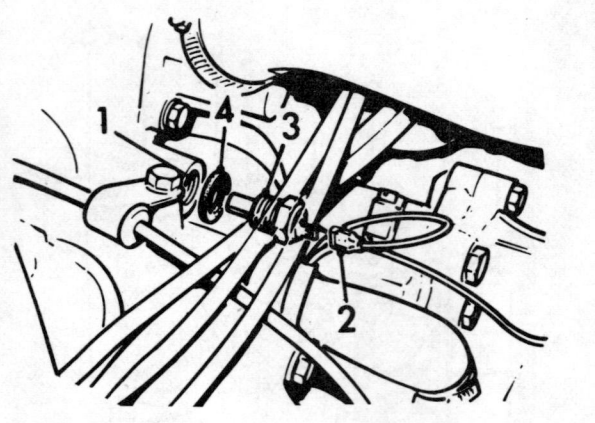

FIG 12:19   The coolant temperature transmitter

Key to Fig 12:19   1 Manifold   2 Lead   3 Transmitter
4 Seal

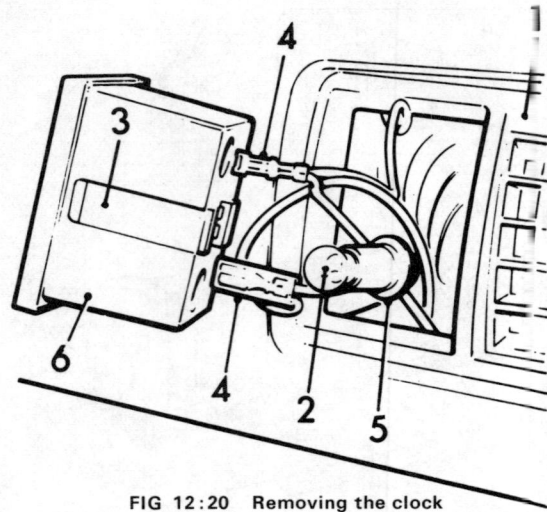

FIG 12:20   Removing the clock

Key to Fig 12:20   1 Facia   2 Bulb   3 Clip   4 Lead
5 Bulb holder   6 Clock

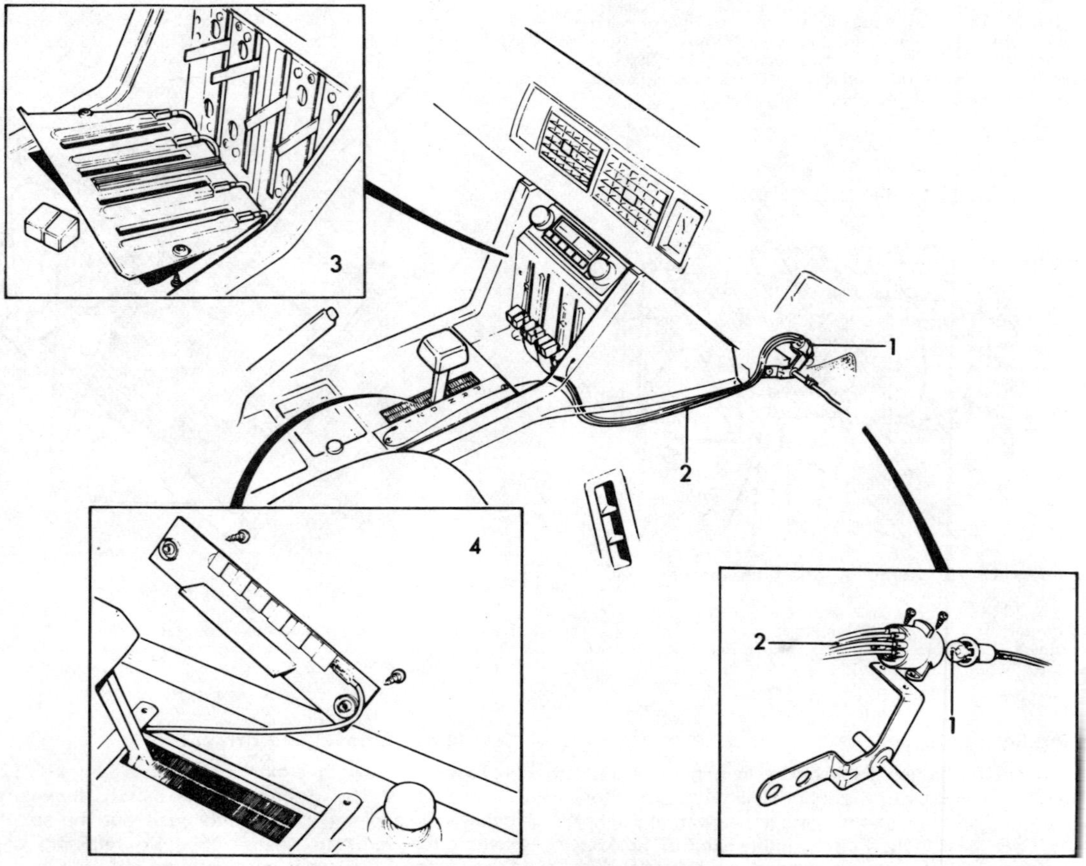

FIG 12:21   Fibre optic system

Key to Fig 12:21   1 Bulb   2 Fibre elements   3 Heater control panel   4 Selector panel (automatic transmission)

Clock removal and fitment:

The clock is not adjustable. Small discrepancies can be corrected by resetting the hands. A defective clock should be renewed. Disconnect the battery, open the glovebox and push out the clock from the facia. Refer to **FIG 12:20**. Disconnect the electrical leads 4, withdraw the bulbholder 5 and dismount the clock 6.

Reverse this sequence when fitting the replacement.

12:12 Fibre optic system

The layout of the system in an automatic transmission model is shown in **FIG 12:21**. This has five fibre elements 2. The manual transmission model version has four fibre elements. The single light source bulb 1 is mounted on the glovebox hinge assembly adjacent to the heater. If there is no illumination at all the end points, check the fuse 21-22 (19f) and the light source bulb. If illumination is absent at an individual end point, suspect a broken or an uncoupled fibre element.

12:13 Door locks

The feed for the door locking system is via an in-line fuse (3 in **FIG 14:1**). Current passes through a lock or an unlock resistor to charge the lock or the unlock capacitor. When a control switch (either an external door key switch or the internal switch in the driver's armrest) is closed, the lock or the unlock capacitor discharges through the lock or the unlock relay which actuates the five lock solenoids. A time delay of at least three seconds is required to recharge the capacitor before a repeat actuation of the solenoids can be made.

Control assembly removal and fitment:

The assembly is located in the righthand side of the luggage compartment as shown in **FIG 12:22**. Disconnect the battery, pull away the carpet, remove four screws and one star washer, manoeuvre the control assembly through the aperture and disconnect the six terminals colour coded in **FIG 12:23**.

Fitment is the reverse of this sequence.

Solenoids:

Refer to **Chapter 13, Section 13:8**.

Relays:

The relays are 8 and 9 in the wiring diagram **FIG 14:1**. Access requires removal of the control assembly as described earlier. Identify the relevant relay (see **FIG 12:23**) from the colours of the four connections as follows. Lock relay; brown, brown/red, green/black, green/slate. Unlock relay; brown, brown/red, blue/black, blue/orange.

To remove a relay, disconnect two connectors, pull back two rubber covers, remove two nuts and spring washers and remove four harness tags. Remove two nuts, spring washers and bolts to release the relay noting that the second relay will also be released but will remain captive by its wiring.

Fitment is the reverse of this sequence.

Resistors and capacitors:

The resistors are 4 and 5 and the capacitors are 6 and 7 in **FIG 14:1** the wiring diagram. Access requires removal of the control assembly as described earlier. To improve

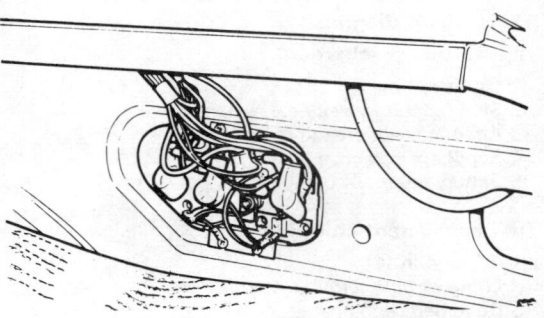

FIG 12:22 Location of lock control unit

access to the resistors, pull back two rubber covers, remove two nuts and spring washers and remove four harness tags. Identify the relevant resistor or capacitor by tracing the brown/red wire from the relevant relay (identified as described earlier), identify the wiring connections and disconnect the relevant resistor or capacitor.

Fitment is the reverse of this sequence.

12:14 Window lifts

No procedures are prescribed for the repair or overhaul of the electrically operated optional equipment window lifts and, in the event of a motor failure, a replacement assembly should be fitted. Access requires removal of the door trim from the relevant door as described in **Chapter 13, Section 13:8**.

Relays:

Refer to **Section 12:3**.

Rear isolation switch:

Refer to **Section 12:11**.

Thermal cut-out switch:

The location of this switch is shown in **FIG 12:2**.

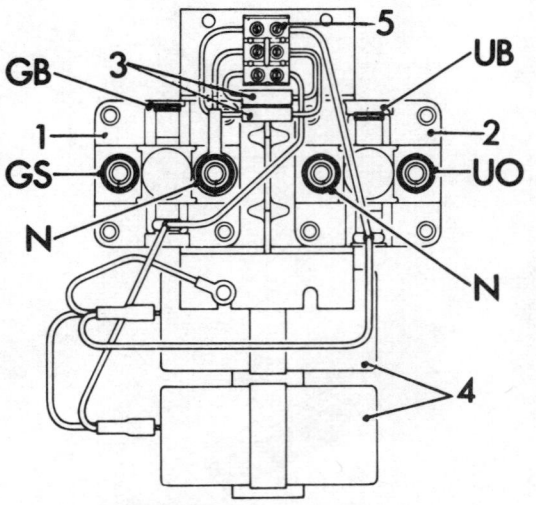

FIG 12:23 Lock control unit

Key to Fig 12:23   1 Relay (lock)   2 Relay (unlock)
3 Resistors   4 Capacitors   5 Terminal block

12:15 Fault diagnosis

(a) Battery discharged

1 Lights left on
2 Short circuit in electrical system
3 Alternator not charging
4 Regulator defective
5 Battery internally defective

(b) Insufficient charging rate

1 Check 4 in (a)
2 Loose or dirty terminal connections
3 Drive belt slipping

(c) Battery overcharged

1 Check 4 in (a)

(d) Alternator output low or nil

1 Check 4 in (a) and 3 in (b)
2 Drive belt broken
3 Stator and/or rotor windings defective
4 Slip rings worn, burned or shorted
5 Brushes worn or sticking

(e) Starter motor lacks power or will not operate

1 Battery discharged; cable connection loose
2 Starter switch, relay or solenoid defective
3 Brushes worn or sticking
4 Commutator worn, burned or shorted
5 Pinion engagement mechanism defective
6 Armature and/or field coils defective

(f) Starter motor rough or noisy

1 Retaining bolts loose
2 Damaged teeth on pinion or ring gear

(g) Lights inoperative or erratic

1 Battery discharged; bulbs burned out
2 Faulty earth connection; discontinuity in wiring
3 Defective switch or relay; fuse(s) blown

(h) Wiper motor sluggish

1 Defective motor
2 Seized linkage pivot

(j) Washer inoperative

1 Blocked jet(s)
2 Empty tank
3 Pump or motor defective

(k) Gauge inoperative

1 Transmitter disconnected or defective
2 Gauge defective
3 Fuse blown; wiring discontinuity

(l) Warning light inoperative

1 Check 1 and 3 in (k)
2 Bulb blown

(m) Fibre optics system inoperative

1 Check 3 in (k); 2 in (l)
2 Fibre element(s) uncoupled or broken

CHAPTER 13

THE BODYWORK

13:1 Bodywork finish

Large-scale repairs to body panels are best left to expert panel beaters. Even small dents can be tricky, as too much hammering will stretch the metal and make things worse instead of better. Filling minor dents and scratches is probably the best method of restoring the surface. Use a modern filling compound and work to the manufacturer's instructions. The touching-up of paintwork is well within the ability of most owners, particularly as self-spraying aerosol cans of the correct colours are now readily available. Paint may change colour with age and it is better to spray a whole wing or panel rather than to touch-up a small area.

Before spraying, remove all traces of wax polish with white spirit. More drastic treatment will be required if silicone polish has been applied. Use a primer surfacer or a paste stopper or a filler according to the amount of filling required, and when it is dry, rub it down with 400 grade 'Wet or Dry' paper until the surface is smooth and flush with the surrounding area. Spend time on getting a good finish as this will control the final effect. Apply the retouching paint keeping it wet in the centre and light and dry round the edges. After a few hours drying, use a cutting compound to remove the dry spray and finish off with a liquid polish.

Take great care when working with hydraulic brake fluid not to spill any on the paintwork.

13:2 The bonnet

Removal and fitment:

Disconnect the battery. Disconnect the leads to the bonnet lamp and switch and pull the harness clear of the body. Pull the washer tubing from the T-piece. Support the bonnet and mark round the hinge positions. Remove the split pin and washers and uncouple the support stay from the bonnet. Remove the four bolts and two adjuster plates from the hinges and lift off the bonnet.

Fitment is the reverse of this sequence. Align the hinges to the marked positions and check the alignment of the bonnet with the body before finally tightening the hinge bolts fully.

Bonnet catch:

To adjust, pull back the spring, loosen the locknut and, using a screwdriver, turn the shaft in or out as appropriate. After checking, tighten the locknut.

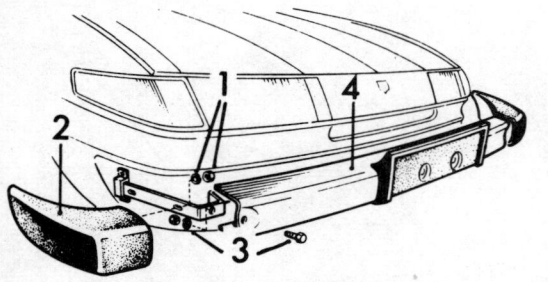

FIG 13:1   Removing a front bumper

Key to Fig 13:1   1 Nut and washer   **2** Bumper end piece
3 Bolt, nut and washer   **4** Bumper

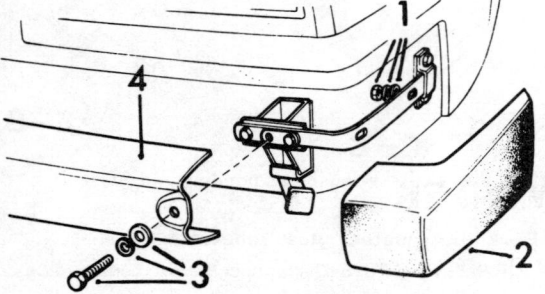

FIG 13:2   Removing a rear bumper

Key to Fig 13:2   1 Nut and washers   **2** Bumper end piece
3 Bolt and washers   **4** Bumper

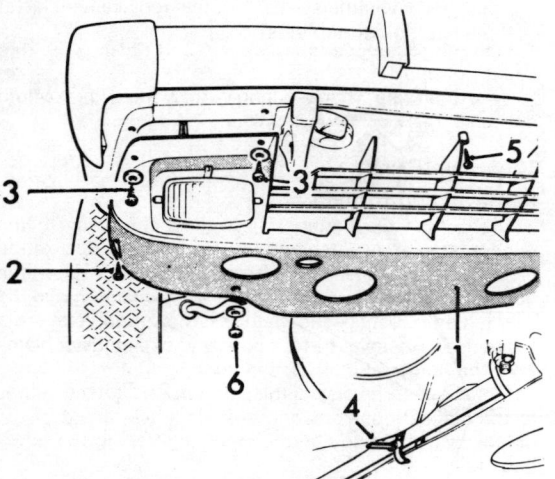

FIG 13:3   Removing the underbelly panel

Key to Fig 13:3   1 Underbelly panel   **2** Screw   **3** Screw
and washer   **4** Support strap   **5** Screw   **6** Screw and
washer

Bonnet lock:

Removal is covered in **Chapter 12, Section 12:6**.

Bonnet release cable renewal:

Remove the trunnion from the cable, loosen the pinch bolt and detach the cable from the lock. Open the glovebox and disconnect the cable from the bracket beneath the facia. Withdraw the cable through the grommet in the bulkhead and collect the nut and washer. **Do not close the bonnet with the cable release removed or inoperative.**

Fitment is the reverse of this sequence.

13:3 The bumpers

Bumper removal and fitment:

Refer to **FIG 13:1** in the case of a **front bumper** or to **FIG 13:2** in the case of a **rear bumper**.

Remove the four sets of nuts and washers 1 and detach the bumper ends 2 from the brackets. Support the bumper. Remove two sets of bolts and washers 3 and dismount the bumper 4.

To fit, reverse this sequence.

13:4 Underbelly panel

Removal and fitment:

Disconnect the leads from both fog lamps. Refer to **FIG 13:3**. Remove two side screws 2 and four screws and washers 3 from the forward edge of the panel 1. Remove two support straps 4 which secure the panel to the anti-roll bar, support the panel and remove two screws and washers 5 from the centre of the grille. Remove two screws and washers 6 from the rear edge of the panel and dismount the panel.

Fitment is the reverse of this sequence.

13:5 Windscreen

The windscreen glass moulding is electrically bonded to the glass and to the body aperture flange. The finishers are embedded into the moulding. The procedures for bonding the Solbit moulding require the use of a variable output transformer which can provide 11 amps at 28 volts for up to two hours. Precise location of the glass and finishers is essential as, once bonded, adjustment is not possible. The glass fitment procedures should not be attempted by an inexperienced owner who should have the glass fitted by a specialist. Notes on the bonding times etc are, however, given later to guide those who may be able to engage the professional services of an experienced assistant. The procedure for the removal of the old glass is less complex.

Removing old glass:

Protect the instrument panel, facia and interior trim from broken glass by covering with a sheet. Remove the windscreen wiper arms (see **Chapter 12, Section 12:6**) and dismount the interior mirror. Refer to **Section 13:11** and remove the trim pads from the forward posts. Carefully prise out the two corner finishers. From outside and starting at the top righthand corner, cut a hole through the old Solbit moulding and feed a wire through to an assistant. Keeping the wire clear of the body and as close

as possible to the glass, 'saw' through the old Solbit. Carefully knife out the remaining Solbit from the aperture and from the finishers. Reject the finishers if they are distorted or will not clean up satisfactorily. Finally clean off the finishers and the body flange with methylated spirit.

Notes on fitting new glass:

Kit RTC 2063 (sealing strip) is essential and, if the finishers are not serviceable, kit RTC 2064 (finishers) will also be required.

Position the spacers from the sealing strip kit at 150 to 230mm (6 to 9in) from the forward pillars and offer up the glass to the aperture for a trial fitment. There must be sufficient Solbit along the whole length of the gap into which the finishers are embedded and under the glass for a watertight bond (see **FIG 13:4**). Use methylated spirit to clean the new glass and use glass lifters. Apply a thin coat of primer to the aperture flange including any small areas of residual Solbit and to the inner face of the glass (this should not be more than 13mm (0.50in) wide). Allow the primer to dry for one minute.

Before removing the Solbit from the pack, apply the specified current for 15 to 90 seconds (depending upon the temperature and the shelf-age of the Solbit) but do not overheat or it will be difficult to remove from the pack and to handle.

Position the Solbit and apply the specified current. After about 90 to 120 **seconds**, fit the glass and apply pressure to it. The bond line (seen through the glass) should not be less than 7mm (0.25in) wide during the early stages of the heating cycle. Switch off the current after 90 to 120 **minutes** and allow the glass to cool for 10 to 15 minutes before removing the spacers and embedding the finishers. If, at this stage, the finishers and glass are proud, additional pressure may be applied.

13:6 Backlight and quarterlight glass

Although the glass shapes are different and preparatory work differs, the procedure instructions for removing the glass and fitting new are common to both.

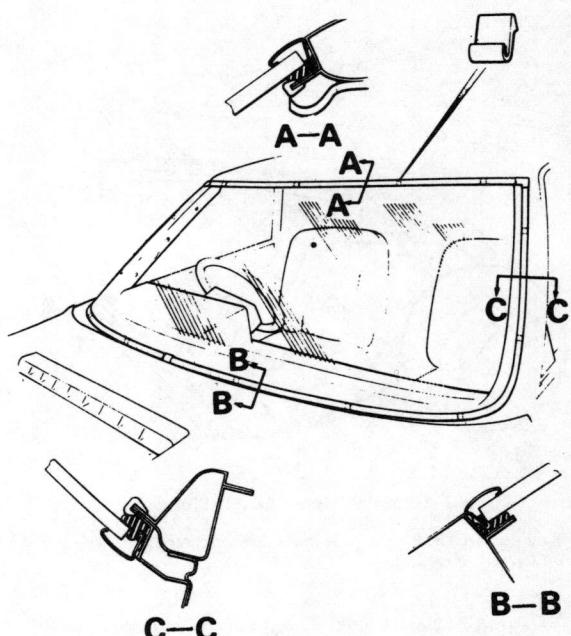

FIG 13:4   **Windscreen bonding and finishers**

Backlight (heated) glass renewal:

1 Refer to **FIG 13:5**. Disconnect the two harness plugs 2 from the heater element.

2 Using a thin-bladed tool, break the seal between the glass and the weatherstrip and between the weatherstrip and the body flange. Dismount the glass by pushing outwards.

3 Remove the weatherstrip and finishers from the old glass and clean off old sealing compound from the body flange and the weatherstrip. Reject unserviceable finishers or weatherstrip and obtain replacement kit(s) (see later for kit numbers).

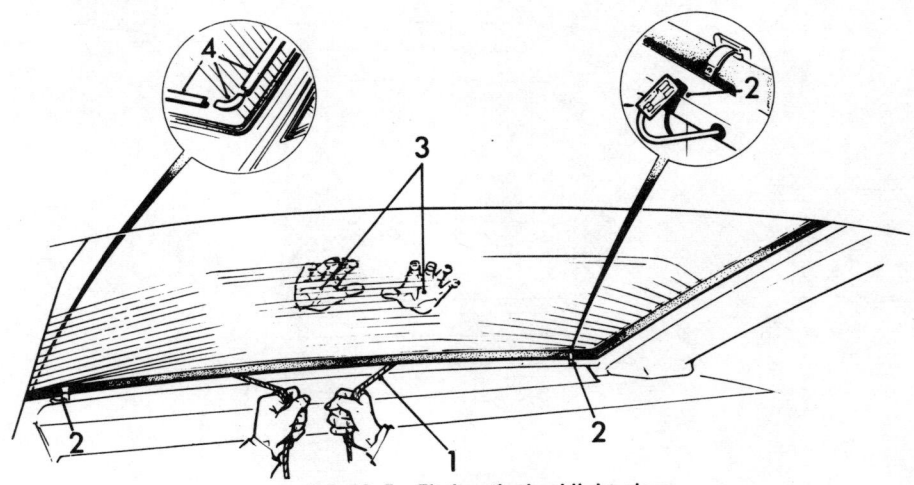

FIG 13:5   **Fitting the backlight glass**

Key to Fig 13:5   1 Cord   2 Heater connecting plug   3 Applying hand pressure   4 Finishers

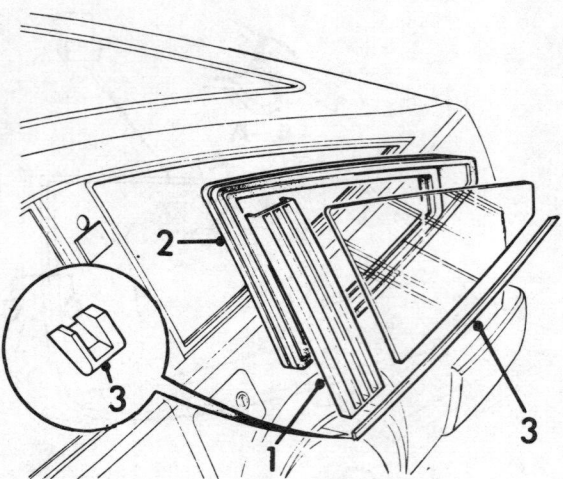

FIG 13:6   Fitting a quarterlight glass

Key to Fig 13:6   1 Capping   2 Weatherstrip   3 End cap and waist moulding

4 Apply Seelastik sealing compound to the weatherstrip glass channel and fit the weatherstrip and finishers to the glass. Insert a strong cord (see 1 in **FIG 13:5**) into the weatherstrip inner channel with the ends protruding from the lower centre edge.

5 With an assistant on the outside of the car applying steady hand pressure, pull the cord ends to lip the weatherstrip over the body flange.

6 Seal the outer channel of the weatherstrip to the body flange with Seelastik and reconnect the two harness plugs.

Quarterlight glass renewal:

1 Refer to **Chapter 8, Section 8:10** and remove the squab wing. Refer to **Section 13:11** and remove the relevant post trim pads and cappings. Lift out the parcel tray and the relevant parcel tray extension.

2 Refer to **FIG 13:6**. Carry out operations 2, 3, 4 and 5 of the backlight glass renewal procedure on the quarterlight.

3 Seal the outer channel of the weatherstrip to the body flange with Seelastik and refit the cappings, trim pads, squab wing etc.

Weatherstrip and finisher kits:

Backlight kits are: BRC 37, weatherstrip; RTC 2052, finishers. Quarterlight kits are: BRC 202, righthand weatherstrip; BRC 203, lefthand weatherstrip; BRC 2470, plate (not handed); BRC 2551, clip (not handed).

13:7 Doors

The procedure instructions for the removal and fitment of a front or a rear door are identical. If, however, radio speakers are fitted to front doors, the relevant speaker must be disconnected and dismounted.

Door removal and fitment:

Disconnect the battery. Refer to **Section 13:8** and remove the door trim. Disconnect the multi-point plug and connectors. If fitted, disconnect and dismount the radio speaker from a front door. Support the door and remove six nuts, spring and plain washers and clamping plates from inside the door. Dismount the door.

Fitment is the reverse of this sequence. Align the door before finally tightening the hinge fixings.

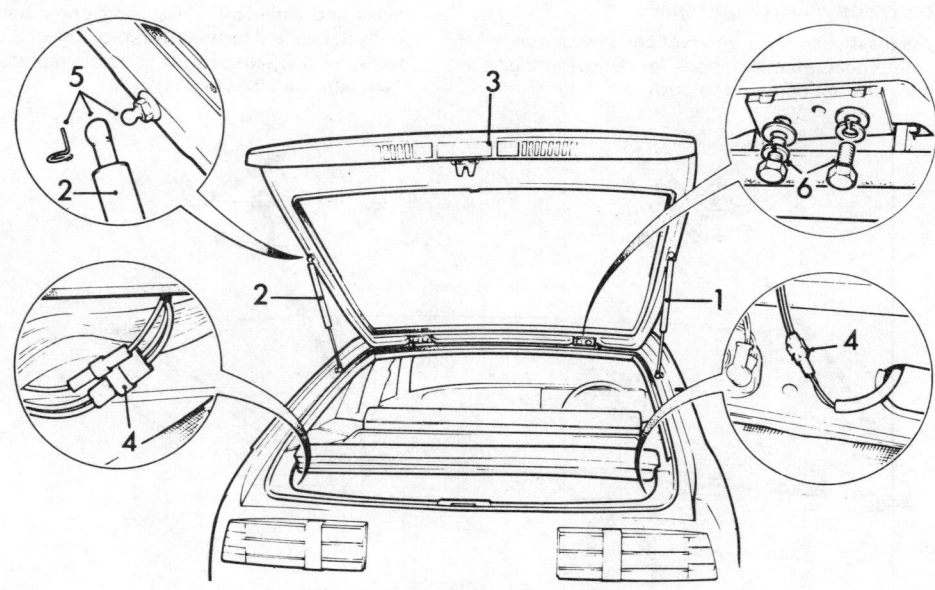

FIG 13:7   Removing the tailgate

Key to Fig 13:7   1 and 2 Stay   3 Tailgate   4 Connectors   5 Stay ballpin and clip   6 Bolts

Tailgate removal and fitment:

Disconnect the battery. Open and support the tailgate. Refer to **FIG 13:7**. Pull away the carpet, disconnect the harness plugs 4, attach suitable lengths of string to them to facilitate refitting and pull each harness and grommet through the aperture on the tailgate closing face. Detach the clips 5 and separate the stays 1 and 2 from their ball pins. Remove four bolts and washers 6 and dismount the tailgate.

Fitment is the reverse of this sequence. Align the tailgate before finally tightening the hinge bolts.

13:8 Door trim, locks and fittings

Door trim removal and fitment:

Unclip the regulator handle plastic cover at the pivot end, remove the retaining screw and pull the handle off with its cover and bezel. Remove the screw from inside the door pull moulding to release the trim at this point (on the driver's door this also releases the master locking switch protecting ramp). Refer to **FIG 13:8**. Insert a large screwdriver 1 as shown. Ensure that (as at 1) the blade passes **over** the spring clip and **between it and the inner door panel** and prise the clip out of engagement. Repeat this at the other clips. Raise the door trim to release it from the channels 2 and lift it off.

Fitment is the reverse of this sequence. Align all the spring clips with their locations before pressing the trim into position.

Door locks, removal and fitment:

Each lock solenoid is integral with its inner latch assembly and cannot be renewed separately. In the case of a **front** lock, refer to **FIG 13:9**. In the case of a **rear** lock, refer to **FIG 13:10**.

On **front** and **rear** doors, close the window glass and remove the door trim as described earlier. Refer to **Section 13:9** and remove the window regulator. Remove the tie bracket 2. Remove the outer latch unit 3.

On **rear** doors, pull the rubber moulding 8 out of the channel and tape it to one side. Remove the screw 9 and the bolt, plain and spring washers from the bracket inside the door to release the rear 'cheater' channel. Remove the channel.

On **front** and **rear** doors, unclip the latch release rod 4 (on **front** doors also unclip the lock operating rod) from the outside handle. Remove two screws, plain and shakeproof washers holding the interior locking control 5 (note that, on refitting, the coloured dot is forwards). Pull the interior locking control away from the inner door panel and disconnect the clip to release the operating rod 6.

On **rear** doors, disconnect clip 11 which retains the locking rod to the lock lever and withdraw the rod. Unscrew the safety lock knob 10.

On **front** and **rear** doors, disconnect clip 7 which retains the operating rod to the remote control release. Pull out multi-plug(s) (one on **rear** doors, two on **front** doors). Remove the lock inner latch assembly with its operating rods (two on **rear** doors, four on **front** doors) and solenoid wiring attached.

Fitment is the reverse of the removal sequence in each case.

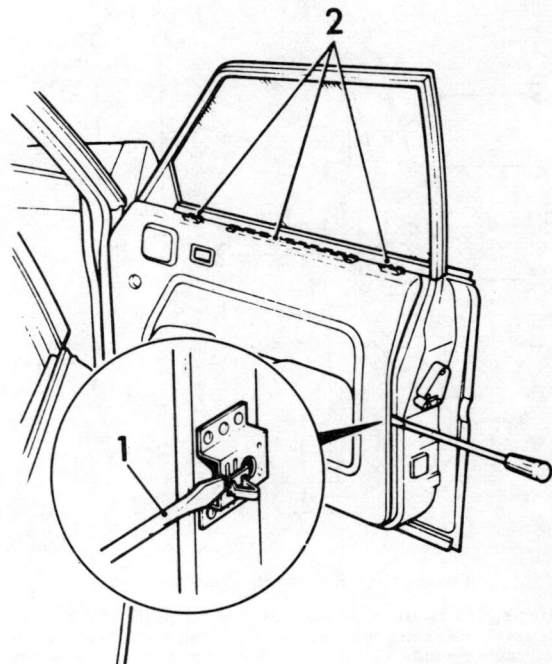

FIG 13:8   Removing the door trim panel

Key to Fig 13:8   1 Screwdriver blade   2 Channels

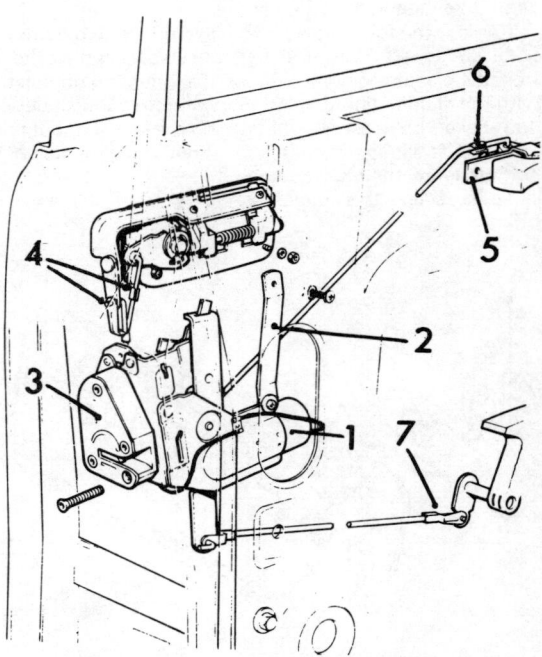

FIG 13:9   Removing a front door lock

Key to Fig 13:9   1 Solenoid   2 Tie bracket   3 Outer latch   4 Latch release rod and lock operating rod   5 Interior locking control   6 Operating rod   7 Clip

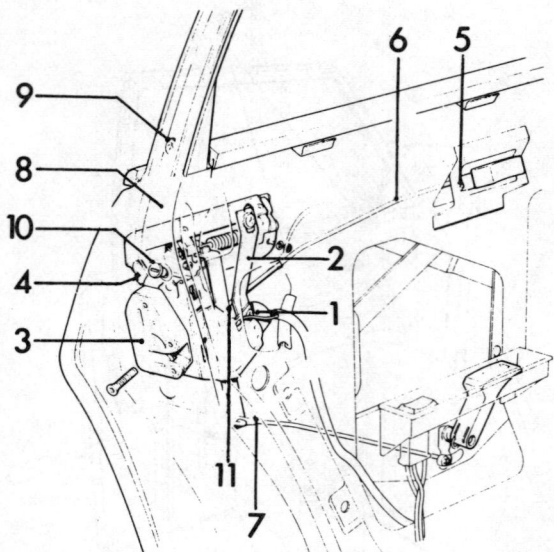

FIG 13:10   Removing a rear door lock

Key to Fig 13:10   1 Solenoid   2 Tie bracket   3 Outer
latch   4 Latch release rod   5 Interior locking control
6 Operating rod   7 Clip   8 Rubber moulding   9 Screw
10 Safety lock knob   11 Clip

Tailgate lock removal and fitment:

The lock solenoid is integral with the lock assembly and
cannot be renewed separately.

Remove the four screws which secure the two number
plate illumination units. Remove four screws and washers
from the plastic moulding, release the moulding complete
with the illumination units. Remove the two long screws
and shakeproof washers which retain the lock. Lift out the
lock and its wiring. Uncouple the three inside connectors
and withdraw the lock assembly.

To fit, reverse this sequence.

Front door barrel lock removal and fitment:

Close the window glass. Remove the door trim as
described earlier. Refer to **Section 13:9** and remove the
window regulator. Refer to **FIG 13:9** and remove the tie
bracket 2. Remove the bolt, plain and shakeproof washers
holding the bottom of the rearmost glass channel. Pull the
rubber moulding out of the channel and tape it to one side.
Remove the channel. Refer to **FIG 13:11** and remove
items 1 to 4 in that order. Withdraw the barrel lock 5 and
collect the 'O' ring 6.

To fit, reverse this sequence. Do not omit to fit the 'O'
ring.

Door lock striker:

The components of a door lock striker are shown in **FIG
13:12**. Two screws secure the striker assembly to a plate
inside the door pillar. Adjustment is made by loosening the
two screws 1, repositioning the striker horizontally and/or
vertically as required and retightening the screws. It should
be possible with a correctly set striker to press a closed
door fractionally against its seals **beyond the latched
position**.

Tailgate striker:

Remove the four screws which retain the righthand sill
moulding. Remove the three retaining screws, plain and
shakeproof washers and dismount the striker.

To fit, reverse this sequence noting that, for adjustment,
the striker is moved as required in the vertical slots.

13:9 Door glass and regulators
Glass removal and fitment:

On **front** and **rear** doors, remove the regulator as
described later. Unclip the interior sealing strip from the
window sill (five clips). Unclip the interior waist rail
moulding (four clips).

On **rear** doors, remove the screw from the rear edge of
the door frame (this retains the upper 'cheater' section of
the rearmost glass channel). Remove the bolt, plain and

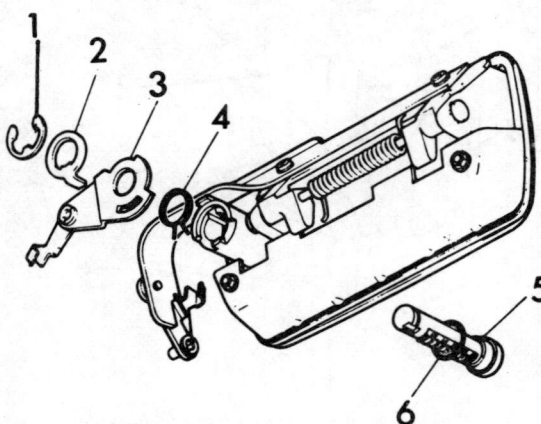

FIG 13:11   Removing a barrel lock

Key to Fig 13:11   1 Circlip   2 Indexing plate   3 Operating
lever   4 Indexing spring   5 Barrel lock   6 'O' ring

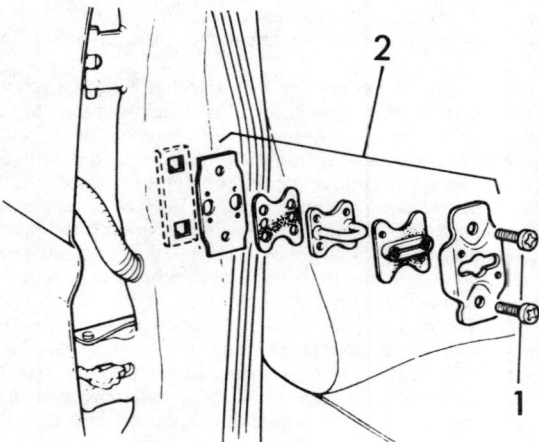

FIG 13:12   Components of a lock striker

Key to Fig 13:12   1 Retaining screws   2 Striker assembly

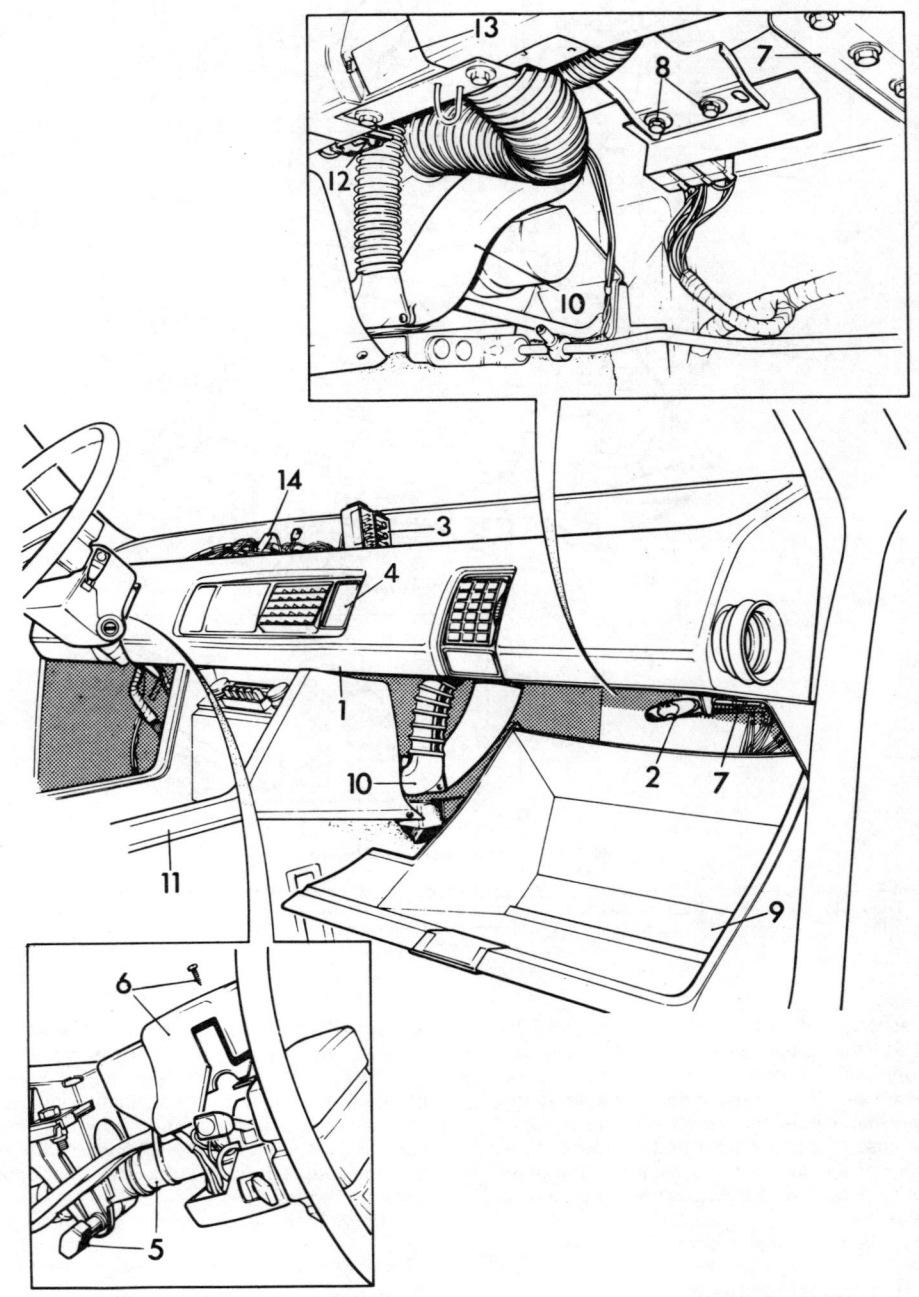

FIG 13:13   Removing the facia

Key to Fig 13:13   1 Facia   2 Bonnet latch release   3 Fuses   4 Clock   5 Steering column   6 Upper nacelle and retaining screw   7 Bracket   8 Bolts   9 Glove box   10 Duct   11 Console   12 Connectors   13 Map light   14 Harnesses

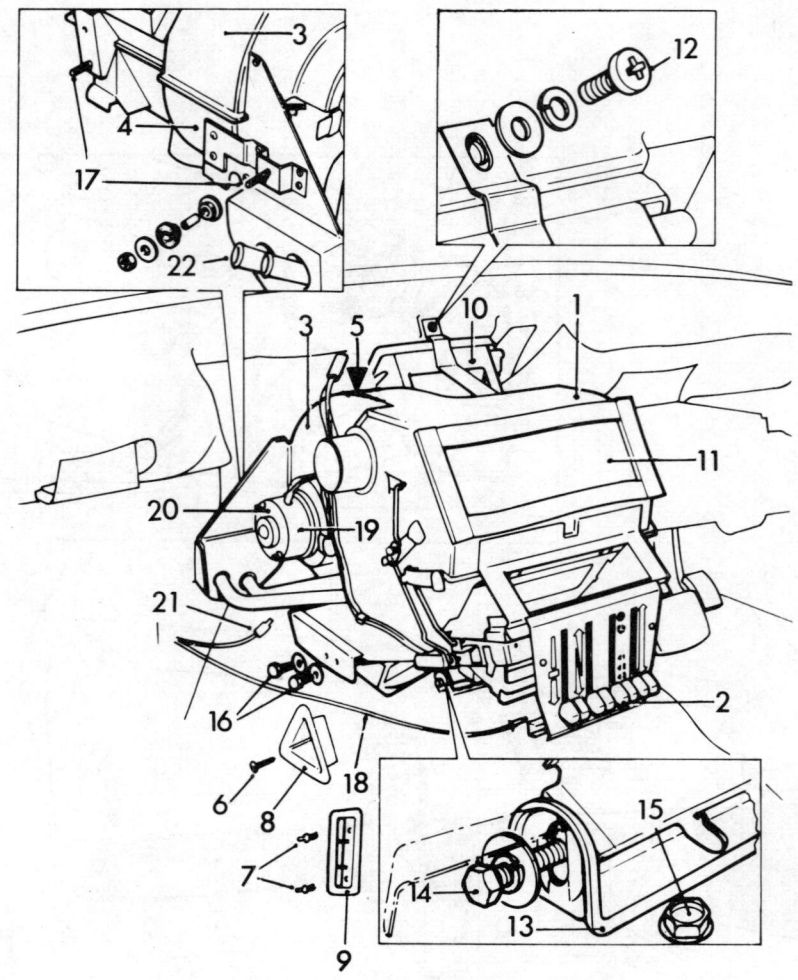

FIG 13:14   Removing the heater

shakeproof washers holding the bottom of the rearmost glass channel. Pull the rubber moulding out of the channel and tape it to one side. Remove the channel from the door.

On **front** and **rear** doors, remove the tape holding the glass to the door frame. Raise the glass, tilting it upwards at the rear in the case of a **front** door and upwards at the front in the case of a **rear** door and withdraw the glass from the outside taking care that it does not get scratched against the door frame.

To fit, reverse the removal sequence in each case.

Regulators, removal and fitment:

The procedure instructions are the same for a **front** and for a **rear** door.

Close the window glass and tape the glass to the top of the door frame. Remove the door trim as described in

Section 13:8. Remove the four bolts which secure the regulator (in the case of a **front** door, the rearmost bolt also retains the door pull moulding). Slide the scissor linkage horizontally backwards and forwards as required to disengage the lifting studs from the horizontal glass support and support plate channels. Lift the regulator assembly out of the central aperture. Check that the glass is securely held by the tape.

Fitment is the reverse of this sequence.

13:10 Facia, gloveboxes and console
Glovebox removal and fitment:

Detach the support straps from the glovebox, remove two screws from inside the box and detach the box from the spigots on the pivot bracket.

To fit, reverse this sequence.

Facia removal and fitment:

Disconnect the battery. Refer to **Section 13:2** and disconnect the bonnet release cable from beneath the facia. Refer to **Chapter 12, Section 12:11**, dismount the instrument panel and remove the clock from the facia. Refer to **Chapter 10, Section 10:6** and remove the steering wheel. Remove the steering column upper nacelle. Remove the gloveboxes as described earlier.

Refer to **FIG 13:13**. Remove six bolts and washers securing the facia 1 to the body brackets 7. Remove two bolts and washers 8 securing the facia and relay bracket to the bulkhead. Pull the demister vents 10 clear of the heater and detach the side vent and pull it clear of the steering column 5. Disconnect the glovebox lights and the map light 13. Carefully manoeuvre the facia out of the car while feeding the wiring harness 14, speedometer cable etc through the apertures in the top of the facia.

Fitment follows the reverse of this sequence.

Console:

Refer to **Chapter 6, FIG 6:11**.

13:11 Post trim pads and cappings

Post trim pads:

The forward post upper pads are each retained by two screws and cup washers. The lower pads are each retained by two press studs.

The upper central post pads are each retained by the safety belt fixings. Prise off the bolt cover and remove the swivel bolt and wavy washer. The interior lamp can be manoeuvred through the pad aperture. The lower pad is retained by two screws and is spigotted at the upper end. For access to the screws, unclip the carpets.

After removing the seat squab wing, the rear post pad may be removed by pulling away the pad and disengaging the upper clip and then the lower clip. The lower pad is retained by two drive fasteners.

The rearmost (sloping) pad is removed by removing the single screw and pulling the pad forwards to disengage the rear clip.

Quarterlight capping:

This exterior capping is 1 in **FIG 13:6**. Removal requires drilling out of the four blind rivets along the forward edge. The two tongues on the rear edge can then be disengaged from the weatherstrip channel.

To refit, engage the tongues in the weatherstrip channel and blind rivet the forward edge to the post.

13:12 Heater

If the heater blower does not operate, check that the fuse 3-4 (19j in **FIG 14:1**) is intact and that the relay 48 in **FIG 14:1** and located behind the glovebox (see **Chapter 12, Section 12:3** and **FIG 12:2**) is not defective. With the heater unit in situ, access to the resistor unit (the location is indicated by the arrow 5 in **FIG 13:14**) requires the removal of the facia as described in **Section 13:10**. Access to the motor, matrix etc requires removal of the heater unit. Proceed as follows.

Removal and fitment:

1 Disconnect the battery. Drain the cooling system as described in **Chapter 4, Section 4:3**. Identify and disconnect the inlet and outlet hoses (14 in **Chapter 2, FIG 2:2**). Remove two nuts, plain and spring washers from the heater fixing studs (17 in **FIG 13:14**) located through recessed holes in the padded front bulkhead behind the engine and in line with each rocker cover.

2 Refer to **FIG 13:14**. Remove the screws 6 holding the triangulated air duct covers 8 (one on each side of the transmission tunnel). Press out the plastic rivet centres 7 to release the rectangular air duct covers 9.

3 Refer to **Chapter 6, FIG 6:11** and remove the console. Lift the carpet and remove the screws (two each side of the tunnel) holding the air ducts. Remove the facia as described in **Section 13:10**.

4 Remove bolt 12 which retains the top bracket to the bulkhead and collect the plain and spring washers. Remove two bolts 14, plain and spring washers from the support bracket 13 (one each side). Remove two bolts 15, plain and shakeproof washers. Remove four bolts 16, plain and shakeproof washers.

5 Lift the heater rearwards until studs 17 are clear of the bulkhead. Pull out the radio aerial 18. Refer to **Chapter 12, Section 12:12** and uncouple the fibre optic elements.

6 Remove the motor cover 20 and disconnect the red feed wire under the motor. Disconnect the earth wire 21 under the heater. Blank off the inlet and outlet pipes 22 to prevent spillage of residual coolant from the matrix. Lift out the heater unit.

Fitment is the reverse of this sequence. On completion, refill the cooling system as described in **Chapter 4, Section 4:3**.

NOTES

APPENDIX

TECHNICAL DATA

Engine   Fuel system   Ignition system   Cooling system
Clutch   Transmission   Suspension   Steering   Brakes
Electrical equipment   Capacities   Dimensions
Torque wrench settings   Wiring diagrams

HINTS ON MAINTENANCE AND OVERHAUL

GLOSSARY OF TERMS

INDEX

Inches	Decimals	Milli-metres	Inches to Millimetres — Inches	Inches to Millimetres — mm	Millimetres to Inches — mm	Millimetres to Inches — Inches
$\frac{1}{64}$	.015625	.3969	.001	.0254	.01	.00039
$\frac{1}{32}$	.03125	.7937	.002	.0508	.02	.00079
$\frac{3}{64}$	.046875	1.1906	.003	.0762	.03	.00118
$\frac{1}{16}$	.0625	1.5875	.004	.1016	.04	.00157
$\frac{5}{64}$	.078125	1.9844	.005	.1270	.05	.00197
$\frac{3}{32}$	.09375	2.3812	.006	.1524	.06	.00236
$\frac{7}{64}$	.109375	2.7781	.007	.1778	.07	.00276
$\frac{1}{8}$	.125	3.1750	.008	.2032	.08	.00315
$\frac{9}{64}$	.140625	3.5719	.009	.2286	.09	.00354
$\frac{5}{32}$	.15625	3.9687	.01	.254	.1	.00394
$\frac{11}{64}$	.171875	4.3656	.02	.508	.2	.00787
$\frac{3}{16}$	.1875	4.7625	.03	.762	.3	.01181
$\frac{13}{64}$	.203125	5.1594	.04	1.016	.4	.01575
$\frac{7}{32}$	.21875	5.5562	.05	1.270	.5	.01969
$\frac{15}{64}$	.234375	5.9531	.06	1.524	.6	.02362
$\frac{1}{4}$	.25	6.3500	.07	1.778	.7	.02756
$\frac{17}{64}$	.265625	6.7469	.08	2.032	.8	.03150
$\frac{9}{32}$	.28125	7.1437	.09	2.286	.9	.03543
$\frac{19}{64}$	.296875	7.5406	.1	2.54	1	.03937
$\frac{5}{16}$	.3125	7.9375	.2	5.08	2	.07874
$\frac{21}{64}$	.328125	8.3344	.3	7.62	3	.11811
$\frac{11}{32}$	.34375	8.7312	.4	10.16	4	.15748
$\frac{23}{64}$	.359375	9.1281	.5	12.70	5	.19685
$\frac{3}{8}$	.375	9.5250	.6	15.24	6	.23622
$\frac{25}{64}$	.390625	9.9219	.7	17.78	7	.27559
$\frac{13}{32}$	.40625	10.3187	.8	20.32	8	.31496
$\frac{27}{64}$	.421875	10.7156	.9	22.86	9	.35433
$\frac{7}{16}$	.4375	11.1125	1	25.4	10	.39370
$\frac{29}{64}$	.453125	11.5094	2	50.8	11	.43307
$\frac{15}{32}$	.46875	11.9062	3	76.2	12	.47244
$\frac{31}{64}$	.484375	12.3031	4	101.6	13	.51181
$\frac{1}{2}$	.5	12.7000	5	127.0	14	.55118
$\frac{33}{64}$	.515625	13.0969	6	152.4	15	.59055
$\frac{17}{32}$	.53125	13.4937	7	177.8	16	.62992
$\frac{35}{64}$	.546875	13.8906	8	203.2	17	.66929
$\frac{9}{16}$	.5625	14.2875	9	228.6	18	.70866
$\frac{37}{64}$	.578125	14.6844	10	254.0	19	.74803
$\frac{19}{32}$	.59375	15.0812	11	279.4	20	.78740
$\frac{39}{64}$	.609375	15.4781	12	304.8	21	.82677
$\frac{5}{8}$	.625	15.8750	13	330.2	22	.86614
$\frac{41}{64}$	.640625	16.2719	14	355.6	23	.90551
$\frac{21}{32}$	.65625	16.6687	15	381.0	24	.94488
$\frac{43}{64}$	.671875	17.0656	16	406.4	25	.98425
$\frac{11}{16}$	.6875	17.4625	17	431.8	26	1.02362
$\frac{45}{64}$	.703125	17.8594	18	457.2	27	1.06299
$\frac{23}{32}$	.71875	18.2562	19	482.6	28	1.10236
$\frac{47}{64}$	.734375	18.6531	20	508.0	29	1.14173
$\frac{3}{4}$	.75	19.0500	21	533.4	30	1.18110
$\frac{49}{64}$	.765625	19.4469	22	558.8	31	1.22047
$\frac{25}{32}$	.78125	19.8437	23	584.2	32	1.25984
$\frac{51}{64}$	.796875	20.2406	24	609.6	33	1.29921
$\frac{13}{16}$	.8125	20.6375	25	635.0	34	1.33858
$\frac{53}{64}$	.828125	21.0344	26	660.4	35	1.37795
$\frac{27}{32}$	.84375	21.4312	27	685.8	36	1.41732
$\frac{55}{64}$	.859375	21.8281	28	711.2	37	1.4567
$\frac{7}{8}$	.875	22.2250	29	736.6	38	1.4961
$\frac{57}{64}$	.890625	22.6219	30	762.0	39	1.5354
$\frac{29}{32}$	.90625	23.0187	31	787.4	40	1.5748
$\frac{59}{64}$	.921875	23.4156	32	812.8	41	1.6142
$\frac{15}{16}$	.9375	23.8125	33	838.2	42	1.6535
$\frac{61}{64}$	.953125	24.2094	34	863.6	43	1.6929
$\frac{31}{32}$	.96875	24.6062	35	889.0	44	1.7323
$\frac{63}{64}$	.984375	25.0031	36	914.4	45	1.7717

UNITS	Pints to Litres	Gallons to Litres	Litres to Pints	Litres to Gallons	Miles to Kilometres	Kilometres to Miles	Lbs. per sq. In. to Kg. per sq. Cm.	Kg. per sq. Cm. to Lbs. per sq. In.
1	.57	4.55	1.76	.22	1.61	.62	.07	14.22
2	1.14	9.09	3.52	.44	3.22	1.24	.14	28.50
3	1.70	13.64	5.28	.66	4.83	1.86	.21	42.67
4	2.27	18.18	7.04	.88	6.44	2.49	.28	56.89
5	2.84	22.73	8.80	1.10	8.05	3.11	.35	71.12
6	3.41	27.28	10.56	1.32	9.66	3.73	.42	85.34
7	3.98	31.82	12.32	1.54	11.27	4.35	.49	99.56
8	4.55	36.37	14.08	1.76	12.88	4.97	.56	113.79
9		40.91	15.84	1.98	14.48	5.59	.63	128.00
10		45.46	17.60	2.20	16.09	6.21	.70	142.23
20				4.40	32.19	12.43	1.41	284.47
30				6.60	48.28	18.64	2.11	426.70
40				8.80	64.37	24.85		
50					80.47	31.07		
60					96.56	37.28		
70					112.65	43.50		
80					128.75	49.71		
90					144.84	55.92		
100					160.93	62.14		

UNITS	Lb ft to kgm	Kgm to lb ft	UNITS	Lb ft to kgm	Kgm to lb ft
1	.138	7.233	7	.967	50.631
2	.276	14.466	8	1.106	57.864
3	.414	21.699	9	1.244	65.097
4	.553	28.932	10	1.382	72.330
5	.691	36.165	20	2.765	144.660
6	.829	43.398	30	4.147	216.990

TECHNICAL DATA

Dimensions are in mm unless otherwise stated

In certain cases inch equivalents are given in brackets. If inch equivalents are not quoted refer, if necessary, to the Metric Conversion Tables on page 140

ENGINE

Engine:

Type	V8, 4-stroke, OHV, pushrod operation
Capacity	3528cc
Bore and stroke	89.90 × 71.12
Compression ratio	9.35:1
Compression pressure	9.5 kg/sq cm (135lb/sq in)
Cylinder numbering:	
Lefthand bank	1 (front), 3, 5, 7
Righthand bank	2, 4, 6, 8

Crankshaft:

Main bearings	5, Vandervell shell-type
Material	Lead-indium
Journal diameter	58.412 − 0.013
Bearing clearance	0.025 to 0.061 (0.0010 to 0.0024)
Axial float	0.10 to 0.20 (0.004 to 0.008)
Big-end journals:	
Diameter	50.812 − 0.012
Pilot bearing diameter	19.060 + 0.025

Connecting rods:

Big-end bearings	Vandervell shell-type
Axial float	0.15 to 0.36 (0.006 to 0.014)
Material	Lead-indium
Bearing clearance	0.015 to 0.056 (0.0006 to 0.0022)
Length between centres	143.81 to 143.71

Pistons .. .. | Aluminium alloy, W-slot skirts

Clearance with bores:	
Top land	0.65 to 0.81 (0.0255 to 0.032)
Skirt top	0.018 to 0.033 (0.0007 to 0.0013)
Skirt bottom	0.008 to 0.043 (0.0003 to 0.0017)
Oversize, standard bore (one only)	0.025 (0.001) above standard

Piston rings .. .. | Two compression, one oil control

Top compression	Chrome parallel faced
Second compression	L-profile (marked T or TOP)
Compression ring widths	1.56 to 1.59
Gap	0.43 to 0.56 (0.017 to 0.022)
Side clearance	0.08 to 0.13 (0.003 to 0.005)
Oil ring	Composite, type 98-6
Width	4.81

Gudgeon pins:

Length	72.67 to 72.79
Diameter	22.22 − 0.008 (0.8749 − 0.0003)
Fit with small-end	Interference press fit
Clearance in piston	0.003 to 0.008 (0.0001 to 0.0003)

Cylinder heads .. .. | Aluminium alloy

Bolt lengths:	
Long	97.03 (3.820)
Medium	66.55 (2.620)
Short	54.86 (2.160)

Valve seats	..	..	..	..	Brico alloy 318 inserts
Inlet, standard OD	..	..	..	..	42.769 − 0.033
Exhaust, standard OD	..	..	..	..	36.944 − 0.028
Oversizes (two)	..	..	..	..	+ 0.25 and + 0.50
Seat profiles	..	..	..	..	See **FIG 1 : 8**

Valve guides:

Oversize (one only)	..	..	..	..	÷ 0.025
Fitted height above step	..	..	..	..	19 (see **FIG 1 : 6**)

Valves:

Face angle	..	..	..	..	45°
Overall length	..	..	..	..	116.58 to 117.35
Inlet stem diameter	..	..	..	..	8.641 to 8.666 at head
Increasing to	..	..	..	..	8.654 to 8.679
Clearance in guide	..	..	..	..	0.025 to 0.076 at top
Decreasing to	..	..	..	..	0.0127 to 0.0635
Overall head diameter	..	..	..	..	39.75 to 40.00
Exhaust stem diameter	..	..	..	..	8.628 to 8.654 at head
Increasing to	..	..	..	..	8.641 to 8.666
Clearance in guide	..	..	..	..	0.038 to 0.089 at top
Increasing to	..	..	..	..	0.05 to 0.10
Overall head diameter	..	..	..	..	34.226 to 34.480

Valve timing:

					Inlet	*Exhaust*
Opens (degrees)	..	..	..	..	30° BTDC	68° BBDC
Closes (degrees)	..	..	..	..	75° ABDC	37° ATDC
Opening duration	..	..	..	..	285°	285°
Peaks at (degrees)	..	..	..	..	112.5° ATDC	105.5° BTDC

Tappets	..	..	..	..	Self-adjusting, hydraulic

Valve springs:

Length under load:			
40.05 (1.577)	..	..	31.78 (70lb) ± 5%
34.29 (1.350)	..	..	59.02 (130lb) ± 5%
30.15 (1.187)	..	..	79.9 (176lb) ± 5%

Camshaft:

Valve lift	..	..	..	..	9.9 inlet and exhaust
Drive	..	..	..	..	Inverted tooth chain

Lubrication system:

Pump	..	..	..	..	Gear type
Pressure at 2000rev/min	..	..	..	..	1.97kg/sq cm (28lb/sq in)
Oil filter	..	..	..	..	Full flow, disposable
Filler cap	..	..	..	..	Sealed
Recommended oil:					
Ambient temperature:					
Below −12°C (10°F)	..	..	..	5W/20, 5W/30 or 5W/40
Above −22°C (−8°F)	..	..	..	10W/30, 10W/40 or 10W/50
Above −12°C (10°F)	..	..	..	15W/40 or 15W/50
Above 0°C (32°F)	..	..	..	20W/40 or 20W/50

Flywheel:

Minimum thickness	..	..	..	..	29.33 (1.155) overall

Breather system	..	..	..	..	Self-consuming
Filter	..	..	..	..	Disposable

FUEL SYSTEM

Fuel pump	..	..	..	..	Submerged in fuel tank
Type	..	..	..	..	Electrical
Carburetters	..	..	..	..	Two SU HIF-6
Bore	..	..	..	..	44.57
Needle type	..	..	..	..	BAK

Jet size	..	..	..	..	..	0.100in
Float level	..	..	..	..	..	0.50 to 1.50 (see page 38)
Choke orifice	..	..	..	..	..	1.20
Piston spring	..	..	..	..	..	Colour coded: yellow
Damper oil	..	..	..	..	..	SAE 20

Idle speed .. .. 725 to 775rev/min
Fast-idle speed .. .. 1100 to 1200rev/min
CO content of exhaust:
   At idle speed .. .. 3.0% to 4.5%
Filter .. .. In-line, disposable

IGNITION SYSTEM

Firing order 1, 8, 4, 3, 6, 5, 7, 2
Ignition timing .. .. Crankshaft datum
  Static .. .. 6° BTDC
  Dynamic .. .. Inclusive of static advance
     1200rev/min .. .. 10.0° BTDC
     1800rev/min .. .. 17.5° BTDC
     2600rev/min .. .. 22.0° BTDC
Sparking plugs:
  Type .. .. Champion N12Y
  Points gap 0.80 (0.032)
Ignition system .. .. Lucas 'Opus' electronic
  Polarity .. .. Negative earth only
Distributor .. .. Lucas 35 DE8
  Pick-up air gap .. .. 0.36 to 0.41 (0.014 to 0.016)
  Angle .. .. 45° ± 1°
  Rotation .. .. Clockwise
  Characteristics .. .. Distributor shaft datum
     300rev/min .. .. No advance to occur
     600 .. .. 1.0 to 3.0° advance
     900 .. .. 4.5 to 7.0
     1300 .. .. 7.0 to 9.0
     2200 .. .. 9.5 to 11.5
     2800 .. .. 10.0 to 12.0
     0in Hg (vacuum) .. .. .. 0 to 0.5° advance
     1.4 .. .. 0 to 0.5
     2.4 .. .. 0 to 1.0
     4.3 .. .. 0 to 3.0
     7.0 .. .. 3.0 to 6.0
     10.0 .. .. 6.0 to 9.0
     20.0 .. .. 7.0 to 9.0
Coil .. .. Lucas 22C12
Ballast resistor .. .. 9 BR
  Part no .. .. Lucas 41673, Rover ERC 3310

COOLING SYSTEM

Type .. .. Pressurised 'no loss'
Radiator .. .. Vertical flow
Pressure cap .. .. On expansion tank
  Pressure .. .. 1.05kg/sq cm (15lb/sq in)
Circulation .. .. Impeller pump assisted
Thermostat:
  Fully open at .. .. 82°C (180°F)
Fan .. .. 7 blades
  Diameter 405
  Drive .. .. Viscous coupling

Coolant .. .. Solution of antifreeze
  Specification .. .. Meeting BSI 3150
    Proportions .. .. See tabulation on page 50
    Type .. .. With inhibitor for aluminium engines
    Approved brands .. .. Smith's Bluecol U, Shellsafe, etc.

CLUTCH

Type .. .. Single dry-plate
  Diameter 240
  Spring .. .. Diaphragm
Release operation .. .. Hydraulic
  Fluid specification .. .. SAE J1703d
  Recommended brands .. .. See page 53

TRANSMISSION

Manual .. .. 5 forward speeds and reverse
  Engagement .. .. Synchro on forward speeds
  Gear ratios:
    1st 3.321:1
    2nd 2.087:1
    3rd 1.396:1
    4th .. .. 1.000:1, direct
    5th .. .. 0.833:1, overdrive
    Reverse 3.428:1
  Lubrication .. .. Splash and oil pump
  Oil specification .. .. Hypoid 75W
Final drive ratio 3.08:1

Miles/hr at 1000rev/min:

	5th gear	4th gear
195/70 HR tyres	27.8	23.1
185 HR tyres	28.5	23.7
Denovo tyres (195/65 HR375)	27.4	22.7

Automatic .. .. Borg Warner type 65
  Gear ratios:
    1st 2.39:1
    2nd 1.45:1
    3rd 1.00:1
    Reverse 2.09:1
  Torque converter .. .. Three-element
  Converter range:
    1st .. .. 2.39:1 to 4.97:1
    2nd .. .. 1.45:1 to 3.02:1
    3rd .. .. 1.00:1 to 2.08:1
    Reverse .. .. 2.09:1 to 4.35:1
Final drive ratio 3.08:1
Miles/hr at 1000rev/min .. .. .. 11.1 to 23.2
Propeller shaft .. .. Two constant velocity joints

SUSPENSION

Tyre pressures (lb/sq in):

Tyre type:	Front	Rear
185 HR	26 * * *	26 * * or 30 *
195/70 HR	26 * * *	26 * * or 28 *
Denovo	23 * * or 26 *	23 * * or 28 *

 * More than 4 up
** 1 to 4 up, no luggage

Wheels:
- Standard .. .. Pressed steel
- Optional .. .. Cast alloy with 195/70 tyres
- Diameter 14in
- Rim section 6J

Front suspension .. .. Independent
- Type .. .. MacPherson struts
- Springs .. .. Coil (offset to strut CL)
- Dampers .. .. Integral hydraulic telescopic
- Bump stops .. .. Incorporated in struts
- Wheel hub .. .. Runs on two taper roller bearings
- Geometry:*

	Unladen	Laden
Kingpin inclination	13° – 30′	10° 15′
Camber angle	Zero	+ 55′
Castor angle	2°	2°

- Anti-roll bar .. .. Also acts as trailing arms

* Reference only (see page 97)

Rear Suspension .. .. Live axle
- Springs .. .. Coil
- Dampers .. .. Self-levelling telescopic
- Axle location:
  - Longitudinal .. .. Trailing arms
  - Transverse .. .. Watts linkage

STEERING

Type .. .. Rack and pinion
- Make .. .. Berman power assisted
- Geared at.. .. .. 2.7 turns lock to lock
- Hydraulic pump .. .. Vane type
- Pressure at full lock:
  - At idling .. .. 32kg/sq cm
  - At 1000rev/min .. .. 67 to 70kg/sq cm
- Off load pressure:
  - At idling .. .. 4kg/sq cm
- Hydraulic fluid .. .. ATF type F (as for automatic transmission)

Wheel alignment .. .. Zero to 3.17 (0.125) toe-in

BRAKES

Operation:
- Pedal .. .. Hydraulic dual line
- Hand .. .. Mechanical on rear wheels

Front brakes .. .. Caliper disc
- Disc diameter 258

Rear brakes .. .. Drum
- Drum diameter 228
- Drum width 57

Brake servo .. .. Direct acting
- Boost ratio 3.08:1

Master cylinder .. .. Tandem pistons
- Primary piston .. .. Front brakes
- Secondary piston.. .. .. .. Rear brakes

Hydraulic fluid .. .. SAE J1703d
- Recommended brands .. .. .. See page 53

ELECTRICAL EQUIPMENT

Battery	12-volt
Earthing system	Negative earth
Fuses	See page 118
Relays	See pages 118 and 119
Starter motor	Lucas 3M 100 PE
Engagement	Positive
Solenoid	Rover part no RTC 342
Pull-in coil	0.25 to 0.27 ohms
Hold-in coil	0.76 to 0.80 ohms
Brushes	Rover part no GSB 112
New length	18.0
Renew at	9.53
Commutator:	
Skimming thickness	3.56 minimum
Shaft end float	0.25 maximum
Bearing renewal	Mandrel diameters
Commutator end cover	11.118
Drive end bracket	12.012
Alternator	Lucas 23 ACR
Polarity	Negative earth only
Brushes	Rover part no GGB 504
New length	12.7
Renew at	5.0 (free protrusion)
Stator winding	3-phase, delta
Field winding	3.20 ohms at 20°C
Regulator	Lucas 14TR
Control voltage	14-volt
Output	55 amp
Rectifier	6 diodes (3 live, 3 earth)
Field winding supply	3 diodes

CAPACITIES

	Litre	Imp.	USA
Fuel	65.9	14.5 gals	17.4 gals
Engine:			
Sump and filter	5.4	9.5 pints	11.4 pints
Sump (drain/refill)	4.7	8.25 pints	9.9 pints
Manual gearbox (from dry)	1.53	2.7 pints	3.2 pints
Automatic transmission:			
With cooler	6.96	12.25 pints	14.7 pints
Rear axle (from dry)	0.91	1.6 pints	1.91 pints
Reservoirs:			
Brakes		As required	
Power steering	1.56	2.75 pints	3.3 pints
Clutch		As required	
Windscreen washer	1.70	3.0 pints	3.6 pints
Cooling system (with heater) ..	11.1	19.5 pints	23.4 pints

DIMENSIONS

Overall length	4699
Overall width	1768
Overall height	1340 (unladen)
Track:	
Front	1500
Rear	1490
With Denovo tyres	10 less than standard

Wheelbase ..	..	..	..	..	..	2815
Ground clearance		..	..	..	..	155 (nominal)
Weight (basic)	..	..	..	..	..	1351kg (no optional extras)

TORQUE WRENCH SETTINGS

Torques are in kgm with lb ft equivalents in brackets

Engine:

Chainwheel to camshaft	6.2 (45)
Connecting rod bolt	4.8 (35)
Clutch to flywheel	2.75 (20)
Crankshaft pulley bolt	22.1 (160)
Cylinder head bolts:	
Bolt nos 1 to 10 (**FIG 1 :4**)	9.7 (70)
Bolt nos 11 to 14 (**FIG 1 :4**)	6.9 (50)
Exhaust manifold to heads	2.2 (16)
Flywheel/drive plate to crankshaft	8.3 (60)
Starter ring to drive plate	3.5 (25)
Inlet manifold to heads	4.0 (30)
Main bearing cap bolts:	
Rear bolts	9.7 (70)
All others	7.6 (55)
Manifold gasket clamp bolt	2.0 (15)
Oil relief valve cap	4.0 (30)
Oil sump drain plug	4.8 (35)
Oil sump to cylinder block:	
Rear setscrews	2.4 (17)
Other setscrews	1.1 (8)
Rocker cover to head	0.7 (5)
Rocker shaft bracket to head	4.0 (30)

Engine mountings:

Bracket front to lower fixing	6.9 (50)
Bracket front to upper fixing	2.5 (18)

Ignition system:

Sparking plugs	1.7 (12)
Distributor clamp bolt	1.9 (14)

Manual gearbox:

Bottom cover to clutch housing	1.0 (7)
Clutch housing to engine and sump bracings ..	5.0 (37)
Clutch housing to casing..	8.0 (59)
Clutch housing to block and plate	2.9 (21)
Clutch fulcrum pin	5.0 (37)
Cover plate to housing	2.0 (15)
Cover plate to extension housing	0.6 (4.5)
Drive flange to mainshaft	20.7 (150)
Extension/centre plate/main case	2.9 (21)
Pivot bracket to centre plate	2.9 (21)
Front cover to main case	2.9 (21)
'J' pin to selector shaft	2.0 (15)
Mounting bracket fixings..	2.9 (21)
Magnetic drain plug	3.6 (26)
Oil pump to extension case	1.0 (7)
Reverse:	
Lever pin to centre plate	2.9 (21)
Baulk plate to extension case	1.0 (7)
Remote control to extension case	2.0 (15)
Spool retainer to main case	1.0 (7)

Torsion spring:
    Brackets to extension case 1.0 (7)
    Adjuster locking 2.0 (15)

Propeller shaft:
  Coupling bolts 5.0 (37)

Rear axle:
  Bearing retaining plate 5.0 (37)
  Differential bearing caps 10.0 (75)
  Crownwheel bolts 12.3 (89)
  Extension casing:
    To axle housing 5.0 (37)
    Mounting bracket 5.0 (37)
    Drive flange 16.6 (120)
  Seal housing 5.0 (37)
  Filler/level plug 3.6 (26)

Front suspension:
  Anti-roll bar:
    To crossmember 4.4 (32)
    To bottom link 9.8 (71)
    Clamp 5.7 (41)
  Bottom link ball joint 4.9 (36)
  Brake caliper to strut 7.6 (55)
  Disc to hub 5.7 (41)
  Crossmember to body 4.0 (30)
  Strut to body 2.9 (21)
  Road spring to strut 4.0 (30)
  Steering arm to strut 7.6 (55)

Rear suspension:
  Levelling unit:
    Top and bottom nuts 6.3 (45)
    Top and bottom locknuts 4.5 (33)
  Crossmember:
    To extension casing 5.6 (41)
    To body outer mounting 4.7 (34)
  Spring retainer to seat 1.2 (9)
  Bump stop to spring cup 2.75 (20)
  Watts linkage to axle 5.6 (41)
  Trailing link:
    Link to fork 5.6 (41)
    Fork to body 5.6 (41)
    Link to axle 5.6 (41)

Steering:
  Wheel to column 2.75 (20)
  Column to dashboard 2.75 (20)
  Coupling setscrews 2.75 (20)
  Rack and pinion to crossmember ..   4.4 (32)
  Ball joint to steering arm 4.9 (36)
  Ball joint/tie rod locknut 6.5 (47)
  Support plate to body 2.75 (20)
  High pressure feed pipe:
    To rack housing 1.9 (14)
    To pump 3.0 (22)
  Low pressure pipe to pump 3.0 (22)

Brakes:
  Brake hoses:
    To bracket locknuts 2.4 (17)
    To pipe unions 1.38 (10)

Brake pipes:
To calipers	..	..	..	..	1.1 (8)
To drums	..	..	..	..	0.8 (6)
To master cylinder	..	..	..	..	1.1 (8)
To pressure valve	..	..	..	..	0.8 (6)
Master cylinder end plug	..	..	..	..	4.5 (33)
Servo to dashboard	..	..	..	..	1.5 (11)

Electrical equipment:
Alternator bracket to head		..	..	..	3.4 (25)
Alternator pivots	..	..	..	..	2.4 (17)
Alternator adjuster link		..	..	..	2.4 (17)
Starter motor bolts		..	..	..	4.8 (35)

General:
$\frac{7}{16}$ UNC	..	..	..	..	6.9 (50)
$\frac{3}{8}$ UNC	..	..	..	..	3.4 (25)
$\frac{5}{16}$ UNC	..	..	..	..	2.5 (18)
$\frac{1}{4}$ UNC	..	..	..	..	1.1 (8)
M12	..	..	..	..	6.3 (45)
M10	..	..	..	..	4.0 (30)
M8	..	..	..	..	2.75 (20)
M6	..	..	..	..	1.1 (8)

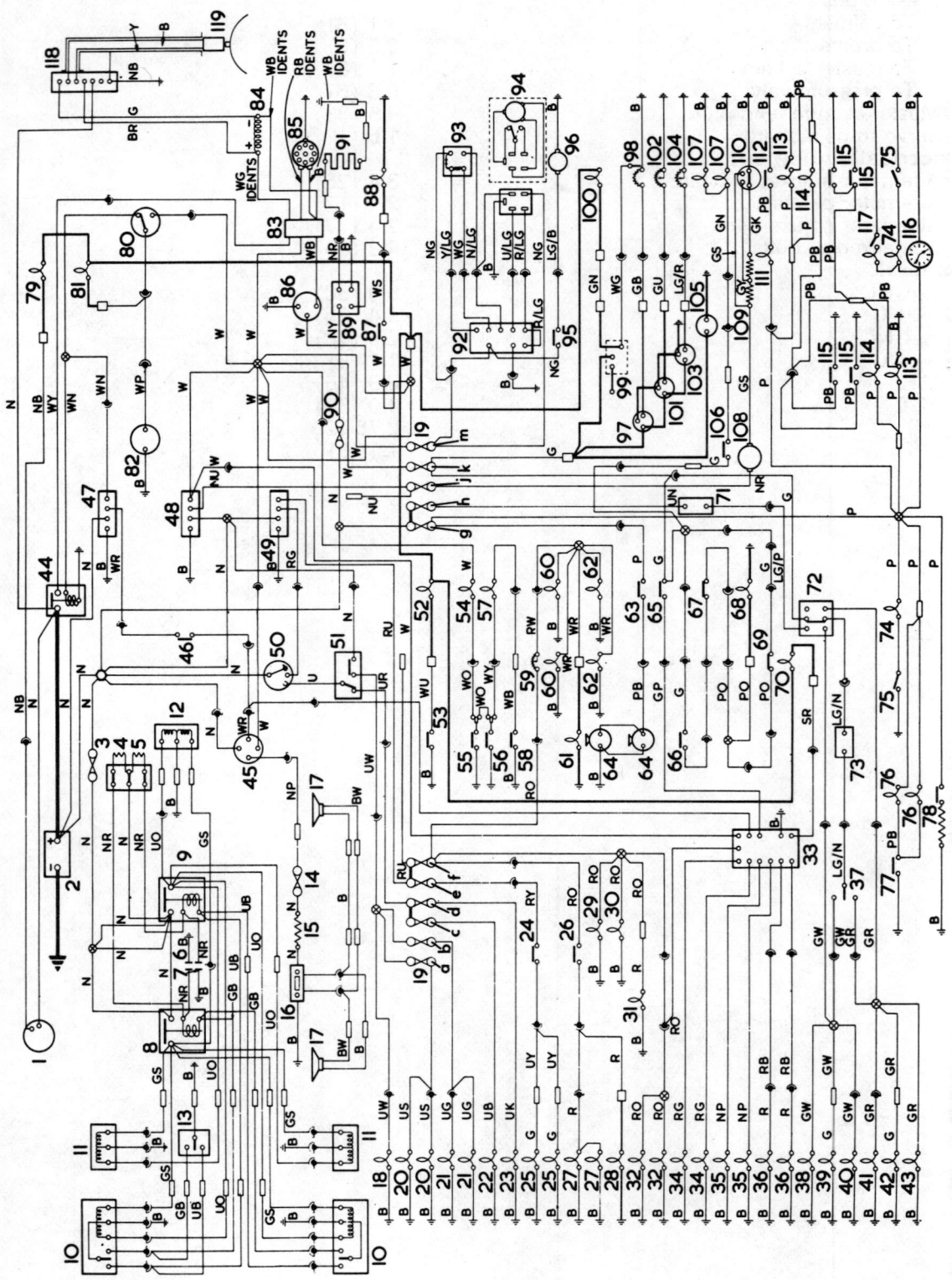

150

Key to Fig 14:1   1 Alternator   2 Battery   3 Door lock fuse   4 Resistor, unlock   5 Resistor, lock   6 Capacitor, unlock   7 Capacitor, lock   8 Relay, unlock   9 Relay, lock   10 Front door lock solenoid and key switch   11 Rear door lock solenoid   12 Tailgate lock solenoid   13 Interior switch   14 Radio fuse   15 Radio choke   16 Radio   17 Speaker   18 Main beam warning light   19 Fuse   20 Righthand main beam   21 Lefthand main beam   22 Righthand dip beam   23 Lefthand dip beam   24 Front fog lamp switch   25 Front fog lamp   26 Rear fog lamp switch   27 Rear fog lamp   28 Rear fog lamp warning light   29 Fibre optic lamp   30 Clock illumination   31 Cigarette lighter illumination   32 Plate illumination lamp   33 Bulb failure indicator   34 Tail lamp   35 Stop lamp   36 Front parking lamp   37 Turn signal switch   38 Righthand flasher warning light   39 Righthand front flasher lamp   40 Righthand rear flasher lamp   41 Lefthand rear flasher lamp   42 Lefthand front flasher lamp   43 Lefthand flasher warning light   44 Starter motor   45 Ignition/starter switch   46 Starter inhibitor switch (automatic transmission only)   47 Starter motor relay   48 Heater motor supply line relay   49 Lighting supply line relay   50 Master light switch   51 Main/dip/flash switch   52 Choke warning light   53 Choke   54 Brake warning light   55 Brake fluid level switch   56 Brake line failure switch   57 Handbrake warning light   58 Handbrake switch   59 Panel rheostat switch   60 Tachometer illumination   61 Instrument illumination   62 Speedometer illumination   63 Horn push   64 Horn   65 Stop lamp switch   66 Passenger's seat switch   67 Passenger's belt switch   68 Seat belt warning light   69 Driver's belt switch   70 Bulb failure warning light   71 Hazard flasher unit   72 Hazard switch   73 Turn signal flasher unit   74 Glove box lamp   75 Glove box lamp switch   76 Engine bay lamp   77 Engine bay lamp switch   78 Cigarette lighter   79 Ignition warning light   80 Oil pressure switch   81 Oil pressure warning light   82 Fuel pump   83 Ballast resistor   84 Ignition coil   85 Ignition distributor   86 Tachometer   87 Heated backlight switch   88 Heated backlight warning light   89 Heated backlight relay   90 Heated backlight fuse   91 Heated backlight   92 Windscreen wiper switch   93 Windscreen wiper delay unit   94 Windscreen wiper motor   95 Windscreen washer switch   96 Windscreen washer pump   97 Fuel indicator   98 Fuel tank unit   99 Fuel warning light delay unit   100 Fuel warning light   101 Temperature indicator   102 Temperature transmitter   103 Oil pressure indicator   104 Oil pressure transmitter   105 Battery condition indicator   106 Reverse lamp switch   107 Reverse lamp   108 Heater motor   109 Heater resistor   110 Heater switch   111 Luggage bay lamp   112 Luggage bay lamp switch   113 'B post' lamp   114 Front door guard lamp   115 Door switch   116 Clock   117 Map lamp   118 Engine diagnosis socket   119 Engine diagnosis timing transducer

Key to cable colour code   B Black   G Green   K Pink   N Brown   O Orange   P Purple   R Red   S Slate   U Blue   W White   Y Yellow

steering system which have been damaged should be renewed, as attempts to repair them may lead to cracking and subsequent failure, and steering ball joints should be disconnected using a recommended tool to prevent damage.

3   It often happens that an owner is baffled when trying to dismantle an unfamiliar piece of equipment. So many modern devices are pressed together or assembled by spinning-over flanges, that they must be sawn apart. The intention is that the whole assembly must be renewed. However, parts which appear to be in one piece to the naked eye, may reveal close-fitting joint lines when inspected with a magnifying glass, and, this may provide the necessary clue to dismantling. Lefthanded screw threads are used where rotational forces would tend to unscrew a righthanded screw thread.

Be very careful when dismantling mechanisms which may come apart suddenly. Work in an enclosed space where the parts will be contained, and drape a piece of cloth over the device if springs are likely to fly in all directions. Mark everything which might be reassembled in the wrong position, scratched symbols may be used on unstressed parts, or a sequence of tiny dots from a centre punch can be useful. Stressed parts should never be scratched or centre-popped as this may lead to cracking under working conditions. Store parts which look alike in the correct order for reassembly. Never rely upon memory to assist in the assembly of complicated mechanisms, especially when they will be dismantled for a long time, but make notes, and drawings to supplement the diagrams in the manual, and put labels on detached wires. Rust stains may indicate unlubricated wear. This can sometimes be seen round the outside edge of a bearing cup in a universal joint. Look for bright rubbing marks on parts which normally should not make heavy contact. These might prove that something is bent or running out of truth. For example, there might be bright marks on one side of a piston, at the top near the ring grooves, and others at the bottom of the skirt on the other side. This could well be the clue to a bent connecting rod. Suspected cracks can be proved by heating the component in a light oil to approximately 100°C, removing, drying off, and dusting with french chalk, if a crack is present the oil retained in the crack will stain the french chalk.

4   In determining wear, and the degree, against the permissible limits set in the manual, accurate measurement can only be achieved by the use of a micrometer. In many cases, the wear is given to the fourth place of decimals; that is in ten-thousandths of an inch. This can be read by the vernier scale on the barrel of a good micrometer. Bore diameters are more difficult to determine. If, however, the matching shaft is accurately measured, the degree of play in the bore can be felt as a guide to its suitability. In other cases, the shank of a twist drill of known diameter is a handy check.

Many methods have been devised for determining the clearance between bearing surfaces. To-day the best and simplest is by the use of Plastigage, obtainable from most garages. A thin plastic thread is laid between the two surfaces and the bearing is tightened, flattening the thread. On removal, the width of the thread is compared with a scale supplied with the thread and the clearance is read off directly. Sometimes joint faces leak persistently, even after gasket renewal. The fault will then be traceable to distortion, dirt or burrs. Studs which are screwed into soft metal frequently raise burrs at the point of entry. A quick cure for this is to chamfer the edge of the hole in the part which fits over the stud.

5   **Always check a replacement part with the original one before it is fitted.**

If parts are not marked, and the order for reassembly is not known, a little detective work will help. Look for marks which are due to wear to see if they can be mated. Joint faces may not be identical due to manufacturing errors, and parts which overlap may be stained, giving a clue to the correct position. Most fixings leave identifying marks especially if they were painted over on assembly. It is then easier to decide whether a nut, for instance, has a plain, a spring, or a shakeproof washer under it. All running surfaces become 'bedded' together after long spells of work and tiny imperfections on one part will be found to have left corresponding marks on the other. This is particularly true of shafts and bearings and even a score on a cylinder wall will show on the piston.

6   Checking end float or rocker clearances by feeler gauge may not always give accurate results because of wear. For instance, the rocker tip which bears on a valve stem may be deeply pitted, in which case the feeler will simply be bridging a depression. Thrust washers may also wear depressions in opposing faces to make accurate measurement difficult. End float is then easier to check by using a dial gauge. It is common practice to adjust end play in bearing assemblies, like front hubs with taper rollers, by doing up the axle nut until the hub becomes stiff to turn and then backing it off a little. Do not use this method with ballbearing hubs as the assembly is often preloaded by tightening the axle nut to its fullest extent. If the splitpin hole will not line up, file the base of the nut a little.

Steering assemblies often wear in the straight-ahead position. If any part is adjusted, make sure that it remains free when moved from lock to lock. Do not be surprised if an assembly like a steering gearbox, which is known to be carefully adjusted outside the car, becomes stiff when it is bolted in place. This will be due to distortion of the case by the pull of the mounting bolts, particularly if the mounting points are not all touching together. This problem may be met in other equipment and is cured by careful attention to the alignment of mounting points.

When a spanner is stamped with a size and A/F it means that the dimension is the width between the jaws and has no connection with ANF, which is the designation for the American National Fine thread. Coarse threads like Whitworth are rarely used on cars to-day except for studs which screw into soft aluminium or cast iron. For this reason it might be found that the top end of a cylinder head stud has a fine thread and the lower end a coarse thread to screw into the cylinder block. If the car has mainly UNF threads then it is likely that any coarse threads will be UNC, which are not the same as Whitworth. Small sizes have the same number of threads in Whitworth and UNC, but in the $\frac{1}{2}$ inch size for example, there are twelve threads to the inch in the former and thirteen in the latter.

7 After a major overhaul, particularly if a great deal of work has been done on the braking, steering and suspension systems, it is advisable to approach the problem of testing with care. If the braking system has been overhauled, apply heavy pressure to the brake pedal and get a second operator to check every possible source of leakage. The brakes may work extremely well, but a leak could cause complete failure after a few miles.

Do not fit the hub caps until every wheel nut has been checked for tightness, and make sure the tyre pressures are correct. Check the levels of coolant, lubricants and hydraulic fluids. Being satisfied that all is well, take the car on the road and test the brakes at once. Check the steering and the action of the handbrake. Do all this at moderate speeds on quiet roads, and make sure there is no other vehicle behind you when you try a rapid stop.

Finally, remember that many parts settle down after a time, so check for tightness of all fixings after the car has been on the road for a hundred miles or so.

8 It is useless to tune an engine which has not reached its normal running temperature. In the same way, the tune of an engine which is stiff after a rebore will be different when the engine is again running free. Remember too, that rocker clearances on pushrod operated valve gear will change when the cylinder head nuts are tightened after an initial period of running with a new head gasket.

Trouble may not always be due to what seems the obvious cause. Ignition, carburation and mechanical condition are interdependent and spitting back through the carburetter, which might be attributed to a weak mixture, can be caused by a sticking inlet valve.

For one final hint on tuning, never adjust more than one thing at a time or it will be impossible to tell which adjustment produced the desired result.

NOTES

GLOSSARY OF TERMS

Allen key   Cranked wrench of hexagonal section for use with socket head screws.

Alternator   Electrical generator producing alternating current. Rectified to direct current for battery charging.

Ambient temperature   Surrounding atmospheric temperature.

Annulus   Used in engineering to indicate the outer ring gear of an epicyclic gear train.

Armature   The shaft carrying the windings, which rotates in the magnetic field of a generator or starter motor. That part of a solenoid or relay which is activated by the magnetic field.

Axial   In line with, or pertaining to, an axis.

Backlash   Play in meshing gears.

Balance lever   A bar where force applied at the centre is equally divided between connections at the ends.

Banjo axle   Axle casing with large diameter housing for the crownwheel and differential.

Bendix pinion   A self-engaging and self-disengaging drive on a starter motor shaft.

Bevel pinion   A conical shaped gearwheel, designed to mesh with a similar gear with an axis usually at 90 deg. to its own.

bhp   Brake horse power, measured on a dynamometer.

bmep   Brake mean effective pressure. Average pressure on a piston during the working stroke.

Brake cylinder   Cylinder with hydraulically operated piston(s) acting on brake shoes or pad(s).

Brake regulator   Control valve fitted in hydraulic braking system which limits brake pressure to rear brakes during heavy braking to prevent rear wheel locking.

Camber   Angle at which a wheel is tilted from the vertical.

Capacitor   Modern term for an electrical condenser. Part of distributor assembly, connected across contact breaker points, acts as an interference suppressor.

Castellated   Top face of a nut, slotted across the flats, to take a locking splitpin.

Castor   Angle at which the kingpin or swivel pin is tilted when viewed from the side.

cc   Cubic centimetres. Engine capacity is arrived at by multiplying the area of the bore in sq cm by the stroke in cm by the number of cylinders.

Clevis   U-shaped forked connector used with a clevis pin, usually at handbrake connections.

Collet   A type of collar, usually split and located in a groove in a shaft, and held in place by a retainer. The arrangement used to retain the spring(s) on a valve stem in most cases.

Commutator   Rotating segmented current distributor between armature windings and brushes in generator or motor.

Compression ratio   The ratio, or quantitative relation, of the total volume (piston at bottom of stroke) to the unswept volume (piston at top of stroke) in an engine cylinder.

Condenser   See 'Capacitor'.

Core plug   Plug for blanking off a manufacturing hole in a casting.

Crownwheel   Large bevel gear in rear axle, driven by a bevel pinion attached to the propeller shaft. Sometimes called a 'ring gear'.

'C'-spanner   Like a 'C' with a handle. For use on screwed collars without flats, but with slots or holes.

Damper   Modern term for shock absorber, used in vehicle suspension systems to damp out spring oscillations.

Depression   The lowering of atmospheric pressure as in the inlet manifold and carburetter.

Dowel   Close tolerance pin, peg, tube, or bolt, which accurately locates mating parts.

Drag link   Rod connecting steering box drop arm (pitman arm) to nearest front wheel steering arm in certain types of steering systems.

Dry liner   Thinwall tube pressed into cylinder bore.

Dry sump   Lubrication system where all oil is scavenged from the sump, and returned to a separate tank.

Dynamo   See 'Generator'.

Electrode   Terminal part of an electrical component, such as the points or 'Electrodes' of a sparking plug.

Electrolyte   In lead-acid car batteries a solution of sulphuric acid and distilled water.

End float   The axial movement between associated parts, end play.

EP   Extreme pressure. In lubricants, special grades for heavily loaded bearing surfaces, such as gear teeth in a gearbox, or crownwheel and pinion in a rear axle.

Fade	Of brakes. Reduced efficiency due to overheating.
Field coils	Windings on the polepieces of motors and generators.
Fillets	Narrow finishing strips usually applied to interior bodywork.
First motion shaft	Input shaft from clutch to gearbox.
Fullflow filter	Filters in which all the oil is pumped to the engine. If the element becomes clogged, a bypass valve operates to pass unfiltered oil to the engine.
FWD	Front wheel drive.
Gear pump	Two meshing gears in a close fitting casing. Oil is carried from the inlet round the outside of both gears in the spaces between the gear teeth and casing to the outlet, the meshing gear teeth prevent oil passing back to the inlet, and the oil is forced through the outlet port.
Generator	Modern term for 'Dynamo'. When rotated produces electrical current.
Grommet	A ring of protective or sealing material. Can be used to protect pipes or leads passing through bulkheads.
Grubscrew	Fully threaded headless screw with screwdriver slot. Used for locking, or alignment purposes.
Gudgeon pin	Shaft which connects a piston to its connecting rod. Sometimes called 'wrist pin', or 'piston pin'.
Halfshaft	One of a pair transmitting drive from the differential.
Helical	In spiral form. The teeth of helical gears are cut at a spiral angle to the side faces of the gearwheel.
Hot spot	Hot area that assists vapourisation of fuel on its way to cylinders. Often provided by close contact between inlet and exhaust manifolds.
HT	High Tension. Applied to electrical current produced by the ignition coil for the sparking plugs.
Hydrometer	A device for checking specific gravity of liquids. Used to check specific gravity of electrolyte.
Hypoid bevel gears	A form of bevel gear used in the rear axle drive gears. The bevel pinion meshes below the centre line of the crownwheel, giving a lower propeller shaft line.
Idler	A device for passing on movement. A free running gear between driving and driven gears. A lever transmitting track rod movement to a side rod in steering gear.
Impeller	A centrifugal pumping element. Used in water pumps to stimulate flow.
Journals	Those parts of a shaft that are in contact with the bearings.
Kingpin	The main vertical pin which carries the front wheel spindle, and permits steering movement. May be called 'steering pin' or 'swivel pin'.
Layshaft	The shaft which carries the laygear in the gearbox. The laygear is driven by the first motion shaft and drives the third motion shaft according to the gear selected. Sometimes called the 'countershaft' or 'second motion shaft'.
lb ft	A measure of twist or torque. A pull of 10 lb at a radius of 1 ft is a torque of 10 lb ft.
lb/sq in	Pounds per square inch.
Little-end	The small, or piston end of a connecting rod. Sometimes called the 'small-end'.
LT	Low Tension. The current output from the battery.
Mandrel	Accurately manufactured bar or rod used for test or centring purposes
Manifold	A pipe, duct, or chamber, with several branches.
Needle rollers	Bearing rollers with a length many times their diameter.
Oil bath	Reservoir which lubricates parts by immersion. In air filters, a separate oil supply for wetting a wire mesh element to hold the dust.
Oil wetted	In air filters, a wire mesh element lightly oiled to trap and hold airborne dust.
Overlap	Period during which inlet and exhaust valves are open together.
Panhard rod	Bar connected between fixed point on chassis and another on axle to control sideways movement.
Pawl	Pivoted catch which engages in the teeth of a ratchet to permit movement in one direction only.
Peg spanner	Tool with pegs, or pins, to engage in holes or slots in the part to be turned.
Pendant pedals	Pedals with levers that are pivoted at the top end.
Phillips screwdriver	A cross-point screwdriver for use with the cross-slotted heads of Philips screws.
Pinion	A small gear, usually in relation to another gear.
Piston-type damper	Shock absorber in which damping is controlled by a piston working in a closed oil-filled cylinder.
Preloading	Preset static pressure on ball or roller bearings not due to working loads.
Radial	Radiating from a centre, like the spokes of a wheel.

Radius rod	Pivoted arm confining movement of a part to an arc of fixed radius.
Ratchet	Toothed wheel or rack which can move in one direction only, movement in the other being prevented by a pawl.
Ring gear	A gear tooth ring attached to outer periphery of flywheel. Starter pinion engages with it during starting.
Runout	Amount by which rotating part is out of true.
Semi-floating axle	Outer end of rear axle halfshaft is carried on bearing inside axle casing. Wheel hub is secured to end of shaft.
Servo	A hydraulic or pneumatic system for assisting, or, augmenting a physical effort. See 'Vacuum Servo'.
Setscrew	One which is threaded for the full length of the shank.
Shackle	A coupling link, used in the form of two parallel pins connected by side plates to secure the end of the master suspension spring and absorb the effects of deflection.
Shell bearing	Thinwalled steel shell lined with anti-friction metal. Usually semi-circular and used in pairs for main and big-end bearings.
Shock absorber	See 'Damper'.
Silentbloc	Rubber bush bonded to inner and outer metal sleeves.
Socket-head screw	Screw with hexagonal socket for an Allen key.
Solenoid	A coil of wire creating a magnetic field when electric current passes through it. Used with a soft iron core to operate contacts or a mechanical device.
Spur gear	A gear with teeth cut axially across the periphery.
Stub axle	Short axle fixed at one end only.
Tachometer	An instrument for accurate measurement of rotating speed. Usually indicates in revolutions per minute.

TDC	Top Dead Centre. The highest point reached by a piston in a cylinder, with the crank and connecting rod in line.
Thermostat	Automatic device for regulating temperature. Used in vehicle coolant systems to open a valve which restricts circulation at low temperature.
Third motion shaft	Output shaft of gearbox.
Threequarter floating axle	Outer end of rear axle halfshaft flanged and bolted to wheel hub, which runs on bearing mounted on outside of axle casing. Vehicle weight is not carried by the axle shaft.
Thrust bearing or washer	Used to reduce friction in rotating parts subject to axial loads.
Torque	Turning or twisting effort. See 'lb ft'.
Track rod	The bar(s) across the vehicle which connect the steering arms and maintain the front wheels in their correct alignment.
UJ	Universal joint. A coupling between shafts which permits angular movement.
UNF	Unified National Fine screw thread.
Vacuum servo	Device used in brake system, using difference between atmospheric pressure and inlet manifold depression to operate a piston which acts to augment brake pressure as required. See 'Servo'.
Venturi	A restriction or 'choke' in a tube, as in a carburetter, used to increase velocity to obtain a reduction in pressure.
Vernier	A sliding scale for obtaining fractional readings of the graduations of an adjacent scale.
Welch plug	A domed thin metal disc which is partially flattened to lock in a recess. Used to plug core holes in castings.
Wet liner	Removable cylinder barrel, sealed against coolant leakage, where the coolant is in direct contact with the outer surface.
Wet sump	A reservoir attached to the crankcase to hold the lubricating oil.

NOTES

INDEX